14-
7F

THE NEW
VICTORIANS

THE NEW VICTORIANS

Poverty, Politics, and Propaganda in Two Gilded Ages

STEPHEN PIMPARE

THE NEW PRESS

NEW YORK
LONDON

Published in the United States by The New Press, New York, 2004
Distributed by W. W. Norton & Company, Inc., New York

LIBRARY OF CONGRESS CATALOGING-IN-PUBLICATION DATA
Pimpare, Stephen.
    The new Victorians : poverty, politics, and propaganda in two
Gilded Ages / Stephen Pimpare.
        p. cm.
    Includes bibliographical references and index.
    ISBN 1-56584-839-X
    1. Public welfare—United States.   2. Public welfare
administration—United States—Evaluation.   3. Poor—
Government policy—United States—History.   4. United States—
Social policy.   5. Lobbying—United States—History.   6. Pressure
groups—United States—History.   7. Political action committees—
United States.   I. Title.

    HV95.P54 2004
    362.5'561'0973—dc22   2003066113

The New Press was established in 1990 as a not-for-profit alternative
to the large, commercial publishing houses currently dominating the
book publishing industry. The New Press operates in the public
interest rather than for private gain, and is committed to publishing,
in innovative ways, works of educational, cultural, and community
value that are often deemed insufficiently profitable.

The New Press
38 Greene Street, 4th floor
New York, NY 10013
www.thenewpress.com

Composition by dix!

Printed in the United States of America

10 9 8 7 6 5 4 3 2 1

*The Gilded Age knew nothing of the Enlightenment;
it recognized only the acquisitive instinct.*

—Vernon Louis Parrington, 1930

CONTENTS

THE NEW
VICTORIANS

PREFACE

The passage of welfare reform legislation in 1996 was welcome and long overdue. We *had* to reform our poor-relief programs, and the public finally demanded that we do so because they were expensive, inefficient, and too riddled with waste, fraud, and abuse. Worse, by seizing income from middle-class taxpayers and giving it to poor mothers, and only unmarried mothers at that (while expecting nothing in return), welfare discouraged work, marriage, and thrift while it subsidized out-of-wedlock births, long-term dependence, and irresponsibility. By teaching children of welfare mothers all the wrong lessons about the need to work and be accountable for their own well-being, welfare trapped people in a cycle of intergenerational poverty and created an underclass, a poverty culture. As a result, entire neighborhoods were beset by crime, stagnation, and despair. Relief harmed the poor. We can see why Lyndon Johnson's War on Poverty, despite good intentions and massive expenditures, inevitably failed: the roots of poverty are ultimately moral and individual, not economic and social, and the federal government is too distant from local conditions to effectively solve these problems. State governments, closer to the people, can do better, but there is an even more effective and ultimately more compassionate way to aid the poor: before the massive modern welfare state that was built from the 1930s to the early 1970s, welfare was voluntary, privately funded and administered, and *personal;* it addressed the moral roots of need, often because religious and community organizations were more centrally involved. That is the model to emulate if we are serious about improving the lives of the dependent poor. And indeed, because it finally took these matters seriously and overcame partisan political intransigence and the pleadings of the poverty industry, welfare reform has succeeded, and quite spectacularly, despite the overwrought predictions of doom from its opponents: welfare reform has saved money, reduced poverty, reduced dependency, encouraged marriage and more responsible childbearing, and has finally given poor women and their children real opportunities to escape poverty and to be self-reliant.

Or so goes the conventional wisdom. It is, like much of conventional wisdom, wrong in almost every respect.[1] Welfare was always a small portion of the federal budget, paid benefits that never lifted recipients out of poverty, and never reached even half of all poor people. Welfare use is not transmitted like a birth defect from one generation to another, although in America people born poor are more likely to remain poor than they are in many other advanced industrialized nations. Women on Aid to Families with Dependent Children (AFDC) typically had fewer children than the average woman, and because benefits were low they often worked, although sometimes at poorly paid "under-the-table" jobs in the informal economy. Most recipients used welfare for relatively brief periods of time (about a year and a half, on average, although many returned) as a transitional program that allowed them to survive while looking for a better job, escaping an abusive relationship, going to school, or caring for their children; those who remained on the rolls longer were, by virtue of their lower educational achievements, or because of disability or illness, usually of little value in the modern labor market. The roots of need are not moral; they are industrial, political, and systemic. Note, for example, that the Federal Reserve Bank has historically considered that when 5–6 percent of the working-age job-seeking population was without work, the United States had reached "full employment": even the most conservative financial and regulatory institutions do not expect the economy to be able to provide enough jobs for everyone. The War on Poverty, which was too poorly funded for us to say that it was fought in earnest, nonetheless achieved real results, notably by reducing poverty, especially among the old. The difference with state-level administration of relief is not that local governments are more effective but that they permit variation in policies and benefits to suit local conditions, which has historically resulted in, among other failures, arbitrary and racially discriminatory practices and policies that are more subject to pressure from business threatening flight to more hospitable climes. There is no evidence that churches or private charity providers per se are more effective than public agencies. And so on. The brief against relief is built on myths, on lies, on the simplistic reading of complicated data and a propensity to reason by anecdote and analogy.

There is, however, some truth to part of the indictment, and this is where the objection to welfare is really rooted: the availability of cash relief, even if modest, allows people to refuse low-wage, low-benefit work.[2] Anti-welfare activists describe this as a "perverse incentive," as a structural failing of relief, a root of dependency. But welfare does not make people dependent. Rather, it allows them the ability to trade one kind of dependence for another, sacrificing dependence on the labor market or a husband or family or the noblesse oblige of private charity for dependence on the state.[3] Relief thereby gives poor women some measure of power, of freedom even, for it provides them with a choice, however limited it may be. Our modern usage of the term *dependence* is loaded, an epithet now reserved only for the poor, but we are all dependent: upon each other, upon our jobs, upon government. We are all needy, although in different ways.[4] Moreover, by removing some people from the labor market poor relief sets something of a floor under wages, helping other workers by pushing up their earning power, if only modestly. The benefits of welfare reach further than the public knows, and much of the apparent opposition to it has been rooted in ignorance of its virtues and its true functions. Welfare can be good for you, even if you never use it. But higher wages, while good for workers, are not so welcomed by their employers.

Which brings me to the explanation I want to offer for why welfare was reformed in 1996. Beginning with the New Deal, in the twentieth century the federal government was increasingly willing to intrude in the private sector with progressive taxation, protections for workers and unions, expansive social welfare programs, and massive new schemes of industrial and financial regulation. As a result, poor and working people fared increasingly well: wages rose and poverty declined. Profitability also declined, however, and business and the corporate classes, feeling under assault, responded and organized, at first quite loosely, to regain influence in politics. They funded lobbying firms, public relations departments, political action committees, and, especially important for our purposes, sophisticated Washington, D.C.–based think tanks to help them advance their cause with Congress, the executive branch, the media, and the public. There were many targets, and welfare was only one among them, but it was an important one. First, welfare violated the basic tenets of capitalist free-market philosophy, and many genuinely believed that it did more harm than good; since these men (and it was mostly men, white men) had little personal experience with poverty, discrimination, or dead-end jobs, they believed that with hard work anyone could advance, and thought welfare an unnecessary crutch. Second, they knew that readily available and moderately generous relief could increase wages (from their perspective, labor costs) because it gave recipients an alternative to low-wage work. Finally, for reasons that had much to do with race, welfare served as a symbolically powerful and politically vulnerable program that could lay the rhetorical groundwork for much broader assaults on more entrenched government interventions in the market on behalf of poor and working people. Over roughly three decades of smart, persistent, well-funded advocacy that began in the early 1970s, these anti-welfare activists achieved their narrow mission by turning public debate away from the questions of poverty that were prominent in the 1960s to the problems of welfare and the state itself, which helped lead eventually to the repeal of AFDC. The broader project of which welfare was only a part is still ongoing—the efforts to undo the social welfare programs that were the hallmark of the twentieth century. This mobilization of the right is the key political narrative of the late twentieth and early twenty-first centuries, a mobilization whose successes are seen not just in the repeal of AFDC but in a host of regulatory, tax, and other regressive policy changes, in a resurgence of the ever more conservative Republican party throughout all levels of the American political system, and in the more corporate-conservative identity of the Democratic party—even, perhaps, in an undoing of the small solidarities in American political culture fostered by the New Deal and the Great Society. In this way, the repeal of AFDC reveals something about a much larger political history, and as Tom Stoppard's *Rosencrantz and Guildenstern Are Dead* gave theater-goers a "worm's-eye view" of *Hamlet,* retelling the tale from the standpoint of two very minor characters and thereby showing us something new about the prince himself, I want to use an examination of the battles against the relatively modest interventions of welfare to give us a worm's-eye view of this larger and more threatening class war.

But these twentieth-century events are only part of the story, for this "unprecedented"[5] assault on American poor relief was not unprecedented at all. It has happened before.

In the wake of the depression of 1873, to respond to challenges posed by the industrialization of the nation, to help alleviate the misery increasingly concentrated in the growing cities, which were full to overflowing with migrants from rural regions of the United States and immigrants from other nations, and to defuse the threat of these "dangerous classes," cities undertook large expansions in their programs of public relief for the poor and unemployed. Simultaneously, as the industrial corporation took form and grew more powerful, states and, increasingly, the federal government were showing themselves newly willing to regulate and restrict its activities and would, from time to time, for various reasons, align themselves with a growing, angry, insistent, and oftentimes violent labor movement. In response, business organized to help secure and increase its power. One of their targets was poor relief, because in addition to it being anathema to them, they found that it allowed workers the ability to decline their offers of what was often very low-wage and dangerous work. They sought to influence public opinion and public policy, and one of the ways in which they did so was through what they called Charity Organization Societies, a very early kind of think tank. The arguments elites used about the dangers of poor relief and the harm it caused the poor as well as the working and middle classes effectively portrayed their narrow class concerns as matters for the public good. And thanks to some three decades of effort, poor relief was ended or cut back in almost 80 percent of large American cities.

Taking these events together, the claim I make in the following pages is that welfare was "reformed" in the Gilded Age and in our New Gilded Age not because relief was corrupt or wasteful, not because the public demanded it, not because a better means of assisting the poor was contemplated, but because of the successful campaigns waged by organized and determined actors who were advancing their own narrow interests. During these periods of profound economic transformation, they used similar arguments to make ending or restricting relief seem an act of compassion, not of cruelty, thus giving political viability and moral legitimacy to their self-serving cause. Such propaganda was disseminated through similar kinds of organizations, Charity Organization Societies in one era and think tanks in another, that functioned as mediating institutions, linking their funders, the media, and the political system. Those funders, business elites who stood to benefit from such campaigns and who continued their financial support as the campaigns achieved success, were behaving rationally and intended these results. While they remained mostly behind the scenes during these battles, their investments allowed ostensibly neutral intellectuals with decidedly Victorian sensibilities to take the stage, reformers who helped, sometimes wittingly, sometimes not, obscure their patrons' economic goals with moral rhetoric; that moral interpretation surely resonated with these business and professional men, but they could identify an economic interest as well, which in moments of candor they would admit, as we will see.

Reformers achieved significant results. Though it would occasionally fail, in the late nineteenth century anti-relief agitation helped lead to the widespread reduction or elimination of "lavish" *outdoor relief* (what we now call welfare) in cities throughout the country, an impressive outcome given organized charities' relatively limited budgets and the opposition they faced, especially in their early years. Late-twentieth-century reformers achieved even more striking successes than their predecessors, rolling back the "explosion" in welfare rolls and elements of the "failed War on Poverty," in part because they had greater resources, well-cultivated influence with politicians, and easy access to a national media, and because, ironically, the New Deal had centralized poor relief, thereby narrowing their target. Their achievement is all the more impressive given the vast body of social science research that gave the lie to their claims. The enactment of similar kinds of work-enforcing policies had similar results, with need among the poor increasing, along with their dependence on the low-wage labor market, public costs rising, and private contractors reaping the financial rewards. These campaigns simultaneously sent a stern message to all marginal and disgruntled workers about the price of idleness, for as Frances Fox Piven and Richard A. Cloward wrote a generation ago, "to demean and punish those who do not work is to exalt by contrast even the meanest labor at the meanest wages."[6] Moreover, such efforts helped to delegitimize a range of government interventions on behalf of the poor and working classes. Both campaigns were battles in much larger wars about the proper role of the state and the legitimacy of its interference in the free market, wars undertaken in response to the very real gains made by poor and working people in the post–Civil War and post–World War II periods.

There is one key difference between these reform epochs. While many charity reformers in the Gilded Age helped convince their cities to abolish or restrict public poor relief and to shift the burden of care to the voluntary sector, as their counterparts have done more recently, they later admitted that they had failed and that they had misdiagnosed the problem. In the aftermath of the 1893 depression, many cities found themselves overrun with the newly unemployed, a growing, angry, dangerous class desperate for food, fuel, and work. Cities found that voluntary charitable efforts were insufficient to confront the need they faced and more expensive than the public relief they had replaced. In fact, it turns out that many campaigns were not battles against public relief at all, but were instead battles against the patronage-driven private relief that rose in the wake of public relief abolition—Gilded Age reformers often fought against the ill effects of *privatization*; and the lessons that "compassionate conservatism" founder Marvin Olasky, President George W. Bush, and other Victorian revivalists would have us draw from this era about the successes of "faith-based" charity are entirely unsupported by the historical record. By the end of the nineteenth century many people who had once been anti-relief activists petitioned local governments to intervene and reinstate relief; many reformers softened or abandoned their opposition to public aid and waged new campaigns to expand public relief and to increase government regulation of the turbulent economy through efforts we now identify with the Progressive Era—struggles for unemployment insurance; state pensions for widows; sanitation, housing, and workplace reforms; controls on monopoly capital; regulations to govern manufacturing; and more. The failure of Gilded Age reforms helped lead to these very different kinds of reforms, reforms that in turn laid the foundation for the New Deal and the construction of the American welfare state. From 1893 through to the early 1970s, moral understandings of poverty largely gave way and were replaced by a more complicated science of social problem solving that took seriously the industrial, environmental, political, and economic causes of deprivation. It is this one-hundred-year-old transformation in understandings of the roots of misery and a tenuous political truce about the proper role of government that the late-twentieth-century mobilization against relief has sought to undo; we have returned to the Gilded Age and readopted a once-discredited discourse in which poverty is a moral failure, aid to the poor itself causes poverty, and government efforts to ameliorate suffering exacerbate it.

The point is not that because comparable reforms failed then, they must fail now, but rather that we are building reforms upon the same assumptions that governed late-nineteenth-century reforms, in much the same way, for many of the same reasons, and the outcome of those similar struggles should inform current debate. More than that, viewing events through the worm's eye can tell us about more than just poor relief or welfare. It can remind us that history does not move only forward and that the advance of time does not always bring with it progress. This is worth emphasizing, for with some few exceptions,[7] those who have devoted their efforts to understanding welfare (cash and in-kind assistance of goods and services to the very poor) and the welfare state (broader protections such as old-age pensions, unemployment and disability insurance, and government-funded health care) have discussed them in evolutionary, progressive, forward-moving terms.[8] From the grudging poorhouse relief of the colonial period to the broader gains of the Progressive Era, then the New Deal and the Great Society, a common story line suggests that over time, and especially in the twentieth century, poor and working people steadily gained protections from the state.[9] It is a tale of progress. But how then do we account for the fact that twice in American history this evolutionary process seems to have moved backward, from 1873 to 1898, when thirty-nine of the fifty largest American cities cut back or eliminated their public cash-relief programs, and from 1973 to 1996, when the campaign that culminated in "welfare reform" finally repealed the New Deal's federal-state guarantee of poor relief to all eligible people? Perhaps an examination of these policy changes can tell us something about how democratic governments can act against the best interests of the majority with relative impunity.

Perhaps it can teach us lessons about the operations of class in the supposedly classless United States and draw attention to sometimes-neglected corners of the American political system and the ways in which influence is exerted behind the scenes. Finally, perhaps it can show that despite the association of propaganda with totalitarian regimes, it is an essential tool of the powerful in democratic polities too, who can use it to deceive a populace into supporting policies that are against their best interests but are in the best interests of an elite minority. This last might seem a particularly timely lesson.

I

Same As It Ever Was

If we can restore the language of morality, reviving such words as illegitimacy and promiscuity, we may also be able to revive such concepts as discipline and self-discipline. Perhaps we may even be able
to revive such archaic ideas as virtue and vice. And if we can remoralize social discourse, we may be able to remoralize social policy.

—Gertrude Himmelfarb,
Harvard Journal of Law and Public Policy, 1996

Too often it will be found that the root of the evil lies in the characters of the poor themselves,—in habits of laziness, shiftlessness, intemperance, or vice, which have reduced them to an irregular and
meagre subsistence. To such people, almsgiving, far from being the
universal remedy, is a simple aggravation of the trouble. For demand and supply are the law of life as well as of trade. In Nature's
economy, strength tends to appear where it is called for; and strength
will degenerate into weakness when another supplies the needs one
could and should supply for one's self. When, therefore, the lazy
man finds that he gets on just as well without working, he will be less
and less inclined to work. So of intemperance; for the drunkard who
finds that, when he fails to provide for his family, his prosperous
neighbors do, is to place a direct premium on drunkenness. Why
should such people care to work to buy their children food and
clothes, when they can get them for nothing for the asking? Moreover, alms to the improvident do not even relieve their material
needs, for by no device can we permanently stand between a man
and his own character. Others can never take as good care of him as
he could take care of himself; and indiscriminate charity is by its very

> nature insufficient and uncertain,—it first encourages a man to be
> idle, and then keeps him on the verge of starvation.
>
> —Mrs. Glendower Evans,
> *National Conference on Charities and Corrections,* 1889

> This we commanded you, that if any would not work, neither
> should he eat.
>
> —St. Paul, 2 Thessalonians 3:10

On September 15, 1995, U.S. secretary of health and
human services Donna Shalala delivered to President
William Jefferson Clinton a study predicting that the
welfare reform legislation being considered by the Senate
would drive over one million American children into poverty.[1]
Less than one year later, on August 22, 1996, Clinton, whose
1992 election campaign famously vowed to "end welfare as we
know it," signed the Personal Responsibility and Work Opportunity Reconciliation Act of 1996 (PRA), legislation in some re-
spects harsher than the bill Shalala had warned him about.[2]
"The current welfare system is fundamentally broken," he said,
"and this may be our last best chance to set it straight." The PRA
repealed the New Deal's Aid to Dependent Children program,
imposed new work requirements upon relief recipients, made
public assistance harder to get, and enacted time limits on its receipt. Senator Daniel Patrick Moynihan of New York, who had
advocated work requirements since the 1960s, nonetheless
called this new law "the most regressive and brutal act of social
policy since Reconstruction."[3] One critic wrote: "We know how
welfare reform will turn out . . . wages will go down, families
will fracture, millions of children will be more miserable than
ever."[4] Yet by 2002, on the eve of the first efforts to reauthorize
the PRA, national rolls had been cut in half and there were

fewer people on welfare than at any time in three decades. Official national poverty rates, even among children, even among African American children, had declined to record or near-record lows. A majority of former welfare recipients had entered the workforce. When reintroducing a reauthorization bill in early 2003, by which time relief rolls had fallen 60 percent from their peak in 1994, California representative Bill Thomas crowed: "Welfare reform has been a huge success. Work is up, dependence and poverty are down and hopes are brighter for the future."[5] Political scientist Lawrence Mead, like many others, noted with satisfaction: "Little evidence of hardship has surfaced."[6] Welfare reform has been widely proclaimed a success.

Some observers have been struck by the similarities between these late-twentieth-century American reforms and the English Poor Laws, especially the harsh New Poor Law of 1834.[7] That comparison can be revealing: inspired by the eighteenth-century writings of Parson Thomas Malthus and his belief that poor relief subsidized the uncontrolled reproduction of the lower classes and protected the poor from the consequences of their own actions, the New Poor Law sought to abolish relief in industrializing Britain and relegate care for the "able-bodied" poor to the workhouse, where they might learn diligence, restraint, and independence, goals much like those of more recent policy events, it is true. But we need not go quite so far back in history or cross the Atlantic to find antecedents. Between 1874 and 1900 one-fourth of the fifty largest American cities (and many smaller ones as well) abolished welfare ("outdoor relief," or "out relief," they called it); one-third reduced their rolls and relief expenditures; and one-fifth offered only in-kind aid like food or coal, but no more cash. Most imposed a new "work test" as a condition for relief, which even to the most "deserving" was given sparingly, if at all. Reformers claimed that no harm had come to the poor. As Levi L. Barbour of Detroit said in 1891: "Quite a number of our large cities provide no outdoor relief,

and their statistics fail to reveal more suffering than exists in other cities which provide a large and yearly-increasing fund for that purpose."[8] Poorhouse populations did not swell, street begging was eradicated, and the moral tone of the cities was improved, they observed with pleasure. By the early 1890s reform was proclaimed a success, just as it would be a century later.

These Gilded Age assaults on poor relief offer a more apt comparison than the English case, for while the resemblance between the Personal Responsibility Act and the Poor Law is real, its source is indirect: it was nineteenth-century American charity reformers such as the formidable Josephine Shaw Lowell, Rev. Stephen Humphreys Gurteen, and Children's Aid Society founder Charles Loring Brace who, long before the PRA, adopted and adapted the principles and programs of the Poor Law to suit Gilded Age America. Lowell even proclaimed the grim *Report of the Royal Poor Law Commission,* which led to the English reforms, "probably the most instructive historical document in existence which relates to pauperism" and devoted her 1884 book *Public Relief and Private Charity* to quoting it at length, extolling its virtues, and demonstrating how its features could be applied in urban America.[9] The Poor Law–influenced ideas espoused by Gilded Age reform leaders and the policies they helped enact would then, much later, serve as models for Marvin Olasky, Newt Gingrich, Charles Murray, and other leaders of the more recent reform movement; among our modern anti-welfare moralists, only historian Gertrude Himmelfarb would find occasion to draw explicitly on English policy. It is from these American Victorians that we have gained our current thinking about poor relief policy; it is from this Gilded Age experience that our New Victorians have borrowed, often quite consciously. That is why there is the faint whiff of Poor Law practice and philosophy in the PRA. The Poor Law first struck American shores not in 1996 but in the nineteenth century, and if we are going to look to the past for insight into contemporary politics and policy making, and in this case I think that we should, then we should first turn our attention to the neglected welfare history of Gilded Age America and not to more distant, foreign events.

TWO GILDED AGES

A comparison of these two late-century reform movements is important because they mark the only sustained and successful assaults on poor-relief programs in all of American history.[10] But it is more than that, for there is something similar about the context in which they took place, something peculiar about these two historical epochs. History does not, of course, repeat itself—although we might remember Karl Marx's warning that history *is* repeated, first as tragedy, then as farce—and much changed in American politics, society, and economy between the Gilded Age and our New Gilded Age; any historical analogy is treacherous, always imprecise and can obscure more than it reveals. The former was a period of nascent industrialism marked by economic and political conditions that were fundamentally different from the latter postindustrial age. The federal government had no relief role in the first era (even states were peripheral players), while debates about the relative roles of states and the federal government were central to our recent reforms.[11] And the late nineteenth century was a period of widespread, often violent protest from workers and poor people demanding that government give them relief or, more commonly, work and higher wages. In the last quarter of the twentieth century, by contrast, and especially during debate over the PRA, poor people and their potential allies were mostly passive. The list could readily be expanded, but suffice it to say that circumstances were different.

Nonetheless, the ends of the nineteenth and twentieth centuries had much in common, as author Kevin Phillips has been at pains to point out. Both eras were marked by the dominance of laissez-faire philosophy and anti-government politics, large-scale economic and corporate restructuring and consolidation, massive tax cuts, a fragile labor movement under attack, concentrated wealth, high individual and corporate debt, and a speculative finance bubble.[12] Both ages saw record influxes of immigrants, many of whom arrived to work long hours in dangerous jobs for low wages. For most families, no male breadwinner's salary was sufficient, so women (and in the late nineteenth century, children) typically worked too. Prison populations exploded, teeming with poor immigrant men in the late nineteenth century and poor black and Hispanic men in the twentieth. The Supreme Court concerned itself with limiting national power over states and protecting private property from public responsibility, while the Congress attended to questions of monetary policy, tariffs, and civil service reform in the late nineteenth century, and budget policy, trade agreements, and campaign finance reform in the late twentieth. In these eras of divided government, in which one political party rarely controlled both the Congress and the presidency, complaints grew that the parties were indistinguishable and beholden to the same corporate interests. Note this stanza from U.M. Fisk's "The Plutocrat's Jubilee," published in the *American Nonconformist* in 1894:

> *We own all the money—we will own the land.*
> *The Courts and the Congress are at our command.*
> *Our fortunes have gone up like beautiful rockets*
> *We've the Dems and Republicans both in our pockets;*
> *And to please the fool people, we make our salam,*
> *And let them choose either—we don't give a damn!*[13]

It sounds curiously like something *The Nation*'s "deadline poet," Calvin Trillin, could have written in the early twenty-first century. And never mind the odd parallels between the contested presidential elections of 1876 and 2000.

But the most startling similarity is surely the economic inequality of both periods. In 1890, the wealthiest 12 percent of the population possessed 86 percent of all wealth, and the top 2 percent earned 50 percent of all income.[14] In 1999, the top 10 percent of the population possessed 71.8 percent of all wealth (while the wealthiest 1 percent owned 40.1 percent), and the top 1 percent earned 50.4 percent of all income. In 1976, by contrast, the wealthiest 1 percent owned 19.9 percent of all wealth.[15] The only other time in which wealth was as concentrated as these two periods was in 1929, just prior to the stock market crash.[16] Cities especially revealed the stratification of American society, from the vast mansions of the Vanderbilt set to the squalid, crowded slums of Five Points, or think more recently of dot-com millionaires' mammoth new Silicon Valley houses while homelessness reached record levels.

Others before me have noted the extremes of the late nineteenth and twentieth centuries. The Nexis news database, for one crude but suggestive measure, records from just 1995 to 1997, the years surrounding the PRA, hundreds of stories in major American newspapers that explicitly compared the 1990s to the Gilded Age, in articles about immense mergers, growing corporate power, ineffectual antitrust laws, robber barons and Bill Gates, old and new mugwumps, regressive tax policies, and tariff or trade policy wars. One article compared House Speaker Newt Gingrich to President McKinley's cunning strategist Mark Hannah and, alternately, to the nineteenth century's most influential social Darwinist, William Graham Summer; others reported on lavish parties, extravagant new restaurants, and the grand new houses of the twentieth century that made Gilded Age Newport mansions "look like servants quarters."[17] The *New Yorker* later published an anthology of turn-of-the-twenty-first-century articles from its pages titled simply *The New Gilded Age*. And *plutocracy* returned quietly to our political vocabulary.

This is more than superficial likeness. Both are pivotal eras of systemic change: the late nineteenth century marked the full flowering of American industrialization, and the late twentieth century the end of that era and the burgeoning of a (still-evolving) postindustrial economy. At the heart of both was a struggle to redefine the legitimate role of the state and to redraw the lines separating economic and political power, separating the public from the private: as political economist William Tabb wrote, "Globalization has put pressure on workers the same way the emergence of the national economy did a century earlier. These transformations, as capitalism moves into new stages of its development, are profoundly unsettling."[18] Or, as Henry George wrote in 1879, "The 'tramp' comes with the locomotive, and almshouses and prisons are as surely the marks of 'material progress' as are costly dwellings, rich warehouses, and magnificent churches."[19] Grand rewards for the few came with new miseries heaped upon the many, and the concentration of capital and the rise in power of those who controlled it enabled late-nineteenth-century corporations to extract and acquire new authority and legal privilege without the obligations that had previously attended them, as it does again today.[20] That new freedom from government and over labor was neither inevitable nor an inevitably "efficient" outcome, as business historian Alfred Chandler would have it; it was the result of a contest in which the private prevailed over the public (until, beginning in the Progressive Era, those gains were rolled back, controls were imposed, and the balance of power was shifted, for a time).[21]

RHETORIC OF REFORMS

Regimes seeking to limit the disruptive potential of such division must either repress dissent or disarm it; totalitarian dictatorship or military rule are means to maintain such injustice, but to sustain (and exacerbate) such aristocratic class division in a putatively classless, democratic society is more complicated, and more discreet forms of control are required.[22] Those with wealth and power who sought to protect their status and enlarge their gains needed, among other things, some cohesive rationale, a dominant story that could explain the need for what might seem to be unjust and undemocratic outcomes. "Trickle-down economics" was one such story. Reformers who sought to roll back the already limited aid available to poor people created another kind of story, one in which relief did not reduce poverty but caused it, one in which the roots of need were moral, not industrial, one in which failure was the fault of the individual alone. There was less need for such elaborate public justifications from the 1930s to the 1970s because American society was less evidently split: the booming post–World War II economy distributed its bounty so that wages and living conditions of working people and the poor improved rather steadily and the privileged classes seemed willing (if grudgingly so) to share their wealth, even at the expense of their net income or corporate profits.[23] Not so in the Gilded Ages. The privileged fought more aggressively to increase their relative wealth and power; thanks to their efforts economic gains were more unevenly distributed and the immiseration of the many could reasonably be seen to be the price paid for the advancement of the few. Thus, historian Richard Hofstadter explained the Gilded Age rise of social Darwinism—the application of survival-of-the-fittest and natural-selection theories to economics, public policy, and charity—by observing that

> changes in the structure of social ideas wait on general changes in economic and political life. In determining whether such ideas are accepted, truth and logic are less important criteria than suitability to the intellectual needs and preconceptions of

[dominant] social interests. This is one of the great difficulties that must be faced by rational strategists of social change.[24]

These ideas took hold and came to prominence because they served a purpose that fit the times. That industrialist Andrew Carnegie identified himself as Herbert Spencer's "disciple" (it was Spencer, not Darwin, who coined the phrase "survival of the fittest") and that Summer was exceedingly popular among businessmen are measures of the usefulness of such ideas in the Gilded Age and of the assurance they provided: "Successful business entrepreneurs apparently accepted *almost by instinct* the Darwinian terminology which seemed to portray the conditions of their existence," reported Hofstadter. As one Standard Oil lawyer blithely observed, there is poverty only "because nature or the devil has made some men weak and imbecile and others lazy and worthless, and neither man nor God can do much for one who will do nothing for himself."[25] Reformer Josephine Shaw Lowell agreed: "we must start with the fundamental principle that all relief of bodily wants by outsiders is in itself bad," and that to avoid this injury poor relief must be withdrawn and, instead, "paupers and paupers' children may be re-educated and redeveloped into self-respecting men and women," just as Malthus had recommended, just as so many have recently.[26] This is at the center of Charles Loring Brace's *The Dangerous Classes* and the core of his comprehensive reeducation and reacculturation program for children, institutionalized in the Children's Aid Society and made famous by its "orphan trains," which took tens of thousands of poor children, many not orphans at all, and shipped them off to more pastoral settings. Brace, who was a friend of Darwin's, read *Origin of Species* thirteen times.[27]

In the already chaotic mid-nineteenth-century world, the arrival of evolutionary theory shook the foundations of theological thought, but later it served a political function by bridging the gap between laissez-faire ideology, which demanded that the government not interfere in the market, and cultural and religious impulses for social welfare, which required aid to the poor on moral grounds; it was a "scientific" means to recast charity as an immoral intervention, and inaction as the more moral response. As one relief reformer commented, "Harsh as the law of survival of the fittest may appear, it is the law."[28] This may seem like tough love indeed, but it is in the best interest of the poor, and in the interest of society as a whole. Unlike Carnegie, reformers who found homes in nineteenth-century charity organization societies or twentieth-century think tanks were not necessarily acolytes of Spencer or Sumner or Malthus, but they deployed these theories to help formulate a "rationalization of the *status quo*" and an assault on the protections afforded poor and working people.[29]

How much of this rationalization was conscious and how much merely the reflexive, instinctive action of people seeking to justify their privileged place in the world is unclear. Many of those most responsible for constructing the philosophical foundation for anti-relief campaigns likely did believe that they were helping the poor, but as Bronislaw Geremek wrote about the repressive poor-relief policies of the Middle Ages, "History abounds in examples of schemes to thrust happiness upon men by force."[30] Arguing that offering assistance to poor people only deepens their poverty and insisting that economic self-sufficiency, even if it results in suffering, is the route to moral health and a rise from poverty, charity reformers of the late nineteenth and late twentieth centuries sought to thrust happiness upon poor people by taking away what meager cash, food, or fuel was available to them. As Lowell urged: "We should be willing to suffer ourselves and see our poor friends suffer to save them from this fearful permanent evil," the evil of out-relief.[31] Besides, wrote well-born, well-to-do Lowell, "we exaggerate the importance of physical suffering," for "hunger and cold are not so pressing or so sharp as they are represented to be," and we "must accept the statement that there has been nothing eaten for twenty-four hours rather as a fanciful way of describing the general poverty than as the exact truth."[32] Charity organization member Jacob Riis, famous for his photographs of the slums, suggested, "There is enough of real suffering in the homes of the poor to make one wish that there were some effective way of enforcing Paul's plan of starving the drones into the paths of self-support: no work, nothing to eat."[33] The Heritage Foundation's Robert Rector argued that there was no real hunger or poverty in late-twentieth-century America, and besides, any such need could be salutary, a spur to industry.[34] Marvin Olasky somberly reminded us that the word *compassion* is from the Latin, meaning "with suffering."[35]

Suffering is compassion. This is not intuitive, and charity organization societies had to fight hard to convince the public, especially the old-money elites and the churches, of the evils of any almsgiving apart from their proposed system of rigorous investigation and moral education. So too did the modern think tanks and their reformers struggle to overcome the ideas that seemed prevalent by the 1960s: that poverty was a blight on democratic society, that it could be alleviated, and that state intervention was an essential component in doing so. They succeeded, for here we are again, building public policy on unfounded, discredited, racist, and eugenicist social philosophy, unlearning the lessons of the twentieth century. While the rhetoric of reform was elaborate and extended well beyond any simplistic social Darwinism and was not by itself enough to compel the repeal of relief, it was a necessary condition for it. Had policy makers and the public believed what a century of increasingly sophisticated social science has proved true—that poverty is rooted chiefly in industrial and economic causes beyond the control of the poor—then repeal would have been much harder to achieve. What both ages' anti-relief reformers had in common was the insistence that poverty was the result of immoral or unwise behavior, and that remoralizing the poor must be the principal focus of any effective program. It was therefore not the state, business, markets, tax policy, education, discrimination, or any other politically controllable aspect of society that required alteration, and therefore a reorganization of power relations, but the poor themselves.

Late-twentieth-century policy has been built on nineteenth-century knowledge. Hofstadter predicted this, in a way: "A resurgence of social Darwinism . . . is always possible so long as there is a strong element of predacity in society."[36] We have entered that new predatory era. While the policies of the Progressive Era through the New Deal and Great Society generally conceded that poverty was the problem to be addressed and government intervention in the market was to be an integral part of the solution to it, in the Gilded Age and our New Gilded Age, efforts to relieve poverty were the problem and, oddly enough, the cause of poverty itself. The success of the Personal *Responsibility* Act was thus often judged in the press and by policy makers in terms of how many people were driven from the welfare rolls, not by whether their poverty had been reduced or their standard of living improved, just as the charity organization societies proclaimed their effectiveness in their annual reports by demonstrating that with each passing year they offered assistance to fewer people than they had the year before. Dependence and pauperism were the evils to be remedied, not poverty: "the focus must be on changing and saving people,"[37] lectured Gingrich, to find ways to overcome, insisted Mead, the "fundamental incompetence" of poor women.[38]

The sheer futility of trying to help the poor with material aid was a central theme of both eras' reformers and a key component of their brief against relief. Just as journalist Mickey Kaus observed in a 1992 anti-welfare book that "giving people money only gives people money," one writer in 1886 sighed,

"Out-door relief inevitably becomes, in a greater or less degree, a mechanical, hard, and unfeeling grant of codfish, of oatmeal, of potatoes, of coal,—in the worst cases, of money." [39] Consider this from William Slocum's 1892 address to the National Conference on Charities and Corrections (NCCC):

> Indiscriminate almsgiving is a crime against society. It is opposed to the divine order. It saps the very foundation of the self-respecting home. It destroys the best element of true society. It destroys citizenship and those active powers of the human soul that put it in sympathy with the divine ideal . . . almsgiving, while it may, in a way, express charity, has not the essence of charity. [40]

Compare it with this, from a 2000 Heritage Foundation report by Robert Rector, their chief welfare analyst:

> One-way handouts usually hurt those they are intended to help. True charity begins by requiring responsible behavior from the beneficiary as a condition of receiving aid. True charity seeks to generate in the recipient the virtues, commitment, and self-discipline necessary for success in society, rather than passively subsidizing ever-escalating levels of social pathology . . . what is needed is transformation in the realm of ideas, a change in the current philosophical foundations that govern both government and private aid to the poor. [41]

These were hardly new ideas, nor were they unique to these epochs—late-nineteenth- and late-twentieth-century relief antagonists employed tropes with centuries-long pedigrees. Nor is this to suggest that there was no opposition to anti-relief rhetoric, for there were dissenting voices across both eras. But pro-relief ideas and voices did not dominate; it was the vision of relief articulated by Slocum and Rector that set the terms of the

debate, and the reassertion of Gilded Age, Victorian conceptions of charity and poor relief was an explicit goal of many of
our New Victorian moralists and anti-welfare reformers. As
Mead urged in 1994: "Researchers might return to a discourse
about poverty more like that of a century ago," when "debate
chiefly was about the mentality or morality of the poor and how
they might be reformed by special institutions, such as the
work house or the mental hospital."[42] He advocated a "New
Paternalism" that would use the power of the state to compel
upright behavior from the wayward poor, which had much in
common with Rev. Gurteen's agenda of moral reforms pursued
in late-nineteenth-century Buffalo.[43] The Hudson Institute's
Joel Schwartz, writing after the enactment of the PRA, told
readers: "The virtues of diligence, sobriety, thrift, and familial
responsibility were unhesitatingly commended to the poor in
the mid-nineteenth century . . . [and] are actually more appli-
cable today as remedies for poverty than they were when the
moral reformers first espoused them."[44] Murray, whose 1984
polemic *Losing Ground* remained influential into the 1990s debate, and Rector, by most accounts among the greatest influences during the drafting of reform legislation, each found
occasions to refer us back to the supposed golden age of nineteenth-century private charity. Himmelfarb also harkened
back: "contemplating our own society, we may be prepared to
take a more appreciative view of Victorian moralism—of the
'Puritan ethic' of work, thrift, temperance, cleanliness; of the
idea of 'respectability' . . . of the reverence for 'home and
hearth'; of the stigma attached to the 'able-bodied pauper' "
and of the spirit of voluntarism.[45] She argued that only a return
to the traditional virtues—chastity, charity, fidelity, thrift,
work, self-discipline—could keep modern society from spinning apart; by re-creating a sense of shame in receiving relief, as
the English Poor Law did, self-reliance and thus a healthier society would result. And then there is Olasky, who insisted that

in America "during the nineteenth century, a successful war on poverty was waged by tens of thousands of local, private charitable agencies . . . [they were the] platoons of the greatest charity army in American history."[46] His 1992 book *The Tragedy of American Compassion* explicitly encouraged policy makers to emulate the supposed successes of the personal, private, "faith-based" charity of the Gilded Age. "Many lives can be saved," he promised, "if we recapture the vision that changed lives up to a century ago."[47]

That vision is easily identified. As poverty research pioneer and charity organization society member Robert Hunter said: "The sins of men should bring their own punishment, and the poverty which punishes the vicious and the sinful is good and necessary."[48] Nineteenth-century reformers told salacious, cautionary tales about the sinfulness of relief recipients that were made familiar again by Ronald Reagan, who warned us of the welfare queen, lolling about, living her life on the dole, and breeding a nest of predatory, dependent paupers. Said Reagan, "She has eighty names, thirty addresses, twelve social security cards and is collecting benefits on four nonexistent deceased husbands. . . . Her tax-free cash income alone is over $150,000."[49] At the National Conference on Charities and Corrections of 1877, R.L. Dugdale presented a paper on "The Jukes," a multigenerational tribe of degraded, drunken, illegitimate, and licentious paupers who in seventy-five years, he said, had together cost the public well over $1 million. Inspired by the Jukes, at the NCCC the following year Indiana's Oscar McCulloch presented his own study, "Tribe of Ishmael: A Study in Social Degradation." These paupers and their descendants, he claimed, "underrun society like devil-grass." Dugdale and McCulloch lingered on the effects of sex and alcohol with a prurient fascination that seems all too familiar among the New Victorians of the late twentieth century. Here's Senator John Ashcroft, some years before becoming attorney general under

George W. Bush, speaking to celebrate the then-impending welfare reform:

> There is also the story of Ernesto Ventura. He is at least the fourth generation of a welfare family that includes about 80 welfare recipients and takes up nearly $1 million a year annually in welfare funds. . . . At the time of his abuse, his mother was 26, pregnant, and the mother of six children by five different fathers. She was a drug addict supported by welfare.[50]

As part of their efforts to undo relief, many reformers have worked hard to portray welfare recipients as the irredeemable poor, members of a culture of poverty or an underclass, and the connection with Spencer is inescapable: to identify a separate culture of poverty is to define a whole class of the unfit.[51] It is the inability or unwillingness of the ghetto poor to change culturally transmitted pathologies—as anthropologist Oscar Lewis described some of them, "present-time" orientation, early sexual activity, female-centered families, lack of impulse control—that is the chief cause of their high rates of violence, out-of-wedlock births, welfare dependency, and poverty. This culture-of-poverty notion was widely promulgated in the late twentieth century,[52] and as popularized by Ken Auletta's *The Underclass* and even Michael Harrington's *The Other America,* it became rhetorical shorthand for describing an immobile, black, dangerous, intergenerational ghetto class nourished by welfare payments.[53] Whether there is a culture of poverty and what its functions might be for the urban poor are ultimately irrelevant here—the *idea* of a permanent underclass is useful for opponents of relief, just as Spencer and Malthus are useful, for it places the solution to such problems outside of government intervention.[54]

This stigmatization of the poor was elaborated in even bolder ways. For Hunter and for so many others, pauperism, "like parasitism," was "a disease of character," a natural illness that marked the poor as a special class of the sick. Disease metaphors were common; historian Kenneth Kusmer called it "the rhetoric of contagion."[55] Wrote Buffalo Charity Organization Society General Secretary Frederick Almy in 1900, "Pauperism is far too contagious a disease to be tolerated with safety. When once contracted, it becomes rapidly virulent, and the epidemic spreads from room to room in a tenement and from house to house in a street."[56] Slocum told the 1892 Conference on Charities that "pauperism is a disease . . . it must be destroyed."[57] Moreover, "the presence in the community of certain persons living on public relief, has the tendency to tempt others to sink to their degraded level," for it is "infectious," observed Lowell.[58] For Social Gospel proponent Washington Gladden, relief was a "cancer that is eating out the heart of our social morality."[59] Brace wrote, "When this disease of pauperism is fairly mingled in the blood of children, their condition is almost hopeless."[60] We have again sought to understand poverty or, more typically, welfare receipt as symptomatic of disease with what Sanford Schram and Joe Soss call a discourse of "disorder, sickness and infantilism"; to take an extreme example, in the wake of the PRA one welfare office prescribed the antidepressant Prozac for its applicants, offering a pharmaceutical "cure" for welfare dependence.[61]

Or as Almy said, "Alms are like drugs, and are as dangerous; they create an appetite which is more harmful than the pain which they relieve."[62] George Gilder observed many decades later that "excessive welfare hurts its recipients, demoralizing them or reducing them to an addictive dependency that can ruin their lives."[63] Economist William Niskanen in the *Cato Journal* called relief a "narcotic" (as FDR had decades earlier).[64] For Samuel Bishop relief was a "poison."[65] Moses King's 1893 *Handbook of New York* proudly reported, "Thousands of active philanthropists are daily saving New York from the poison of its depraved and degraded humanity and the venom of pauperized peasant immigration."[66] More recently, George Vaillant offered "a psychiatric viewpoint" by which he described poverty as both an addiction and a disease, and proposed various treatments to cure it, and would no doubt be pleased with the pharmaceutical treatments described above.[67] These understandings of poverty have precedence even in law; in 1837 the U.S. Supreme Court in *City of New York v. Miln* allowed New York to bar poor people from the city, citing "the moral pestilence of paupers." Not until 1941 in *Edwards v. California* would they overturn that decision, arguing, "We do not think that it will now be seriously contended that because a person is without employment and without funds he constitutes a 'moral pestilence.' "[68] But contended it would be again.

Recipients were compared unfavorably to animals, too, for "as vultures flock to the carrion, drunken and shiftless paupers crowd the cities having the largest poor-fund. They are all entitled, they think, to a share, and they want it."[69] Alfred Crozier of Grand Rapids said in 1897, "Instead of finding employment for the poor woman who begs for temporary help, you give her alms. It is easier, and perhaps cheaper. But you have poisoned her soul. Her children are now taught lies by their mother, and sent out under fictitious names to forage on the public. You have converted that once happy though poor home into a nest of paupers, breeding like vipers, and multiplying their accursed species."[70] Barbour told the NCCC, "A swarm of bees, it is said, when removed to a tropical clime, learn that winter never comes, and soon cease to lay up a store of honey. So the pauper, learning that there is a fund for his support, basks in the sunshine of constant expectation, neither toiling nor spinning."[71] This remains familiar. During welfare reform debate in the House of Representatives, John Mica of Florida, arguing that "we have upset the natural order. . . . We have created a system of dependency," suggested that the logic of signs posted in his state that commanded "Do Not Feed the Alligators" might be applied to welfare and its recipients. Later that day Representative Barbara Cubin of Wyoming again emphasized the dangers in feeding wild animals, the harm that came from her state's "wolf welfare program," and the similar danger of interfering with the natural order and creating dependence by offering welfare to the poor.[72]

Efforts to isolate and stigmatize the poor—and thereby discourage the middle class from identifying with them—have taken more predictable forms as well. Race pervaded late-twentieth-century discussions of welfare just as fears of the foreign-born permeated relief debates in the nineteenth century. As Murray wrote: "AFDC evolved into the *bête noire* of the social welfare system. By the fifties it had become embarrassingly, outrageously clear that most of these women were not widows. Many of them had not even been married. Worst of all, they didn't stop having babies after the first lapse. They kept having more. This had not been part of the plan. The most flagrantly unrepentant seemed to be mostly black, too."[73] Similarly, in 1876 the first of many papers claiming that it was immigrant children who most burdened public coffers was presented at the national charities conference, while Theodore Roosevelt Sr. recommended a year later that relief funds be reallocated to ship the "generally shiftless" and improvident Negro back to the South.[74] Between 1880 and 1892, the New York State Board of Charities forcibly repatriated 1,879 European paupers, at a cost of $41,000.[75] It was a renewed terror of overpopulation by the unfit.

The portrayal of welfare mothers as sexually rapacious beings reproducing a brood of future thugs, all with the help of the public purse, was another shared theme: "The paramount goal of welfare reform," observed Rector, "was to reduce illegitimacy and restore marriage."[76] In fact, one of the proclaimed welfare goals of Gingrich's Contract with America was to "discourage illegitimacy and teen pregnancy by prohibiting welfare to minor mothers," and the very first words of Title I of the PRA declared, "Marriage is the foundation of a successful society."[77] Murray had long advocated "group homes" for unwed pregnant teens, and famously wrote, "Illegitimacy is the central social problem of our time, and . . . its spread threatens the underpinnings of a free society . . . the main reason for scrapping welfare is to reduce the number of babies born to single women."[78] As American moralist William Bennett told the House Ways and Means Committee in 1995, "Welfare may not cause illegitimacy, but it does make it economically viable. It sustains it and subsidizes it. And what you subsidize, you get more of. Welfare is illegitimacy's economic life-support system."[79] Traditional Values Coalition lobbyist Andrea Sheldon threatened during the welfare reform debate that if any bill didn't squarely address illegitimacy, "then you don't have anything."[80]

These are not new goals of American poor relief policy. Some Philadelphia public officials as early as 1827 complained that it was unmarried mothers who were the principal users of relief, and in 1835 the city briefly eliminated pensions to women because they "fostered dependence and vice and discouraged women from taking up wage labor jobs outside their homes."[81] Lowell wrote later when urging the passage of a state law that would have committed any poor woman with two illegitimate children to a reformatory that "the very character of the women must be changed. . . . The unhappy beings we are speaking of need, first of all, to be taught to be women; they must be induced to love that which is good and pure, and to wish to resemble it; they must learn all household duties; they must learn to enjoy work; they must have a future to look forward to, and they must be cured, both body and soul, before they can be safely trusted to face the world again."[82] Hysteria over sex and marriage traveled a line from Malthus and Lowell to Murray and Gilder and the Heritage Foundation.[83] But while such rhetoric has focused upon the dependence of women, especially black or "foreign" women, it is their *independence,* from men and from low-wage work, that seems to be the real target.

The insistence upon work in lieu of relief is at the core of reformers' worldview, tethered to the promise of upward mobility. Stories like those in the novels of Horatio Alger loomed large in the relief narratives of the late nineteenth and late twentieth centuries, demonstrating that any industrious young man could rise to join the better classes and reinforcing the idea that welfare was unnecessary, an enabler of immoral and irresponsible behavior. Alger was a key figure in Newt Gingrich's videotaped college course, *Renewing American Civilization,* the myth updated to include Oprah Winfrey, Clarence Thomas, and Arnold Schwarzenegger as paragons of the boundless opportunity available to the diligent and virtuous.[84] Alger's novels do not live up to the myth of them, however, for it is not hard work alone that enables the poor street urchin to rise to commanding heights. Rather, improbable coincidence and blind luck, an almost mystical and magical luck, are always central elements.[85] American class mobility in the nineteenth century has often been exaggerated, and despite the much-touted example of Carnegie and his rise from poverty to power broker, he was atypical. Corporate and political leaders were, with rare exception, native-born, Protestant, of British heritage, and the sons of businessmen or professionals; between 1880 and 1890, at best 12 percent of Boston's blue-collar workers advanced to white-collar jobs.[86] Yet the myth persists, and American mobility continues to be exaggerated. The United States, for example, today offers less income mobility than do Germany, France, the United Kingdom, Denmark, Finland, and Sweden. Our exit rate from poverty is among the lowest of advanced nations, with a substantially higher likelihood that those who do escape will return within five years. The typical low-wage worker in an advanced European economy earns over 40 percent more than he or she would in the United States, while in 1998 only a Portuguese worker was likely to work more hours than an American. Over 26 percent of American workers earned poverty-level wages in 1999, and American poverty rates continue to rank the highest among OECD nations.[87] The Alger cult, like any effective ideology, like the rest of the rhetoric of reform, obscured the reality of the world we inhabited then and obscures the world we inhabit now, a world in which, for many, hard work does not offer an escape from poverty.[88]

But this rags-to-riches mythology was essential to the claims of reformers. If we believe that there is truly equality of opportunity in America, then any inequality of outcomes must be a problem of individual failure, and government interference is inappropriate favoritism. In such a world, government can only be a neutral arbiter by refusing to intervene, allowing the marketplace (of politics, of ideas, of economy) to decide the rightful, deserving victors. Diligence alone is salvation, or as Gilder put it, "The only dependable route from poverty is always work, family and faith."[89] Like so much anti-relief philosophy, the relentless focus upon the individual and her supposed moral failure distracts attention from the much more powerful forces and actors that limit such mobility to the few. Those who do nonetheless overcome such formidable obstacles are then held out as exemplars, never far from the photo op when a politician celebrates reform.

Contemporary anti-relief reformers still hold tight to these ideas. Mead conceded that work may be difficult to obtain, "dirty," and offer few rewards to poor people with little education and few marketable skills, yet he nonetheless insisted that "employment is a school of virtue" and has argued that "poverty may be due not so much to a lack of opportunity, as to a lack of enforcement of social norms such as the work ethic."[90]

He noted elsewhere, "Reluctantly, policymakers have begun to accept that work must be enforced as are other civilities such as obedience to the law or tax payment . . . the solution to the work problem lies in *obligation,* not in freedom. . . . The great question is how to get more of the employable poor to participate in the economy, in any kind of job, not how to improve those jobs."[91] Olasky has made the same argument, that true freedom is hard work, that in the nineteenth century "freedom was the opportunity for a family to escape dire poverty by having a father work long hours and a mother sew garments at home."[92] As Murray has observed, "to sustain [upward] mobility, the United States has depended on the willingness of the poor to make investments—of time, energy, psychic commitment, and money. Because these investments are being made by people with very little to spare in the first place, investing means that an already difficult existence must be made even more difficult."[93] New York mayor Rudolph Giuliani argued that the job centers he proposed to replace welfare offices would transform the city and former welfare recipients, because instead of offering cash or Medicaid or food stamps, "the first thing we try to do is to find you a job, because we really care about you, we really love you and we really understand the human personality a lot better than the people who brought us dependency."[94] As the words over one medieval workhouse proclaimed, *labore nutrior, labore pector:* "by work I am nourished, by work I am punished."[95] In the reformers' lexicon, justice is inaction, obligation is freedom, liberty is responsibility, and work is love.

MISUSES OF PUBLIC OPINION

This late-twentieth-century resurgence of Gilded Age interpretations of and responses to poverty and relief is important, as is the rhetoric used by policy makers and pressure groups, yet the production of policy ideas, the creation of public opinion and the sources of "conventional wisdom" have been absent in most accounts of welfare policy making.[96] Yet without them, our understanding is too limited. Welfare reform did not rise to the top of the national political agenda in the 1990s because "the public demanded policy change," as many analysts have put it.[97] Anti-welfare activists set out decades earlier to alter opinion.[98] They tapped into resonant, almost archetypal ideas about poverty and about poor people, about women, of self-sufficiency and the work ethic, and of ethnic or racial stereo-types, and created with them a rationale, a political logic, a philosophical foundation for their preferred policies. Their arguments were then repeated so often in an environment in which alternative messages were so rare that the public, quite predictably, followed the lead of elites and accepted those arguments as fact.[99] As public opinion expert Robert Shapiro and his colleagues wrote about work requirements, "the public consensus is a broadly sweeping and vague preference in search of a viable policy,"[100] and polls are notorious for the ambivalence and confusion they record, with respondents consistently supporting "aid to the poor" while at the same time opposing "welfare."[101] Growing opposition to the supposed expense of welfare was evident only after Clinton's anti-welfare campaign rhetoric was disseminated, reached its peak when news coverage of the issue peaked, and had already begun to fade by 1997.[102] Nor can we explain nineteenth-century relief withdrawals by saying that "public clamor compelled a change," despite the claims of charity reformers and later historians.[103] To the contrary, public opinion was initially allied against reformers and their charity organization societies and only began to change after their anti-relief campaigns had become widespread and the subject of much laudatory newspaper coverage.[104]

Contrary to another bit of conventional wisdom, politicians can and do ignore public opinion, seeking instead to manipulate it, or prime it, in order to "create the *appearance* of responsiveness . . . to find the most effective means to move public opinion closer to their own desired policies."[105] Public opinion did not drive reform; reform drove public opinion. To be sure, we cannot explain these policy outcomes without describing the specific political circumstances that enabled these reforms to "succeed" when they had failed so often before, but we cannot adequately explain those micro-politics without understanding the ways in which the very context within which reform was debated and understood had been altered.[106] People have *always* been ambivalent about poor relief, after all, and governments have for centuries celebrated work while they blamed the poor and punished their poverty: in the Middle Ages, Venice sentenced those caught begging without a license to imprisonment or public whipping, Rouen required all the dependent poor to identify themselves by wearing yellow crosses on their sleeves, and the gallows were often erected next to the poorhouse to make the link between poverty and punishment unmistakable.[107] Antipathy to public relief and efforts to stigmatize and punish the poor have been documented throughout American history; as I've noted, even Franklin Delano Roosevelt characterized relief as a "narcotic."[108] To point to our "exceptional" and racialized political culture or American opinion aligned against welfare is thus to identify constancy, not change, and to identify public antipathy to welfare as a cause for policy change is therefore illogical. The more useful question, it seems to me, is to ask why it is that only twice have such common sentiments so governed policy making and resulted in a retrenchment of relief.

Part of the answer is that it matters which voices dominate debate. Political scientist Vivien Schmidt, comparing Britain with New Zealand, the Netherlands with Germany, and different regimes within Italy and France, argued that successful modern implementations of regressive welfare policy change have depended upon the use of what she calls "transformative communicative discourse."[109] Effective discourse helped democratically elected government actors "justify policies that go against the immediate or perceived interests of [their] own constituency" to benefit a narrower set of more powerful national or international interests, she found. So too, I argue, for the United States. Such transformative discourse—such rhetoric, such propaganda—is one means by which the institutionalized and entrenched resilience of the modern welfare state can be overcome,[110] allowing the state to rescind benefits without resistance from those who would be harmed.[111] Ideas really do matter, and they were made to matter in similar ways in both Gilded Ages.

Relief reform was not a democratic political response to public dissatisfaction with failed programs. Instead, reformers portrayed their actions as a reaction to public backlash against the "indiscriminate relief" of the 1870s or the "failed War on Poverty" ninety years later. Mead, to take one example of this, asserted, "Controversy about welfare arose because of rising welfare rolls."[112] That is a common claim, but it presumes far too much: it implies that there was only one way to interpret the fact of rising relief rolls, only one possible meaning to attach to the event. But we could imagine other interpretations, other meanings, other ways to understand this fact. Perhaps in noting the expansion of welfare since the late 1960s, which occurred in part because many of the discriminatory practices that had kept eligible black women off the rolls were ended by the Supreme Court, leaders might have concluded that larger welfare rolls more accurately measured true need in the United States, and thereby increased their determination to reduce poverty. Or they might have taken pride in the new racial inclusiveness of government programs that now protected more of the most vulnerable workers from the worst features of the low-wage labor market. Or they might have asked how many in need were still not receiving the benefits for which they were eligible, and set out to enroll them as well. Rising rolls could have been interpreted as a mark of success, not of failure; rising rolls need not have been identified as a political problem and did not necessitate rising antipathy to welfare—that was only one of many possible outcomes. The "fact" of rising rolls had no single independent meaning—such facts do not exist independent of interpretations of them.[113]

None of these or other alternative stories about rising relief rolls came to prominence, of course, and part of my task is to explain why. Public antipathy to welfare, or, to be more precise, the *perception* of public antipathy to welfare, was created. It was created in the latter period by think tanks, foundations, and politicians of both parties with the help of a complicit (if sometimes unknowingly complicit) mass media, and in the former period by the charity organization societies, the chambers of commerce, sympathetic politicians, and partisan newspapers. Reformers then pointed to such opinion as one justification for enacting their proposed policy changes. Relief reform was in part the result of a successful propaganda campaign, the outcome of an effort to sell ideas to the public and, more importantly, to policy makers, about how the most effective means of assisting poor people was not to extend aid to them but quite the reverse—to cut off public aid and compel work. The arguments used to justify relief withdrawal—that giving cash, food, or shelter to poor, hungry, or homeless people would only impoverish, injure, and debase them—have always had adherents. These ideas have always been taken seriously by some, but never by so many. Never have they so formed the basis for public policy as they did in the late nineteenth and late twentieth centuries. But whatever its failings, and they are legion, poor relief, by setting a floor for wages and by allowing some, for a time, to refuse low-wage work, is a boon not only to those who receive it but to all low- to midrange workers. This is the dirty little secret of welfare.[114] Antirelief activists succeeded, in both eras, in convincing the working classes that they were being exploited, funding expensive welfare out of their own pockets, and that it was against their own best interests to do so. It's an old story, pitting one subordinate class against another to better secure power, but no less effective for its familiarity.

2

Rise of the Reformer

Ideas have consequences only when they are connected to action.

—Paul Weyrich, founder,
The Heritage Foundation

Although they are lead actors in my story, late-nineteenth-century anti-relief reformers were supporting players in a much larger drama: the mobilization of business and professional men to secure their power over a disruptive laboring class and dissuade city governments from intervening in the market on its behalf. Poor relief was the reformers' narrow target, and this chapter examines the creation of charity organization societies, the institutions that would serve as their home. It also describes a similar late-twentieth-century movement by business to roll back the gains that the poor and working classes had made in the post–World War II period, a mobilization that is now well documented.[1] By the late twentieth century an elite minority seemed to want to undo the New Deal and the Great Society and return us to the Gilded Age, to a pre-1900 "night watchman state." While welfare is the focus here, it was not just AFDC that was under assault—major regressive changes were made in the 1990s to the 1933 Glass-Steagall Act, which separated banking and finance; the Telecommunications Act of 1934, which inhibited media monopolies; the estate tax, on behalf of which Vanderbilt once spoke so eloquently; and a host of other progressive tax policies and corporate regulations. (The Bush administration and Congress continued this redistribution.) That the 1990s returned income inequality to pre–New Deal levels is one measure of the movement's success. Welfare reform is another—it marked the repeal of Title IV-A of the Social Security Act of 1935, the very bulwark of the American welfare state. By June 2000, there was a lower percentage of Americans on welfare (2.1 percent) than at any time since 1964 and fewer people receiving benefits (5.7 million) than at any time since 1968.[2] The welfare "explosion" of the late 1960s and early 1970s had been rolled back, just as Gilded Age reformers succeeded in rolling back the relief explosions that came in the wake of post–Civil War depressions. But this time, instead of the charity organization societies and their business benefactors aiding the cause, it was the foundations of Richard Mellon Scaife, Joseph Coors, and Lynde and Harry Bradley and think tanks such as the Heritage Foundation, the Hudson Institute, and the American Enterprise Institute.

THE FIRST THREAT

Insecurity was pandemic: thanks to industrialization, large migrations to the cities, and unpredictable economic cycles, unemployment, poverty, and the demand for assistance increased significantly throughout the 1800s. "If scattered and impressionistic evidence can be trusted," historian Alexander Keyssar cautiously observed in his study of Massachusetts, "this period [1870–1920] probably witnessed a slight overall increase in the incidence of serious deprivation among the unemployed" because of the ways in which urbanization left fewer and fewer people with the means of self-support.[3] Many resisted the changes wrought by this new economy by reporting irregularly to work, moving from job to job, staging shutdowns and slowdowns, drinking at work, and ostracizing or punishing co-workers who worked too fast.[4] Resistance took on more violent and threatening forms, too, especially during the frequent depressions that marked more than half of the last twenty-five years of the century. Little wonder that Nell Painter called her history of the era *Standing at Armageddon.*[5]

Such upheaval and transformation demanded an expanded role from the state. By building infrastructure (canals and roads) and providing public goods (clean water and sewers), by protecting the labor supply (through education or liberal immigration policies), and by suppressing newly created class conflict (by centralizing power, or with recently established police forces, the courts, or militias), government sought to meet the needs of those industrialists and financiers who were making their cities centers of power and wealth. But they also sought to appease workers, who began to look more to government as a countervailing power against capital, and simultaneously expanded aid to the poor and unemployed.[6] Outdoor relief expenditures increased dramatically. In 1835, 40 percent of all relief in New York was provided as "indoor relief" (in poorhouses, asylums, workhouses, or labor colonies); by 1859 that had dropped to 19 percent, with the rest as out-relief in cash, coal, or food. While real per-recipient expenditures declined 60 percent from the 1820s to the late 1850s (as did the average time people spent on relief), *total* expenditures more than doubled. Nationwide, from 1850 to 1860, rolls rose 76 percent. While relief was offered in New York to 1.13 percent of the state's population in 1823, it was offered to 6.8 percent by 1859.[7] Moreover, while indoor relief declined and outdoor relief rose as a percentage of the total aid offered, the share of relief going to the elderly and to children declined, while the share going to less sympathetic unemployed men and to the foreign-born rose.[8] Then, from 1860 to 1870 the total amount New York spent on outdoor relief nearly doubled.[9] By the winter of 1867–68, outdoor relief expenditures in Brooklyn had reached $125,000, causing great outcry in the press.[10] Public out-relief expenditures in Philadelphia increased fivefold from 1830 to 1870, nearly doubling from 1850 to 1870; total expenditures climbed 1,000 percent.[11] Many cities expanded their poor relief even further in response to the depression of 1873–78, straining their budgets while still leaving great needs unmet. Churches, private aid societies, and wealthier individuals complained that they could not meet the demands for assistance they received from the poor masses who could not get aid from the city. Simultaneously, complaints abounded about the "indiscriminate charity," public and private both, that the depression called forth.

When state actions were insufficient to suppress discontent or appease the poor, as they often were, or when those efforts favored the lower classes, private organizations formed, and employers launched a counteroffensive with associations that made weapons of the courts, the military, and the press.[12] Much as late-twentieth-century business interests created and funded an infrastructure designed to influence opinion and policy, as we shall see, so too did Gilded Age reformers. By the 1870s, many elites had begun to form a more unified, "self-conscious" class identity, which enabled them to better mobilize against taxation, against universal male suffrage, and against relief.[13] In 1878, reports Samuel Rezneck, one writer in the *Atlantic Monthly* issued a call for business to implement "a program of positive 'propagandism,' which would profit men of property to spend a million dollars in the next three years for the preparation and circulation of broadsides among country papers, repeating the simple truths on such topics as debt, paper money, economy, and thrift."[14] Whether they heeded this particular call or not, late in the century businesses began that propagandism campaign. Corporations began hiring "publicity experts" to introduce their "facts" into newspaper coverage. Standard Oil, seeking to overcome public criticism, wrote articles that they paid newspapers to publish as objective reporting, and crafted other pieces that appeared, unattributed, as editorials. The Mutual Life Insurance Company paid rates as high as $5 a line for such placements. J.P. Morgan and Company used public relations firms and press agents to secure placement of their carefully crafted articles in papers as part of "its hidden struggle for public support."[15] In the late-century proceedings of the National Conference on Charities and Corrections there is ample evidence that reformers understood that part of their mission was persuasion. When opposing its turn-of-the-century decision to create a committee on legislation, for example, William Folwell noted:

> the office of the Conference is to arouse and lead public sentiment—to create a soil and an atmosphere in which legislative projects may generate and develop spontaneously. The Conference, by engaging in the framing of particular bills, and steering them to passage through legislative bodies, would abandon its wide sphere of influences to drop into narrow grooves of routine. Such associations may be all-powerful as organizations of influence, but weak and ridiculous when they undertake to compass their ends by the employment of power.[16]

As historian Martin Sklar rightly suggested, we might think of early industrial-era corporations not as an interest group but as a social movement that launched its battle for power

> in market and property relations, in the law and jurisprudence, in party politics, in government policy and legislation, in foreign-policy making, and in scholarly modes of thought. Their efforts assumed the organizational forms of trade and civic associations, single-issue groups and committees, reform clubs, electoral party politics, lobbying, publications ranging from newsletters and newspapers to periodicals and books,

and conferences and conventions. . . . Corporate capitalism, that is, had to be constructed.[17]

Gilded Age actors sought ways to use their influence to make rebellious workers even more dependent upon the emergent industrial order. Historian Robert Wiebe confirms that business organizations "formed front organizations through which they conducted their lobbying,"[18] and the charity organization society was born as part of this first "corporate reconstruction of American capitalism," to help resist the losses stemming from and the threats posed by the gains of the lower classes and to combat the "misconception," as one partisan put it, that "capital oppresses labor and seeks to deprive it of its natural rights."[19]

THE BIRTH OF THE COS

One of charity organization's first historians, Frank Dekker Watson, called their creation "a protest against the methods of administration of public outdoor relief then obtaining which was viewed as a tool of unscrupulous politicians, wasteful of the taxpayers' money and pauperizing in its effects. Historically, the administration of public outdoor relief had from the beginning of the movement been foreign to the spirit and methods of charity organization."[20] *Charities Review,* the late-century journal of the New York Charity Organization Society, described the effort this way: charity organization "looks to permanent cure of distress, not to its mere temporary alleviation, and . . . seeks to effect that cure in the only way in which it can be effected, by understanding the disease before attempting to treat it: Charity, like medicine, is hardly an exact science, but the time has gone by when we should try to cure human misery with quackery." Charity organization was determined to apply "scientific" methods to charity: to make assistance to poor people rational, systematic and coordinated. "There must be no sentiment in the matter," Gurteen wrote. "Let the head hold in check the heart."[21] Thus, New York COS Secretary Devine would construct an intricate, evolving typology built upon "seventy-five illustrative cases" to guide his "Friendly Visitors" in determining who should receive what kind of relief, under what circumstances, and for what duration; it testifies to their belief that charity could become a profession with clear laws, articulated principles, and specific solutions to specific problems.[22] The movement has historically been described as either a benevolent if misguided attempt to apply rational principles to charity[23] or a darker effort to control the poorest classes.[24] There is truth in both approaches.

The key principle of the COS was that theirs was to be "charity in its original meaning of 'love,' not charity in its debased meaning of 'alms.' "[25] Its infamous motto, inspired by Octavia Hill of the London COS and first used in the United States by Robert Treat Paine of Boston, was "Not Alms, But a Friend."[26] "Almsgiving and dole giving are hurtful," wrote Lowell, another who was influenced by Hill, "therefore they are not charitable."[27] Cash aid was dangerous, even cruel: it fostered dependency, took away incentives to work, and offered false hope for a better future; it might minimize momentary suffering, but it could never get at the causes of poverty, which were chiefly moral. Charity organization societies urged that relief be administered privately to reduce the power of patronage in relief giving and to lodge its administration in institutions that would better discriminate than government or the churches between the "worthy" and "unworthy" poor.[28] They argued that private charity could offer better assistance than public agencies, with moral uplift in lieu of cash, and do it more cheaply and efficiently. Further, they claimed that private relief affected the recipient differently: "There is not so much cringing, and there is more gratitude,"[29] for "the gift without the giver is not only bare, it is an active agent of injury."[30] In the homes of the poor, Gurteen wrote, one would find "an immorality as deep as its poverty." The solution was not money but "to bring back the rich into such close relations with the poor as cannot fail to have a civilizing and healing influence," offering sympathy, moral education, and what French journalist and Society of St. Vincent de Paul founder Sylvain Bailly in 1830 called the "alms of good advice."[31] Besides, charity organizationists argued, as reformers do again today, public relief inhibits the private spirit of giving.[32]

While these institutions called themselves societies for organizing charity, those most lauded by the NCCC functioned as organizations for denying charity and enforcing work. An 1886 survey of twelve cities showed that only 9 percent of all applicants were deemed worthy of ongoing relief; 25 percent were worthy of temporary relief; 40 percent were judged to be in need of work, not relief; and a full 26 percent were unworthy of any consideration. In this last category often fell those judged intemperate and therefore unsuitable even for enforced work. The NCCC of 1887 reported than an examination of nearly thirty thousand COS cases in twenty-five cities showed that 40 percent of all applicants needed work, not relief.[33] James Hyslop reported that 46 percent of all New York COS applicants in 1892 were deemed unworthy, while the average was 22 percent in Indianapolis from 1882 to 1894.[34] Only as the century neared its close would the presumption fade that work was available to all those without it.

There is an irony at the very heart of the COS's role in relief policy. Public opinion was largely against the COS in its early years. It was characterized as "The Society for the Suppression of Benevolence,"[35] and "The Society for the Paying of Salaries to Philanthropists Who Need Money" by the editor of the *New York Morning Telegraph;*[36] its motto was mocked as "Neither Alms nor a Friend," and the poet John Boyle O'Reilly wrote famously that "organized charity scrimped and iced/in the name of a cautious, statistical Christ."[37] One New York State legislator, frustrated by their influence, called them "extra blue-blooded, finely scented, Puritan-Mayflower-Salem-witchcraft stock."[38] The Buffalo COS complained soon after its founding of "the discouragements" it had, including "the ignorance of our citizens as to its objects and its aims; [and] to the hostility of the official keepers of the public purse, fearing an interference with their prerogatives."[39] Yet some while after the movement launched its years-long argument against relief in the 1870s, fighting to change opinion about the proper roles of public relief and private charity and about the nature of need itself, opinion about the COS and about the urban poor did begin to change.[40] That it did so while COS leaders increasingly questioned the wisdom of their behavioral and moral approach to understanding and "curing" poverty is the irony.

Charity organization was not the innovation many of its advocates claimed. In 1617, St. Vincent de Paul established the Ladies of Charity, women of the upper classes who would visit and comfort the poor, just as the COS's friendly visitors would. As de Paul said, "To send money is good, but we have not really begun to serve the poor till we visit them."[41] Cotton Mather in his 1710 treatise *Bonifacius* admonished that one must visit and comfort the poor, "and if it be needful, bestow your alms upon them," "provided it be done with discretion," and "keep, Sir, a list of 'em."[42] Creating that list—a master file with the names of all who applied for relief from any participating agency—was one of the means by which COSs coordinated relief and ensured that no one sought aid from multiple charities. New York's Society for the Prevention of Pauperism, established in 1817, sought to "uplift the poor" through moral education, and cited "the numerous charitable institutions of the city" (along with ignorance, idleness, intemperance and "the want of correct moral principle") as among the principal *causes* of poverty, just as the COSs would (just as others have more recently).[43] The Associations for Improving the Condition of the Poor (AICPs) that formed in the 1840s ("a long name for a weary task," noted Riis) were launched with similar goals to those that would characterize the COS:[44] they lodged responsibility for poverty in the behavior of poor people, complained that outdoor relief made recipients "compliant troopers in political campaigns," and argued that private relief was more efficient than public.[45] The first AICP emerged in New York after the brutal winter and economic crisis of 1837–38 to limit the "false and dangerous methods of relief" used by the Society for the Prevention of Pauperism and other early relief agencies. It divided the city into twenty-two districts and 278 sections, and assigned visitors to each (mostly wealthy men, in this case) "to help them [the poor] discover those hidden springs of virtue within themselves from which alone their prosperity might flow."[46] While even then there were some attempts to address the environmental aspects of poverty, with attention to housing, pure milk campaigns, and the establishment of public bathhouses, New York AICP founder Robert Hartley had little doubt as to the problem and the remedy: "To remove the evil, we must remove the causes, and these being chiefly moral . . . they admit only moral remedies."[47] The "less-eligibility" principles enshrined in the English Poor Law, which demanded that relief always be less desirable or less eligible than work, were adopted by the AICP. Their *Visitor's Manual* urged that they must "give assistance, both in quantity and quality, inferior, except in case of sickness and old age, to what might be procured by labor."[48] By 1876, there were twenty-nine AICPs built upon the New York model. But like the settlement-house workers to follow, the more AICP visitors encountered poor people, the harder it was for them to place the full blame for poverty on moral failings, and, as Watson lamented, "remonstrance was often necessary to prevent these visitors from relaxing efforts at moral reform and calling in the discredited system of relying entirely upon almsgiving." The development of American charity organization societies was an attempt to overcome the AICPs' perceived failures: a lack of organization and cooperation among agencies, which left too much room for fraud by the poor; insufficient focus on moral education, despite AICP claims; too few visitors; corruption in both the government and in private agencies; and what was often characterized as "lavish" outdoor aid—the AICP had "sunk into a sea of almsgiving."[49] Charity organization would for some forty years try to put into practice what the AICP could only hold as ideals, and would succeed, if only for a time, in provoking a massive reordering of the relief system.

The first American COS was established in the Germantown neighborhood of Philadelphia in 1873 to manage the appeals being made to wealthier citizens for food and money. The first city-wide COS was established in 1877 in Buffalo, New York, by Rev. Gurteen, who had moved to America after a short stay in an East London settlement house.[50] He served brief stints as a student in the city of New York, a lawyer's apprentice in Albany, and a classics instructor at Hobart College before becoming assistant minister of St. Paul's Church in Buffalo, just in time to witness the devastating effects of the depression of 1873. There he drew appreciative audiences and swelled parish coffers with rousing sermons and concise pamphlets damning "promiscuous" almsgiving. He studied the London Society for Organizing Charitable Relief and Repressing Mendicity during a two-month return visit in 1877, and those experiences led him later that year to establish the Buffalo Charity Organization Society in order to regulate and restrict the wanton benevolence of Buffalo politicians and citizens. It was not just Gurteen but a number of "public spirited men" who pushed for the establishment of a COS. Watson says it was therefore "not surprising that the new society early entered upon a crusade for the reduction of public outdoor relief," a testament perhaps to how accepted it was that relief was counter to the interests of business and professional men.[51] Over its entrance was posted a black sign with gold letters that read "Charity Organization Society, Central Office," and along each post that supported it were the words "No Relief Given Here." The COS would, Gurteen promised, foster "true charity, true love, true sympathy" by seeking to "inculcate provident habits among the poor" and "suppress the curses of bastardy." Gurteen divided the city into administrative districts to coordinate the charity work within each, deliberately not doing so by wards, "which should always be avoided in consequence of their political complexion." He would not appoint clergy to the governing council, being "equally opposed to the gift of the coal-ticket and the gift of a tract," and instead selected "all business and professional men, and the very ablest that the city afforded." The society was launched with six Sunday lectures delivered by Gurteen, dutifully reported each Monday by the *Buffalo Courier,* whose editor was one of the society's founders and funders.[52]

One hundred ninety-six American cities had established a charity organization society by 1900, many explicitly imitating Buffalo (one of the businessmen who helped Gurteen finance the launch of the Buffalo COS credited him with helping establish the societies in Boston, Philadelphia, Baltimore, Chicago, and many smaller cities).[53] By 1915 some 327 cities had a COS.[54] Although most observers have described charity organization as chiefly an urban and northeastern movement, by the end of the century there were COSs throughout the country.[55] In the 1890s the National Conference on Charities and Correction and Gurteen would begin to issue calls for the creation of a national organization of COSs, and while that was never achieved in the sense they intended, an American Society for Organizing Charity did come to serve as a network for information sharing in the early 1900s.[56]

The ideology of charity organization was not new; their innovation was in the rational, scientific, administrative approach they designed to implement it, a strategy built in part upon their appraisal of the failures of their predecessors, and the effectiveness with which COSs disseminated their ideas and fought to see that they influenced debate and the shaping of public policy. Perhaps the most important difference between the charity organization movement and other campaigns against relief is that we can talk of charity organization as a movement—in the last quarter of the nineteenth century anti-relief sentiments gained a force and an institutionalized influence not seen previously and not seen again until the late twentieth century.

A THREAT EMERGES, AGAIN

Many businesses in the 1970s confronted new challenges to their profitability and power, just as their late-nineteenth-century counterparts had. The OPEC oil embargo led to large rises in the prices of energy and other commodities. Government regulation of business had increased: Christian Parenti reported that "between 1964 and 1979 the federal government enacted sixty-two health and safety laws which protected workers and consumers, while thirty-two other laws were passed protecting the environment and regulating energy use."[57] This was a period of intense congressional regulatory activity, as political scientist Theodore Lowi confirmed: "Depending on who is doing the counting, an argument can be made that Congress enacted more regulatory programs in the five years between 1969 and 1974 than during any other comparable period in our history, including the first five years of the New Deal."[58] These included large, costly programs, such as the Occupational Safety and Health Act, the Clean Water Act, and amendments to the Clean Air Act. Relatively strong labor unions and wage growth contributed to profit declines that began in the mid- to late 1960s. Capital gains taxes rose even under Nixon. Increased global competition, the first American trade deficit since 1893, and an economic crisis longer (from November 1973 to March 1975) and deeper than any since the Great Depression were increasingly seen by many businesses as serious long-term threats.[59] American businesses' postwar willingness to "integrate the labor movement" (which, although limited, came about in part because specific economic conditions made it possible for profitability and wages to rise simultaneously) had come with a price: "the bargaining power of workers in the monopoly sector led to increasing economic demands, fully legitimated within the historical agreements reached to co-opt the unions. These demands were subsequently extended to the area of welfare and indirect wages, and became particularly acute in the periods of expansion, contributing to the cyclical deterioration of the ratio of profit to wages."[60] Labor had won ground and expected to win more.

And just as an expansion of relief preceded the Gilded Age assault, so too in the modern period. Between 1960 and 1969, thanks to reduced stigma, court decrees, relaxed eligibility guidelines, and protest by potential recipients, AFDC rolls rose more than 100 percent, 71 percent of that increase taking place between 1964 and 1969; by 1974 they had tripled.[61] Nixon expanded the food stamp program (federalizing benefits and setting minimum benefit levels), while from 1969 to 1972 federal grants to the states for social services rose from $354 million to $1.7 billion. Through 1972, the value of AFDC benefits and the number of Americans receiving benefits had steadily increased; that year also saw the implementation of Supplemental Security Income, a guaranteed income (not unlike the numerous failed proposals for a negative income tax) for the blind, disabled, and elderly. The real value of hourly wages had been growing, too. By the early 1970s, the American poverty rate was lower than it had ever been before, 11.1 percent, and lower than it has ever been since. This was more than just the effects of economic growth; between 1965 and 1972, the pretransfer poverty rate (the number of people poor before counting government programs) declined 9 percent, while posttransfer poverty declined by more than 15 percent. By 1972, government transfer programs (Social Security, particularly) lifted fully 50 percent of the poor above the poverty line.[62]

Yet it was even more than increased regulation, relatively strong unions, an expanded array of welfare state programs redistributing wealth to poor and working people, and the concomitant concerns about declining profitability. Fundamental shifts in public opinion about corporate power seemed evident, perhaps not surprising given the antiestablishment tenor of many social movements of the late 1960s and early 1970s. A 1971 *Newsweek* article was titled "The American Corporation Under Fire"; in the previous year polls reported that public support for business had declined to 33 percent from 70 percent just two years prior.[63] Such opinion could help achieve further inroads by workers and consumers, many feared. Said one executive, "If we don't take action now, we will see our own demise."[64] One Business Roundtable member proclaimed that "the constant cry within the business community was 'How come we can't get together and make our voices heard?'"[65] In 1971 Lewis Powell (whom Nixon would months later nominate to the Supreme Court) wrote a memorandum for leaders of the Chamber of Commerce that was later widely circulated, a call to arms that was much like the 1878 call in the *Atlantic:*

> The American economic system is under broad attack. . . .
> [The assault] is gaining momentum and converts. . . . The
> overriding first need is for businessmen to recognize that the
> ultimate issue may be *survival*—survival of what we call the
> free enterprise system, and all this means for the strength and
> prosperity of America and the freedom of our people.[66]

Powell urged a coordinated, aggressive regime of lobbying, public relations, and media activism, and the long-term funding of conservative professors and textbooks to counter the "ideological warfare against the enterprise system and the values of western society" waged by "the intellectual community," made possible only because, he wrote, "few elements of American society today have as little influence in government as the American businessman." This memorandum "convinced businessmen that they had to become involved in national politics and in Washington policy making," reported John Judis, and convinced beer magnate Joseph Coors, among others, to continue what would become massive investments in institutions of the right.[67] "Strength lies in organization," Powell had written, "in careful long-term planning and implementation, in consistency of action over an indefinite period of years, in the scale of financing available only through united action and national organizations." Irving Kristol (husband to Gertrude Himmelfarb), in a stream of like-minded articles that moved from the conservative readership of *Commentary, Reason,* and *The Public Interest* to the broader audience of the *Wall Street Journal,* the *New York Times,* and the *Washington Post,* urged corporations to respond in new ways, to fund their own think tanks as a counterforce to the Ford Foundation and others, to stop funding foundations and other charities with anti-corporate agendas, to change opinion. Whether it was any of these particular calls that spurred so many businesses and businessmen to action, spurred to action they were.[68]

Businesses and their leaders mobilized much as corporations and their leaders had a century before. They built trade associations and sector-wide organizations like the Business Roundtable (a lobbying group of two hundred CEOs), created public relations divisions within their firms, increased their marketing budgets, and established new offices close to political power in Washington, D.C. They hired K Street lobbying firms to press their claims upon the federal government. Many fought more forcefully against labor: in 1965 42 percent of companies complied immediately when unions filed to be recognized by the National Labor Relations Board; by 1973, only 16 percent did.[69] They formed political action committees (PACs) to help increase their campaign contributions and influence (and increase campaign contributions overall), they took new risks by shifting campaign funding to Republican congressional challengers (forty-three were elected with their help in 1980, though they were unable to immediately sustain that level of success), and they coordinated contributions with other PACs to further maximize their influence.[70] They endowed university chairs for free-market-advocate professors and offered fellowships to like-minded students. They funded magazines and journals of policy and opinion. New members joined the reinvigorated Chamber of Commerce, the National Federation of Independent Businesses (NFIB), and the National Association of Manufacturers (NAM). And they established policy institutes, foundations, and other organizations designed to produce expert research to support their claims and to gain an audience with policy makers, the media, and the public.[71] Among them were those think tanks or "policy-planning organizations"[72] and some lobbying organizations, such as the U.S. Chamber of Commerce, that, like their COS predecessors, sought to cut back poor relief.[73]

While the COS was created specifically to oppose public relief and private charity, this is not so for the new and newly invigorated think tanks of the late twentieth century, which included opposition to relief among many targets. This difference is partly the result of different circumstances. In the late nineteenth century, especially before the consolidation of corporate capital that peaked from the mid-1890s to 1905, local labor markets had greater impact upon business profit, and there was simply less regulation to roll back.[74] By contrast, late-twentieth-century businesses were pinioned, they might fairly argue, by an array of city, state, and federal regulations that governed much of their operations; relief itself was economically less important (although as important symbolically) than it had been for their Gilded Age predecessors. But it was important.

YET ANOTHER THREAT

That business fought its declining power is perhaps not surprising; that it was able to so effectively roll back the hard-fought gains that poor and working people had made is the outcome that will require explanation. As political scientist Charles Noble cautioned, "Business elites everywhere [in the world] have lobbied against legislation to protect wage earners from the discipline of the market. The real question is why business opposition has been so effective" in the United States.[75] His answers—that our decentralized political system affords businesses easier entrée into government decision making, that single-member districts and winner-take-all elections push campaigns toward centrist policies, that deep racial cleavages inhibit the formation of left coalitions, that strong court interventions limit labor power, and that major media are inherently conservative—are, it seems to me, correct. But Noble points us to structural conditions; my concern is with specific actions during a discrete period. And he misses one factor: this corporate mobilization, which would eventually find influence in both the Democratic and Republican parties,[76] magnified its strength because some of its goals coincided with a culture- and religion-based mobilization.

This mobilization of the religious right was also a response to events of the 1960s. While Puritan divine John Winthrop and his generation saw their new colony as a "city upon a hill," the Christian right saw America as a nation atop a mount, a shining example to the world of progress, moral order, and freedom. (William Bennett, for example, offered wistful, long-ing paeans to this lost "golden age," while Ronald Reagan used the image of the shining city upon a hill in his first inaugural address.) Beginning in the 1960s, that belief became harder to hold as the old moral order began to dissolve. In 1960 a Catholic was elected president. Cultural standards of appropriate sexual behavior had begun a radical change, and with them a change in the definition and structure of the family. Women entered the workforce in growing numbers. In 1963, the Supreme Court ruled that forced religious observance in public schools was unconstitutional. Mass unrest and rioting associated with the civil rights movement shook the old racial order; another order was disrupted again with antiwar protests at the end of the decade. Eastern and New Age religions became more visi-ble in the United States and were especially popular among the young, who already displayed radical new acceptance of sex and drug use. Protestant denominations saw declining mem-bership, shortages of seminarians, and deep funding crises.[77] The oil crisis, financial crises in cities, deindustrialization, stag-nant economic growth, rising inflation, and defeat in Vietnam made notions of the nation atop a mount difficult even for the most faithful to believe. And, noted American religion histo-rian Sidney Ahlstrom, "the group most vulnerable to these changes was the fundamentalist Protestants—not because they were fundamentalist, but because they were by region, history, and education the group most rooted in the past, the one with the least capacity for adjusting to change."[78] It is possible that the Supreme Court's decision in 1973 to legalize abortion was the last straw.

The evangelical movement emerged as a response to this transition into a "post-Puritan" age, and its proponents were able to support it with institutions they built early in the cen-tury, after backlash from the Scopes "monkey trial" drove them from the public sphere.[79] In this "wilderness," they began to

build seminaries, private schools, radio networks and later television networks, publishing houses, direct mail agencies, and
new churches. In addition to energetic institution building, this
budding movement was developing a core of well-educated
and well-trained seminarians, educators, and intellectuals.
Evangelicals midcentury returned to what Max Weber called
"this-worldly asceticism."[80] From World War II to the late
1980s there were more "special-purpose" religious organizations formed than in all of the nineteenth century.[81] The now-
familiar litany of the Christian right's organizational strength
is the result. The Moral Majority brashly announced the entrance of this new Christian right into electoral politics, securing between two million and four million votes for Ronald
Reagan. By the early 1980s, Pat Robertson was operating the
fifth-largest cable television company in the nation, Jim Bakker
was overseeing a ministry with over $100 million in annual rev-
enues, and Jerry Falwell was broadcast in 172 markets.[82] By
1997, there were 1,648 Christian radio stations and 257 Christian television stations. Robertson's *700 Club* had a viewership of
some two million people. In 1995, one-tenth of the entire
American music industry was Christian music. In addition to
nonfiction books, a wide array of periodicals, and Christian
novels, the Christian right even established its own wire service, the Evangelical Press News Service, as well as colleges,
law schools, and, finally, think tanks, many of which were created thanks to the opportunity the Christian Coalition and
other politically active religious organizations seized upon by
finding common cause with members of the "intellectual"
right, corporations seeking lower taxes and reduced regulation,
and issue groups such as the National Rifle Association and
anti-abortion organizations.[83] This cultural countermobilization is not in reality an entirely distinct movement from the
corporate countermobilization described above and below;
they have formed an effective political coalition, and the late-

twentieth-century victories of the Republican party were indebted to both, although plagued by the difficulties of placating both constituencies.

THE BIRTH OF THE THINK TANK

The conservative think tanks and anti-relief business organizations of the late twentieth century were a diverse lot, and others have documented their individual histories and attended to their distinct characters.[84] They were no more monolithic than were COSs, and generalizations about them are harder to make than generalizations about organized charity. Most important for our purposes, there are none quite so narrowly focused upon matters of poor relief as were the early COSs. The COSs, moreover, were service organizations as well as producers of policy ideas; they coordinated and limited the distribution of aid to poor people before the advent of public bureaucracies willing and able to do so. Such municipal administrative and service-delivery concerns are not typically the purview of the think tank. But by the end of the twentieth century, these institutions had become central players in politics and policy, their growth as dramatic as the expansion from one lone city-wide American COS in 1877 to over two hundred by 1900. In 1966, there were fewer than seventy think tanks in the United States, yet by 1996 there were over three hundred active in politics.[85] Many think tanks or lobbying organizations that took an active interest in welfare policy were created late in the twentieth century. The Heritage Foundation was founded in 1973, the Cato Institute in 1977, the Manhattan Institute in 1978 (by future Central Intelligence Agency director William Casey), and Empower America in 1993. Others opened their doors much earlier. The U.S. Chamber of Commerce was established in 1912, built from local chambers, which, as we will see, were active in the fight against nineteenth-century out-relief. The Hoover Institution was founded in 1919, the Brookings Institution in 1927, the American Enterprise Institute in 1943 (by 1954 it was led by the Chamber of Commerce's William Baroody), and the Hudson Institute in 1961. Though some of these latter institutions began as "neutral" organizations of expert government advisors, they would increasingly become partisan and ideologically centered organizations when infused with a new sense of mission and new sources of funding in the late postwar era, funding specifically designed to influence public debate, limit government oversight and intervention in markets, and reshape American public policy toward more neoliberal solutions.[86] Weyrich and other founders have made it clear that they intended such results: as Heritage Foundation president Edward Feulner said, "The Left had a finely tuned policymaking machine, and the Right had nothing to match it."[87] Others with similar interests began to fund these institutions when they discovered that they could serve as useful mechanisms for channeling their policy desires toward political solutions.

Some have talked of this growing family of conservative think tanks and other institutions as a capitalist or conservative "policy planning network"[88] or a "conservative labyrinth."[89] Joseph Peschek observed that such institutions help "convert problems of political economy into manageable objects of public policy"; they "help translate class interests into state action."[90] Put even more simply, they helped achieve consensus, not only within but even across organizations, so that by the late 1970s "ultraconservative" and more moderate policy-planning organizations were finding common ground.[91] Michael Useem, focusing upon a more narrow "inner circle" of corporate leaders such as those of the Business Roundtable, suggested that "this politically active core gives coherence and direction to the politics of business . . . those few whose positions make them sensitive to the welfare of a wide range of firms have come to exercise a voice on behalf of the entire business community."[92] Think tanks are less central for David Vogel, merely a "catalyst," accelerating the celerity with which neoconservative ideas were disseminated.[93] William Domhoff added that they offer corporate interests a forum for exchanging and developing ideas and plans, a training ground for advocates, and a recruiting ground for new operatives.[94] Irving Alpert and Ann Markusen argued that such organizations perform "brokerage functions between private capital and the state," producing "policy, ideology and plans."[95] As Michael Allen put it, "Conservative policy-planning organizations function very much like traditional interest groups, but have the advantage of not being perceived by policymakers as interest groups."[96] They thus serve as discrete links between the corporate and political worlds. None of these descriptions excludes any other, and there is truth in all of them. Anti-relief think tanks were each of these things.

Among think tanks' principal functions has been to provide arguments and ideas, and then to translate them into public policy proposals, even occasionally by drafting legislation. More prosaically, their resident scholars wrote books, journal and magazine articles, briefing papers for politicians and their staffs, op-ed pieces, white papers and policy analyses, press releases, lectures, strategy memos, and pamphlets. Some, such as the American Enterprise Institute and Empower America, produced radio and television programs.[97] They maintained vast mailing lists of funders, and banks of policy experts who were made readily available for television and newspaper reporters in need of quick, concise information. They testified before Congress and briefed members or their staffs. Other organizations, including Virginia's Leadership Institute, taught budding conservative journalists and politicos "the art of selling conservatism as compassion" through sophisticated techniques of "political technology" and operated a job bank to place its graduates in position on Capitol Hill,[98] while the Heritage Foundation provided Washington journalists "free training in computer-assisted research and reporting" through its Center for Media and Public Policy to "bridge [the] chasm between conservatives and the media."[99] As with the COSs, this was an effort at persuasion, of propaganda.

Like the charity organization's, "scientific" philanthropy, the trappings of the think tank (white papers, conferences, briefing papers, monographs, etc.) legitimized their staffs and fellows as experts, helping to more effectively influence the media and through them public opinion. In doing so, think tanks obscured the class-based roots of their activity and "allowed business itself to remain nearly invisible," as Piven observed, while providing an efficient mechanism for disseminating their preferred policy prescriptions.[100] This served a vital function: Mark Smith argued that a unified business position on any matter could have negative effects upon its ability to influence policy, so "business elites therefore might more effectively shape public opinion by funneling money into like-minded think tanks than by advocating positions themselves."[101] These were often thus not direct attacks upon the institutions of power but battles for a kind of hegemonic dominance, the dominance of ideas and interpretations.[102] Rector described himself, accurately, as an "entrepreneur of ideas." As a former Bradley Foundation president said: "It's true that many people do not know where certain ideas come from, but the important thing is that they agree with them."[103]

The comparative success of right-wing think tanks over their liberal counterparts in dominating policy debate can be attributed to their focus on a relatively small number of issues, careful selection of issues for "thematic coherence," greater financial resources, more expert use of media and shrewd use of resonant language and sharp sound bites, better funding and cultivation of affiliated "experts," ability to tell better stories, refusal to compromise on ideas or policy, and talent for widely disseminating materials in such a manner as to make their reach and import appear greater than warranted, saturating the marketplace of ideas. The "echo chamber" effect of this last point has been especially important.[104]

Anti-welfare activism was only part of the work of these twentieth-century organizations, unlike the relative single-mindedness of the COSs. But this dense network of well-funded institutions offered corporate and financial interests powerful means of access to policy makers and the means to dominate public and elite debate about a range of issues, poverty and welfare among them, and the tools to help turn their perspective on these issues into policies that would benefit them. That is why this mobilization is important to understanding the welfare retrenchment of the late twentieth century, for its institutions helped push the ideas into the public and political sphere that would later come to define the policy agenda.[105] While it is notoriously difficult to trace the effects of ideas on policy,[106] it is this institutionalized effort to change policy discourse that is central to understanding how a war on poverty became a war on welfare.

WHO CONTROLLED CHARITY ORGANIZATION?

With rare exception, men set policy and held administrative positions at COSs, while native-born, well-to-do women served as their "friendly visitors," the volunteers who offered moral guidance, comfort, education about such matters as household maintenance and child rearing, and, on those occasions when the client was deemed worthy, material relief. While over time women would assume more positions of responsibility and the composition of COS leadership would become more ethnically diverse, for all its presumed concern about bringing the classes closer together, working people and poor people were never incorporated into the COS leadership.[107] Working-class women would, however, be hired as clerks (agents, they were called), which would eventually impact upon COS effectiveness.

The boards and district committees of COSs were, as a rule, like the governing bodies of their predecessors, the Society for the Prevention of Pauperism and the Association for Improving the Condition of the Poor, composed of white, Republican, Protestant men from the business and professional classes. The original board of the New York Charity Organization Society consisted of two lawyers, two physicians, two businessmen, one banker, and Josephine Shaw Lowell. President Robert deForest, who married the daughter of one of the founders of the Metropolitan Museum of Art, was a prominent lawyer and director for banks, railroads, and insurance companies.[108] Robert Goodman found that

> of the 233 chief office-holders and heads of district committees who worked for the New York Charity Organization Society from 1882 to 1905, 150 are identifiable . . . they come almost exclusively from the middle-class business and professional strata and included twenty-six doctors, forty-four lawyers, twenty-six businessmen, seven manufacturers, sixteen merchants, thirteen bankers, nine ministers, seven teachers, one politician and one artist.[109]

Of Chicago's Associated Charity directors from 1886 to 1908 we see much the same pattern: fourteen were merchants (all affiliated with big business, not small concerns); there were ten bankers, seven lawyers, four manufacturers, three managers, three educators, three settlement workers, two ministers, two physicians, and two real estate brokers. Most were between forty and sixty years old and active in the Civic Federation.[110] Gurteen's founding board consisted of the editor of the *Buffalo Courier,* two businessmen, and two lawyers.[111] In New York, many members of the New York Charity Organization Society, State Charities Aid Association, and State Board of Charities, Lowell most notably, overlapped, forming "a kind of 'charity trust' not unlike the 'oil trust' or the 'steel trust' of Gilded Age businesses."[112] The dense interlocking evident among conservative policy-planning organizations (and liberal ones, too) in the twentieth century, in which relatively small numbers of people held positions of power across a range of institutions, were evident in the nineteenth as well. The New York Charity Organization Society's "patrons" included Andrew Carnegie, J.P. Morgan, Mrs. Cornelius Vanderbilt, William Waldorf Astor, August Belmont, and other prominent industrialists or their wives.[113]

Not just the leadership of charity organization societies was of the upper classes. In the Philadelphia society, most of the men who gave time or money to the COS were professional and upper-class native-born whites; the average contributor was a businessman in his late forties or early fifties who was married and resided in a single-family residence in an elite neighborhood with live-in servants. Ten percent served on the board of a bank or insurance company, and 5 percent on the board of a mining or transportation company. They were likely to support the Committee of 100, a reform organization of and for businessmen. Among female friendly visitors, 77.4 percent had live-in servants and only 6.3 percent were employed (not all outside the home); their fathers or husbands were merchants, bankers, lawyers, judges, physicians, clergy, and educators; 57 percent were single or widowed, and their average age was forty-three.[114]

Historian Robert Bremner observed that "charity agents were well aware of the popular feeling that their efforts were designed mainly to protect the pocketbooks of the rich."[115] Kusmer added that businessmen served on boards to refurbish their image by showing their wealth to be part of a system that benefited all, to demonstrate that wealth had social and not just personal value, and to show that they were not blind to the plight of the poor. "Furthermore, charity organization was particularly appealing to them because it did not endanger their economic position. Charity workers, no less than businessmen, were eager to avoid any kind of class analysis; they spoke instead of reconciling class differences and reuniting American society." As one Chicago banker said, the COS served "as a clearing house through which people of philanthropic disposition may make their contributions to charity without any misgivings that they may be misdirected."[116] Even Cleveland COS trustee Frederic C. Howe would come to think that organized charity was "a business enterprise, designed to keep poverty out of sight and make life more comfortable for the rich."[117] For Edward Ross this was the Achilles' heel of private charity—its dependence upon the largesse of the business and professional classes prevented it from acting as it saw fit. "Most of the adverse conditions [of the day] are mixed up with your lucrative business, and you cannot go about to abolish them without having a business interest on your back." Ross reported that two workers who had refused to act as strikebreakers sought assistance from a local COS leader who then reproached the company for its labor practices. "The reply [the COS] got was, 'You people can't complain of having to handle such cases. Don't we contribute $150 a year to your work?' " Ross continued: "A student of mine, after three years of charity organization work, said to me, 'Professor, I've quit. There's nothing *in* it. The game's too thin. We coax money from the people who are the beneficiaries of the abuses that produce the wrecks we deal with. They let us deal with the wrecks, but we can't touch or even show up the conditions that produce them, because that would affect their income.' "[118]

The COSs' dependence upon certain segments of the upper classes is made clear by the laments of COS leaders about being unable to continue operations during the summer because so many left the cities for their country houses. Some COSs, which faced fewer requests for help then than during the winters anyway, simply closed.[119] By May 1882 Lowell would complain that there were not enough men of "*leisure* with the tradition of public service like so many of the 'nobility and gentry' of England. Our young men, those that we can catch, are very good, but usually too busy." [120] This offers some further indication that those involved were not of the old upper class with a sense of noblesse oblige, but a new guard, perhaps a new class of bourgeoisie.[121]

Most COS reformers implemented a charity that, whatever its intent, was in effect an attempt to monitor and change the behavior of their poor petitioners. One of the principal functions of friendly visitors was to recommend whether a family should receive assistance, and in what form, which was clear to those visited: among their challenges, then, was to at least *appear* to be comporting with the desired behavior of their visitor, since fewer than one in three applicants was eventually deemed worthy of relief.[122] They did not take to the streets in protest, and few dared risk outright confrontation, but they did lie to and deceive visitors in order to appear qualified for relief, acting with the passive resistance we might more readily associate with slave stratagems. COS visitors were aware of these subterfuges, and their reports are full of descriptions of supposedly unworthy clients attempting to appear worthy. Indeed, the deceptions that some have documented in charity-client relations attest to a game being played in which charity seekers pretend to comport with the values they know will get them assistance. There was thus a contradiction in the efforts of friendly visitors: while the stated COS goal was to inculcate independence in their poor clients, the power the visitor held over the client fostered their dependence, requiring poor applicants to act as supplicants.[123] As one visitor reported, "Threatened Mrs. G.

that relief would be discontinued if she does not do exactly as she was told. Explained that when she accepted charity, she gave up the right to make any decisions." [124]

While some reformers understood this (charity "divides mankind into lofty patrons and cringing, begging clients," one said), the chasm between visitor and visited could be great. [125] This, from a letter from an Association for Improving the Condition of the Poor visitor in 1873: "The room *dirty* and *disorder,* with some like companion sitting around a table with a pitcher or can of ale or beer, and perhaps already half drunk. I make known my business and of course under the circumstances tell them I can't give any assistance. Then Sir, you may be sure abuse of the first order is heaped on the poor Visitor who finds himself in such a plight." [126] Notice that it's the "poor Visitor" who is "in a plight." [127] Chicago settlement house leader Jane Addams nicely captured the visitor's dilemma: "it often occurs in the mind of the sensitive visitor . . . that she has no right to say these things; that she herself has never been self-supporting; that, whatever her virtues may be, they are not the industrial virtues; that her untrained hands are no more fitted to cope with actual conditions than are those of her broken-down family." [128] Addams wryly observed that the visitor was inevitably frustrated because instead of teaching about things she knew, "like Latin prose," she had to teach what she had not learned from either books or experience. [129]

While a central tenet of COS philosophy was, they insisted, the reunion of rich and poor, the COSs acted to protect the better classes from the dangerous and dependent classes, and to shield business from charity that offered workers leverage against it. Given the COSs' leadership, and presuming that they were rational actors, this is unsurprising. [130] Here is the most explicit admission: presenting a paper at the first convocation of the National Conference on Charities and Correction that was probably written by Charles Loring Brace, R.T. Davis claimed, "Some of the gifts [of charity during the past winter] were no doubt prompted by the selfish prudence of capital wishing to guard against the discontent of the poor."[131] The dangerous effects of such charity were no secret to Brace and those who would soon organize and come to oppose it:

> Mechanics still demanded from $3 to $5 per diem. It was notorious that important trades, such as the building trade, were at a stand-still on account of high wages, and that the employing class could not afford to pay such high rates. Yet no wages came down. Labor was in a struggle with capital against the lowering of prices. Charity assisted labor in the combat. The soup-kitchens and relief associations of various names became thronged with mechanics. . . . The whole settlement of the labor question was postponed by the over-generous charity of the city. . . .
>
> These benevolent institutions also interfered with many kinds of legitimate businesses . . . small eating-houses . . . were almost thrown into bankruptcy by the competition of certain soup-kitchens. . . . In one district, also, a keeper of a laundry, who had ten or twelve girls in his employment, at good wages, found himself stripped of his help in the midst of the winter, these women preferring to live for nothing in the free lodgings.
>
> It had been expected that this industrial crisis would bring down the wages of female servants, since these had remained at a high rate, though all other prices had fallen. The Superintendent of the Free Labor Bureau, however, stated that during all this distress the poor girls who came to his office could not be induced to take situations for less than from $14 to $20 per month, and said that they preferred to live at the charitable institutions until they could get such wages as they chose.[132]

At the tenth annual meeting of the NCCC, President Frederick H. Wines of Illinois told the assembled: "Our task is to diminish the amount of the burden which mankind has to carry and so save expense. It is our duty to scrutinize the demands made upon capital in the name of charity, to detect and expose sham charities, to point out the futility of methods which have often been tried and found ineffectual, to invent better methods to take their place." [133] Or as one of the founders of the social work profession, Mary Richmond, told the conference in 1899, "Businessmen have no time to think about the serious problems of charity. We have come into existence that we may do so." [134] Denver established its COS because "the businessmen of Denver demanded 'that the charitable institutions asking aid in their work should solicit funds through a central agency, and should organize for efficiency and for the prevention of duplication in their work.' " [135] In 1887, John K. Cowen, an attorney for the B&O Railroad, said that the COS "hunts out the fraudulent applicant for relief; furnishes information to those who are benevolently disposed and thus enables them to say to the able-bodied man: 'Do not come unto me, you must work for your living.' " [136] The COSs fulfilled many functions for such businessmen—here it was a way to avoid saying no directly, for one could always blame the local COS. Gurteen argued that one of the essential functions of the district agent ought to be to act as liaison between business and the COS, to keep the COS apprised of local labor needs.[137] Evans agreed: "The visitor's work must then be to try to remove the flaw, to bring the labor to the market where it is in demand, and never to treat an able-bodied workman to a dole of bread till he and his children degenerate into paupers." [138] The Chicago Municipal Lodging House was explicit in one advertisement, which read: "Skilled and unskilled labor to be obtained without charge to employer or employee. . . . Employment is found for the industrious and able bodied. The citizens and housewives of Chicago are requested therefore to refuse alms." [139] By 1909 Devine, with a grant from the fledging Russell Sage Foundation, had designed and established the National Employment Exchange in emulation of local exchanges in New York and other cities. It charged a fee to those seeking work, though not to the employer; its board of trustees was "drawn from the mercantile and industrial classes" and started "with a capital fund of $100,000 donated by New York's wealthiest citizens." [140] Watson noted approvingly that an organization of businesses "in one city" even took over the operation of the COS; this, he observed, was beneficial because a "chamber of commerce or board of trade is a *neutral* body." [141] In Cleveland, by the end of the century some 80 percent of the COS's budget was supplied by Chamber of Commerce members, likely a typical circumstance. [142] Gurteen proudly notes, "At the beginning of the year 1879, some of the leading business men of Buffalo, of their own accord, held a private meeting, when it was unanimously agreed that, in view of the benefit which the Society had been to the city at large, to the poor, to the benevolent and to the tax-payers, they would raise among themselves the $7,000 required for the [COS operating costs for the] ensuing year." [143] In this way, Buffalo businessmen paid the COS to reduce relief, just as they would elsewhere. [144]

Yet COSs were not, in fiscal terms, large enterprises. [145] Most handled relatively few cases (except in the early years of the depression that began in 1893, when almost all were overwhelmed). [146] Most were short-staffed and never able to secure enough volunteer visitors—the notable exceptions were Boston, which in 1886 had one visitor for every five cases (and one for every thirty-four paupers in the city), and Brooklyn, which had one visitor for each eight cases, though only one for every 188 paupers in the city. [147] The COSs raised their modest funding much as charities do today, with mail appeals, advertisements, personal solicitations, membership dues, benefits, tag sales, and targeted requests for donations to be passed on to especially deserving families.[148] Contributors, like William Dean Howells's fictional Silas Lapham, were less likely to have donated out of conviction than out of convention: among certain businessmen, less so of the "old" money of the aristocratic classes, it was simply among the things one did. Howells had reason to know, having served on a COS district committee in New York.[149] Some contributions were means to other ends. As Warner and Coolidge observed, "To contribute to the charities of the localities is one of the means by which social advancement is secured."[150] Munsterberg called it the "charity sport" of social climbing.[151] Even more, wrote Ross, "the popularity-hunter has always appreciated the wisdom of subscribing handsomely to benevolent enterprises. . . . The resort to philanthropy as a means of propitiation becomes more general as the public becomes more and more critical of the ways of business."[152]

The relatively modest budgets and small staff of the COSs did not reflect their influence on local policy makers, for, just as it would be with the think tank, it was their ability to change the opinions of legislators, executives, and the public itself that marked the real source of influence of the COS. It is clear that the COS was dominated, overwhelmingly so, by an identifiable class with identifiable common interests, and it seems fair to conclude that the reformers of the COS were engaged in something other than what they proclaimed, an effort to aid the poor. The same would prove true of the anti-relief think tanks.

Charity organization societies and their wealthy leaders and visitors were not blind to the industrial, environmental, social, and governmental forces and structures that contributed to endemic poverty. They wrote often of the enormous changes, in cities especially, that burgeoning industrialization was bringing to the social order, and believed that they could educate poor people to the means of advancement in this new world. That they were uncertain of how best to address this new and growing crisis should not be surprising. That they were often callused to the real suffering in their midst makes some sense too: "affluence, unless stimulated by a keen imagination, forms but the vaguest notion of the practical strain of poverty," observed Edith Wharton in *The House of Mirth;* or, as Jane Addams put it a few years later, "we credit most easily that which we see."[153]

Charity for the COSs was in part an effort to re-create a sense of community, to rejoin classes being torn asunder, to bring together rich and poor for the sake of both, and a way to avoid the European-like class divisions that seemed to be emerging, to protect them all from what was lost by the move to the city. We see this reflected in the emphasis many reformers placed on garden projects, fresh air funds, farm labor, and programs to remove children from the corrupting influence of the city.[154] By identifying the problems of poverty and pauperism with the loss of what one Scottish reformer had called "natural" charity, by insisting that family, neighbors, and community ties of yore were at the root of successful aid, the COSs almost perceived this truth—that it was the advancement of industrialization and its attendant urbanization that created the conditions that caused poverty in late-nineteenth-century cities, that it was, in a real way, the destruction of those old forms of neighborhood that caused poverty. What they missed was that one could not reestablish those social forms by changing the behavior of poor people—one would have to change the very economic, social, and even geographic forces that caused and were caused by such change. This, though not thought about in quite this way, was perceived by settlement-house leaders such as Addams, and eventually by the COS reformers themselves, who would later help usher in the Progressive Era agenda of environmental and industrial reforms. It is worth emphasizing, however, that the mainstream of neither the settlement nor the COS movement subscribed to arguments, mainly from socialists, that the very industrial order itself must be overturned. Rather, they sought merely to alleviate the worst of the conditions they finally acknowledged it created; that is, they ceased trying to re-create the countryside and focused on changing conditions in the city and helping people adjust to a new world, not return to an old one. It is this transition that marks this era and its struggles.

WHO CONTROLLED THE THINK TANKS?

Leaders of the twentieth-century anti-welfare think tanks had much in common with the leaders of the nineteenth-century charity organizations. In 1990, more than 93 percent of those who sat on two or more boards of twelve key institutions (including the American Enterprise Institute, Brookings Institution, Heritage Foundation, Hoover Institution, National Association of Manufacturers, Business Roundtable, and Chamber of Commerce) were senior corporate executives.[155] In 1994 and 1995, only two of the American Enterprise Institute's thirty trustees were *not* corporate executives; almost 60 percent of those who were executives led Fortune 1,000 firms (while 28 percent of Heritage's trustees did).[156] The overwhelming majority of those who occupied leadership positions among these organizations represented big business; even the Chamber of Commerce came to be dominated by big business.[157] Indeed, when the Business Roundtable and Chamber of Commerce took public positions on issues, they agreed 96 percent of the time in the 1970s; in the 1980s they agreed 95 percent of the time; and they were in 100 percent agreement on all issues by the 1990s.[158] While by the turn of the century women and (to a much

lesser extent) racial minorities could be found among the directors of these think tanks, leadership was still very much the
province of wealthy white men, as it had been with the COSs.

Most of the funding for conservative anti-relief institutions
came from the same few sources: the Lynde and Harry Bradley
Foundation, the John M. Olin Foundation, the Smith Richardson Foundation, the Scaife foundations (Sarah Scaife Foundation, Scaife Family Foundation, Carthage Foundation, and
Allegheny Foundation), the JM Foundation, the Koch family
foundations (Charles G. Koch, David H. Koch, and Claude R.
Lambe Foundations), and the Adolph Coors Foundation. Because of their consistent long-term funding of many of the
same organizations, the Bradley, Olin, Smith Richardson, and
Sarah Scaife foundations came to be known as "the Four Sisters." Their influence was all the more striking given that they
were not the country's wealthiest private foundations.[159] By
2001, none of the Four Sisters was among the fifty largest
American foundations; only Bradley (number seventy-eight)
and Smith Richardson (number ninety-eight) made the top one
hundred, and only Olin was among the one hundred largest
grant makers (at number fifty-one). However, in 1998 all four
were among the top fifty foundations that awarded grants in
Washington, D.C., and all could be counted among the top
twenty-five national grant makers to "public affairs."[160] From
1985 to 2001, the Four Sisters made grants of over $39.4 million
to Heritage, $28.9 million to the American Enterprise Institute,
$10.4 million to the Manhattan Institute, and $3.1 million to
Cato, along with $11.8 million to the Hudson Institute (from
1987 to 1999) and over $4.8 million to Brookings (1986–1999)—
a total of more than $98 million. Of these grants, some $10 million, or 10 percent, specifically targeted welfare initiatives.[161]

Thanks to this support, the budgets of conservative think
tanks grew quickly, especially from 1965 to 1983.[162] What's

more, conservative philanthropists didn't shift funding priorities or set limits on the number of consecutive grants they would make to a single organization, as funders on the left or in the center have typically done. This is important: a steady stream of dependable money allows an institution to devote its resources to influencing policy, not to fund-raising. A report by the Center for Policy Alternatives showed that the American Enterprise Institute, the American Legislative Exchange Council (a state-level business lobby), and the Cato Institute had combined resources 400 percent greater than the Center for Policy Alternatives, the Institute for Policy Studies, the Economic Policy Institute, and the Center for Budget and Policy Priorities, the rough institutional equivalents on the left. That is a failure of foundations to support left-leaning research and advocacy organizations, not a measure of scarce resources. Importantly, conservative foundations focused on the entire "knowledge production process,"[163] from research and its dissemination to media watchdogs such as Morality in Media and Accuracy in Media, and law firms and legal foundations such as Pat Robertson's American Center for Law and Justice, the Washington Legal Foundation, the Pacific Legal Foundation, and the Center for Individual Rights.[164] In the mid-1990s left-leaning foundations contributed less than one-tenth the amount to four leading journals—*The Nation, The Progressive, Mother Jones,* and *In These Times*—that right-wing foundations contributed to *New Criterion, The National Interest, The Public Interest,* and *The American Spectator.*[165] In 2000, the income of Brent Bozell's conservative Media Research Center was eighteen times that of the progressive Fairness and Accuracy in Reporting.[166] Importantly, right-leaning foundations were more willing to fund "goodwill" (public relations) than were left-leaning ones and did not usually fund direct service programs;[167] the result, as People for the American Way commented, was that "progressive groups, local and national, sought to fill gaps in an ever more frayed social safety net while conservative groups invested their resources in further shredding that net."[168] That, it seems to me, was the goal.[169]

The organized charity movement of the late nineteenth century was funded, staffed, and led not by neutral reformers seeking to improve the lot of the poor, but by business and professional men who sought, often explicitly, to limit charity so that the working classes would be less powerful and more dependent upon their employers. This was a battle in a class war. The same can be said for recent anti-relief campaigns. These were quintessentially conservative movements in that they were led by elites seeking to preserve their own prerogatives.[170] Their place in the economic order gave them access to and influence with those in the political order, who, often of the same narrow class, had the compatible goal of preserving as much of the social order as was possible in rapidly changing worlds. In the former period, the COS was one mechanism through which elites sought to regain power eroded by the expansion of the franchise, the growth of municipal government, the rising power of parties, and the press of political machines that grew strong by accumulating loyalties among large numbers of voters. With the decline of patrician city government earlier in the century, when the economic and social elite were the political elite as well, other institutionalized means of representing elite interests were developed. In the latter period, the thinks tanks also served as a counterweight to the more democratic institutions of American politics, which could not always be counted upon to place elite concerns above those of the majority. The creation of think tanks and charity organization societies marks weakness: it was the failure of government to limit relief after the depression of 1873 that led reformers to found many COSs, to do what municipal government could not or would not do for them, just as the Heritage Foundation was established to redirect the energies of the federal government and its democratically elected leaders. This may be why the character of both sets of institutions was anti-state, and why so much of their activity, in relief and other matters, was directed at limiting it: they were created as countervailing powers, to overcome the perceived failure in influence their members suffered.[171] This also helps us understand the opposition many COSs faced from their local governments: they served different constituencies and had different understandings of what the city should do to assist the poor and working classes. Even so, they needed government to enact their policies, and therefore needed to persuade the public and its leaders of the rightness of their cause. They would do just that.

3

Reform: Then Neither Should She Eat

It has been proved, and surely it scarcely needed proving, that no
amount of money scattered among people who are without character and virtue, will ensure even physical comfort.

—Josephine Shaw Lowell,
Public Relief and Private Charity, 1884

That there was a transformation in policy throughout
Gilded Age America is clear. By 1897 there was no
public outdoor relief at all in Brooklyn, Baltimore,
New York, Philadelphia, San Francisco, Kansas City (Missouri), New Orleans, Louisville, Charleston, Portland (Oregon), Denver, Erie, Memphis, St. Louis, Salt Lake City, Peoria,
Atlanta, and Savannah. By the early 1890s, there was no public
outdoor relief in the entire states of Florida and Missouri, nor
in the Utah Territories. Total annual public out-relief was
below (in many cases well below) $10,000 in Springfield (Mass-
achusetts), New Haven, Cincinnati, Indianapolis, Cambridge,
Trenton, the District of Columbia, Wilmington, Saginaw,
Brookline, Albany, Worcester, Lincoln, Providence, Seattle,
Richmond, Somerville, Dayton, Evansville, Allegheny, Jersey
City, Reading, and Hoboken. Still other cities (and many of
those above) offered only in-kind aid—food, clothing, or
coal—but by 1897 dispensed little (under $1,000) or no cash,

including Buffalo, Syracuse, Detroit, Cleveland, Milwaukee, Newark, Minneapolis, Lynn, Bridgeport, Columbus, Fall River, Hoboken, St. Paul, St. Joseph, and Worcester.[1] Thus, of the fifty largest American cities in 1900, twelve (24 percent) had abolished public outdoor relief, sixteen (32 percent) had reduced their rolls and out-relief expenditures, and eleven others (22 percent) offered no cash aid (but in some cases large amounts of in-kind or indoor aid): thirty-nine of the fifty largest cities, or 78 percent, had reconfigured their cash assistance to poor residents during the last quarter of the nineteenth century despite two severe depressions (1873–78 and 1893–98) and one milder one (1882–86).[2] Of the next twenty-five largest cities, fourteen did the same.

Among students of nineteenth-century poor relief, there has been consensus as to why this happened: "Outdoor relief decreased because of a national campaign launched against it" by charity organization societies.[3] For some analysts, there was almost a movement mind at work. Economists Kyle Kauffman and Lynne Kiesling said that Brooklyn abolished outdoor relief "in the sweep of the scientific charity movement."[4] Watson wrote that "the movement came as a natural evolution or its spread would not have been either so rapid or spontaneous," and that COSs sprang up first in large cities and then in small ones.[5] This is not so much explanation as a convenient shorthand, as if to say that there was such widespread public antipathy to relief and such forceful advocacy from the COSs that they together almost willed the abolition of relief. But COSs were created, were founded, were organized. People acted and did so intentionally. There was nothing natural about antipathy to relief; it was cultivated. COSs did not spring up—they were planted and nurtured. And relief did not abolish itself in the sweep of a movement, but it was abolished or cut back by the actions of governments and of people with motives, many of whom used the COSs as means toward their own ends. I em-

phasize this because, as I have noted, this has been an explanation for relief reform in the contemporary period as well, that
the public rose up and demanded change. Not so.

Antipathy to relief has been a constant feature of American
politics, but while anti-relief agitation was evident long before
the creation of COSs, it did not achieve any considerable or
widespread success until the late nineteenth century. Philadelphia was the scene of attacks against relief in 1769, 1774, 1793
(when "outpensions" were briefly abolished), and 1828, when
out-relief was suspended until 1839, in which year it was reinstated thanks to the efforts of publisher Matthew Carey and
other "prominent citizens." In New York, attacks against relief
were launched as early as the 1820s.[6] Throughout the 1820s and
1830s, similar efforts in some other cities were made by AICP
reformers. But few were victorious, and none so successful as
Philadelphia. Not until the last quarter of the nineteenth century did anti-relief mobilizations reach critical mass, perhaps
because of "some special fear born of the depression of 1873,"
perhaps because only then did relief reveal itself (in different
ways in different times in different cities) to be such a threat to
the emerging new industrial order that business and professional men organized to resist it. Their economic goals coincided with the sometimes different goals of charity reformers
seeking to recapture rural community and neighborhood in an
increasingly alien and urban world, forming a coalition of compatible desires that would be seen again in the late twentieth
century when the family-focused reformers of the cultural
right and the work-focused reformers of the corporate-funded
think tanks both fought to restrict the availability of welfare.
There was no such coalition earlier in the nineteenth century,
and there were too few AICPs, with those that did exist being
too poorly funded and too poorly organized to have waged effective campaigns in their own cities, and they certainly did not
have the finances or institutional resources to launch a nation-

wide effort. Even Rev. Joseph Tuckerman's widely praised, model organizational innovations in Boston from the 1830s were of too limited scope to have had much impact.[7]

Not so with the COSs. Whatever their other accomplishments, and they varied from city to city, from year to year, COSs succeeded in setting the terms of the debate about relief in ways that their predecessors had not. This was their signal achievement. COSs were, more than any other institution, responsible for the campaigns against relief in the late century, but the abolition of relief was not inevitable or always even easy—efforts to end aid to the poor failed in some of the largest cities, even when they had strong COS support, while in (a very few) other cities the COS opposed relief repeal. Over the three decades under investigation here, in some cities the COS's role changed from one administration or one depression to the next. Out-relief was sometimes abolished not because the COS demanded it or because the public opposed it, but because partisans found it a useful tool in political skirmishes over resources and symbols.[8] Relief in these cases was part of yet another kind of political drama. The story is complex, and different for each city, and given how few have investigated late-century out-relief, as social-welfare historian Michael Katz and others have observed, I think it useful to examine the explanations of relief repeals that have been offered in the past to try to flesh out the historical record and move us toward a fuller understanding of what happened where, when, and why.

SEARCHING FOR PATTERNS, EXPLAINING REFORM

It is understandable that so many have emphasized a story that credits the COSs for the widespread withdrawal of public outdoor relief, for not only is there much truth in it, as we'll see, but it is the one that charity reformers told at the time, in part, no doubt, to demonstrate to their contributors and supporters that they were succeeding. It is also the narrative that predominates in the only comprehensive institutional histories of COSs, Amos Warner's *American Charities* and Frank Dekker Watson's *The Charity Organization Movement.* "Whether the reason for abolishing outdoor relief in Philadelphia was that of economy or some other, certain it is that the change was made at the direct request of the society, and as the result of sentiment against outdoor relief created by direct agitation," Watson wrote.[9] Warner agreed: "It is not without significance that the movement to do away with public outdoor relief has kept pace with the development of charity organization."[10] New York's Homer Folks, looking back during 1903, said, "In out-door relief, the extreme activity of the associated charity movement in all the leading states of the country has resulted in a very active development of a public sentiment regarding the principles of investigation and co-operation, to the end that helpful relief, instead of harmful relief, is more often given than in the past."[11]

We must, however, reconcile those claims, and they abound, with testimony from other reformers that the COSs were not responsible for some prominent cases of repeal. Kellogg reported, "While this elimination of outdoor relief was not pressed by formal action of our societies, Charity Organizationists claimed the credit of it as a result of their agitation and personal effort, and it was exactly in the line of the principles they advocated."[12] New York COS president Devine's national study of charity organization stated—contradicting Watson—that in Philadelphia, "whatever the motive, it is clear that the change was *not* made at the direct request of the society, or as a result of the sentiment against outdoor relief created by direct agitation."[13] He further asserted that his society played no role in the abolition of relief in New York. Watson, offering a fine example of how confusing all this can be, admitted, "Since these early days there have been *occasional* anti-outdoor relief campaigns conducted by various charity organization societies. . . . [but] there were always directors of the Associated Charities on both sides of the question."[14] Did the COSs cause this nation-wide assault on poor relief, or did they not?

There is a correlation between the presence of a COS and a city's relief policy, although it is an imperfect one. Of the fifty largest cities in 1900, thirty-nine (78 percent) had a COS. Of these, eleven (28 percent) had abolished relief, thirteen (33 percent) had reduced it, and nine (23 percent) offered in-kind aid only. Thus, 84 percent of those cities with a COS offered little or no cash assistance, while the rest—Boston, Rochester, Los Angeles, Scranton, Grand Rapids, and Nashville—kept their relief programs intact despite the presence of an active COS. Boston (along with Indianapolis, usually) was widely praised by reformers as operating the model COS—it was well staffed, had plenty of visitors, effectively coordinated the activities of other charities, and seemed to be well respected and admired within Boston and elsewhere. Yet Boston did not abolish relief. Conversely, eleven large cities (22 percent) had never established a COS or their COS had "lapsed,"[15] yet 55 percent of them also cut back on their public cash relief.[16] In some cities relief abolition *preceded* the formation of the COS, and in the notable cases of New York and Philadelphia the successful campaign against public relief is what led to the formation of the COS.[17] Edward Devine is right to insist that his society had nothing to do with relief abolition in New York: it didn't exist at the time. The presence or absence of a COS is by itself insufficient to account for which cities did and which did not cut back or reconfigure their relief, though the correlation seems strong enough to support the claim that the COS was a central actor.[18]

Others have sought patterns elsewhere. Almy and later Katz noted the correspondence between relief levels and geography: cities with harsh winters were less likely to eliminate aid, they observed, presumably because of the potentially more dire human consequences and the need to keep workers from abandoning cities during winter months to avoid the possibility of labor shortages when work resumed in fair weather.[19] It is true that Chicago and Buffalo did not abolish relief during this period, but New York, Brooklyn, Syracuse, Milwaukee, and Philadelphia did, while Cincinnati and Albany severely contracted their relief programs—all pretty cold places come February. The fact that Atlanta, Richmond, New Orleans, Charleston, Louisville, and Memphis abolished or severely contracted relief along with New York, Philadelphia, and Providence makes north-south hypotheses suspect, too. As Devine notes, New York and Philadelphia abolished relief, but Buffalo and Pittsburgh did not; San Francisco did, but not Los Angeles. This was not generally a regional or state phenomenon but a municipal, and in some cases county, one.[20]

Some say it was a product of population. Warner wrote regarding outdoor aid in the late nineteenth century, "The evils connected with this form of relief have long been a matter of controversy, and in this country the agitation against it has gained headway in almost direct proportion to the density of population. The flagrant abuses of the system in the large Eastern cities led to a concerted movement for doing away with it from 1878 onward."[21] Hunter claimed that, "In no purely rural district has outdoor relief ever yet been abolished."[22] Having a large population does seem to have made a city more likely to have abolished relief, but even of those nineteen cities with the largest populations—two hundred thousand and above—only seven (37 percent) did so.

Could it be a combination of city size and COS presence that offers an explanation? Could the lack of COS presence in small towns explain their lower rates of relief withdrawal? Perhaps.[23] But causation is hard to untangle here, for it is the very factors that fostered and enabled the creation of COSs—ample financing, a pool of volunteers, sufficient charity already operating to require coordination, evidence of waste or indiscriminate giving, an organized and active business and professional community—that contributed to antipathy toward relief. And, more simply, smaller towns and cities, especially those in the West and South, had little entrenched or established poor relief to cut back—smaller cities cut less in part because there was less to cut.[24] But there were nonetheless aggressive campaigns to abolish relief in some smaller cities, and when George Wilson of the D.C. Associated Charities conducted a survey of twenty-two of them in 1900, he concluded that many wanted to abolish relief but feared that their system of private relief was insufficient to meet the need.[25] By 1904, seventy-nine cities with populations between five thousand and sixty thousand had established a COS, yet few had reduced their public relief expenditures. One member of the National Conference of Charities and Corrections in 1879 thought that outdoor relief was, generally, less pernicious in the West because family ties still predominated and unemployment there was "temporary."[26] Brooklyn's future mayor Seth Low thought it less dangerous in rural areas because the appropriate shame was still attached to relief, unlike in large cities.[27] Whatever the reasons, the correlation is poor.

The race or ethnicity of relief seekers does not seem to predict repeal either: in 1890 Boston's "colored" applicants were triple New York's, while its "foreign" population was slightly higher. Baltimore's foreign applicants were almost half (at 37 percent) of the number in New York and Boston. Baltimore and New York abolished relief; Boston did not. The number of New Haven's "colored" applicants was four times greater than New York's (at 8 percent of all applicants to New York's 2 percent), but while New York abolished its program of public out-relief, New Haven merely restricted its relief.[28] Immigration levels and even the proportion of the labor force that was foreign-born offer equally little clear explanatory value.[29]

Rev. Wendte of Cincinnati attributed his city's short-lived[30] relief withdrawal in 1881 to a simple budget crunch: "not by public opinion, but by the stresses of circumstances, we have abolished all out-door relief, save the giving of coal, for ten weeks in the winter."[31] One historian pointed to the rising costs of relief and the need for increased taxation to fund it.[32] This is true; as discussed above, nationally from about 1850 to 1870, relief expenses rose significantly.[33] "If, by abolishing outdoor relief, we can stop the squandering of the public money, and save the taxpayers a half million dollars annually, it should be done at once!" cried one Ohio reformer.[34] New York, whose fiscal health was already weakened by the profligate spending of the corrupt Tweed Ring (temporarily deposed in 1871), was home to (and dependent upon the tax revenues of) many firms that collapsed in the panic of 1873. The Department of Public Charities was singled out for its drain on public finances, and its budget was cut substantially. This was the proximate cause for the first abolition of relief in New York, when it was "temporarily" suspended from July 13, 1874, to January 1875.[35] But the sheer expense of relief doesn't seem to offer a general explanation: many cities that had the largest per-capita relief expenditures were among those that retained or, in some cases, even expanded public outdoor aid late in the century. Those include some of the largest cities (Detroit, Chicago, Boston) as well as the smaller (Scranton, Grand Rapids, Fall River).[36] Similarly, another historian's claim that the "inherent visibility" of outdoor relief in city budgets and tax assessments helps account for the "turn away" from it may be true, but tells us little.[37]

Still, relief, like all budget items, was a resource and was fought over. Katz noted concisely that "local political struggles also shaped the nature of relief." His examination of relief battles in Brooklyn showed that the "abolition of outdoor relief be-

came a symbolic crusade against public spending and waste,"
used to good effect by Republicans seeking to take power away
from Democratic charities commissioners. In other locales, relief was given, said one superintendent, "to accommodate merchants—men who help to elect Overseers of the Poor and
perhaps superintendents."[38] Seth Low noted:

> The system had become furthermore a sore on the body
> politic. The friends of politicians received help whether needy
> or not, and so the system was perpetuated. Families with vot-
> ers were the first served. The "out-door relief" appropriations
> became a vast political corruption fund. Large numbers of the
> population were taught to rely on the county help, and sought
> it for no other reason than that the county gave it. One woman
> received help under nine different names. Many sold what
> they received. Men came from the country every autumn to
> live at the expense of the city during the winter, because the
> city was offering a premium to the idle to come and live in
> idleness. The poor did not get the chief benefit of increased ap-
> propriations.[39]

Many reformers agreed: "Most of the evils and abuses existing here and there in the administration of charitable and penal
institutions are owing in a greater or lesser degree, if not
wholly, to the prevalence of what is commonly called the political spoils system," noted one at the NCCC.[40] This is the crux of
many of the arguments made by charity organization societies—that only (some) private agencies could fairly administer
relief and ensure that it went to those truly in need of it, those
genuinely deserving. An effort was made in the Connecticut
state legislature, for instance, that would have mandated that
all relief be distributed in kind, through purchase orders from
"responsible firms"; it was defeated, reported *Charities Review,*
out of "a natural unwillingness to give up the considerable pa-

tronage which is enjoyed through the present often indiscriminate system of distributing outdoor relief."[41] Relief was associated with patronage and corruption for good reason.[42] That
there was power to be gained from distributing it was made famous by Tammany boss George Washington Plunkitt, who
said, so memorably, "What tells in holdin [*sic*] your grip on
your district is to go right down among the poor families and
help them in different ways they need help. I've got a regular
system for this. . . . If a family is burned out I don't ask whether
they are Republicans or Democrats, and I don't refer them to
the charity organization society, which would investigate their
case in a month or two and decide they were worthy of help
about the same time they are dead from starvation. I just get
quarters for them, buy clothes for them . . . and fix them up."[43]
Even as early as 1857 we can see the political patronage battle
over relief funds. The Chicago *Democratic Press* reported that
some aldermen fought a plan to allow the Chicago Relief and
Aid Society to distribute newly allocated relief funds because
that "would very materially restrict the electioneering finances
of certain members of the council."[44] As one writer said of
Boston mayor Josiah Quincy's similar struggle with ward leaders, "the real issue . . . was not the amount spent but who was to
control the city budget."[45] Relief was a source of power, and
that can tell us something about why skirmishes over relief
happened, but it does not tell us the whole story, and histories
that rightly identified this as a patronage battle have missed
something important.

THE REAL TARGET OF SOME REFORMS

Sociologist Adonica Lui argued that it wasn't the COS that
caused the abolition of relief in New York, but, as suggested
above, the more mundane forces embodied in machine politics,
party maintenance, and state structures. By her accounts, out-

door relief was abolished in 1877 by Tammany mayor William H. Wickham and comptroller Boss Kelly "to withhold patronage resources from the party ranks to achieve internal organizational discipline." Conversely, much later in the century free coal delivery was not abolished, despite the urgings of the AICP and the COS, because Tammany's ties with coal merchants were too strong and because the city's budgeting processes simply didn't give the COS a ready means of influence. When coal distribution was finally abolished in 1898, she wrote, it was not thanks to the COS but instead was "an indirect consequence of the intraparty conflicts of the state Republican party and Greater New York politics" surrounding the consolidation charter that brought the boroughs together to form one city. Thus, "Tammany's decision to cut cash and keep coal relief was an early effort at institutional consolidation, an attempt by the machine leadership to centralize party resources, impose organizational discipline on the district or ward leaders, and, at the same time, build and maintain alliances with the local business community."[46] Kaplan disagrees, and argued some years earlier that instead of an intraparty conflict in which Tammany leaders sought to abolish relief to concentrate power, relief was cut in the mid-1870s as part of a *inter*party downstate-Democrat and upstate-Republican compact to reduce taxes and to weaken Tammany by taking away patronage powers.[47]

But the important point is that they both offer narratives in which the COS played no role in the abolition of public relief. This is to be expected, since the New York COS was not founded until 1882. But what followed in the wake of reform is instructive. In New York, private charities struggled and failed to fill in the gaps left by relief repeal. By 1877, the comptroller's report noted the "alarming increase of taxation within a few years for the support of asylums, reformatories, and charitable institutions in this city," nearly $1 million in 1877.[48] As Kauffman and Kiesling put it, soon after relief was "abolished," the city began "an unprecedented period of assistance in the United States—private charity subsidization from municipal revenues . . . it is clear that New York continued to give outdoor relief in amounts equal to those before their supposed policy change" (see Chapter 5 for more on these issues).[49] By 1880, sixty-six Manhattan agencies gave $546,832 to 525,155 people.[50] The New York COS emerged only after relief had been abolished, in order to regulate the explosion in *private* charity that followed.[51] Public relief was not the target; private charity was.[52]

The tale in Philadelphia is similar. By 1850 private relief expenditures had already outpaced public, with the greatest growth occurring from 1850 to 1870.[53] Then the depression of 1873 hit, and the city faced massive debt. The Common Council "slashed" the budget of the Board of Guardians, those who administered relief.[54] The Philadelphia Society for Organizing Charitable Relief and Repressing Mendicancy (which later became the Philadelphia Society for Organizing Charity) was formed in 1878 to respond to those cuts in public aid that began in 1874 and the profusion of private relief and new relief agencies that followed: by 1878 there were 270 charities and 547 religious organizations, which together raised $1,546,050.[55] The Philadelphia organization was born of a meeting called by twenty-six citizens "to discuss, and, if possible, determine on a method by which idleness and beggary, now so encouraged, may be suppressed, and worthy, self-respecting poverty be discovered and relieved at the smallest cost to the benevolent."[56] Many sought "to protect their charities from the countless impositions practiced upon them"; others would later become members of the Committee of 100.[57] It was "a relief-giving as well as a relief-obtaining society," which caused jealousies from established relief providers and from "the political dispensers of the official relief from the city treasury, who resented interference with so profitable an instrument of political patronage; and professional politicians began to devise means to strangle

the reform at its birth."[58] The city fired its dispensers of poor relief and then suspended relief itself, and turned over all relief to
the COS in hopes of embarrassing them by pointing to the suffering they expected to result from the COS's failure. But, says
Watson, no great increase in relief demand occurred, and the
public almshouse population even decreased. By the end of its
third year the COS had "raised into conditions of self-respect
and self-support" some 1,110 families, totaling 4,000 people.
The council, despite protest from the Guardians of the Poor,
then used the professed effectiveness of the COS as reason to
cut public relief more, and by 1879 all public out-relief was
gone save for Guardians' salaries and medical aid.[59] Here again
we see relief first assaulted before the COS was established,
which came into being not to repeal public relief but to help
limit and control private charity. Relief policy was thereafter a
political drama in which the COS functioned either as an opponent or as a tool to be used for other ends. Once more, we cannot credit the COS per se with relief repeal (although we
should note that here, as elsewhere, many of those most involved in anti-relief campaigns were those who would come to
form COSs).

PROTECTING RELIEF, OPPOSING REPEAL

As both Devine and Katz have previously suggested, local conditions were responsible for whether a Gilded Age city abolished, reduced, expanded, reconfigured, or privatized its relief
programs. The search for simple explanations or for patterns
yields little. But one additional factor that seems to help predict
whether a given city withdrew relief was opinion of its relief
distribution—was it corrupted by politics, ill-managed, and
overgenerous, or relatively "professional" in its operations and
judicious with its funds?

Take Chicago. "With the possible exception of the COS in

New York, no society exerted more influence at the turn of the century on the theory and practice of charity and social work administration," said Kusmer.[60] Yet Chicago was among those cities that did not reduce or eliminate outdoor relief during this period. How might we explain this failure? First is that while Chicago could boast early and consistently influential charities, there was no organization explicitly adherent to COS principles in place throughout the period; charity organization came late to the city. The local COS was organized in 1886 by Gurteen,[61] but the long-standing general relief agency, the Chicago Relief and Aid Society (founded in 1857, it gained power thanks to the voluminous contributions Chicago received after the Great Fire of 1871), would not cooperate with the nascent COS, and "the new society, overshadowed by the older society, was a few years later 'benevolently assimilated' by it and so [the COS] ceased to exist."[62] Alexander Johnson, who took charge of the Chicago COS after a stint as general secretary of the Cincinnati Associated Charities, had accused Relief and Aid of having squandered the Great Fire fund and said it was run at the whim of its board; he urged their executive committee to end relief-giving and turn responsibility for it over to the COS. They refused. Johnson then attempted a hostile takeover and even got seven members of the COS's board appointed to theirs, but he ultimately failed again.[63] The COS fought for control over relief and lost, despite the leadership of a man who would become one of the movement's most accomplished executives.[64] It was not until after 1900 that Chicago really saw the rise of COS methods in its administration and charity.[65] Relief principles won out over COS principles, and, as we will see in the case of the Boston Associated Charities, Relief and Aid consistently insisted that while there were surely cases of fraud and misuse of relief to be found, they were rare, and proclaimed that the "mass of worthy, honest, and economical poor should not be treated as thieves and paupers."[66] The most powerful and prominent charity in the city, which, in the case of Chicago was *not* the COS, defended relief, properly administered. Anti-relief propaganda could get little foothold because relief was perceived to be well administered, beset by little if any corruption, free from political or religious control, and conservative and careful in its giving. Indeed, Relief and Aid was no profligate dispenser of relief, and faced opposition from elite Chicago women who wanted more liberal aid to the poor and who established their own organizations to circumvent the control of this powerful, cautious agency. Even in the wake of the Great Fire, Relief and Aid fought successfully to close a Chicago soup kitchen that had been established and funded by a Cincinnati relief agency.[67] The relatively conservative reputation of Relief and Aid did not make it or its relief practices an easy target for anti-relief reformers, as Alexander Johnson discovered.

There was a similar dynamic in Cleveland, where in 1897 its Associated Charities lamented its failure to compel the city to abolish relief and turn its provision over to them. Here, the charity organizationists did not speak with one voice and were divided into two camps, one supporting the "privatization" plan and the other reluctantly opposing it for fear that they would be unable to take over relief and that sufficient funding was unavailable. Besides, reported the superintendent of the Associated Charities, "the outdoor relief as administered at present is as carefully done as we could wish. The investigators are old and experienced, who see to it that only the really needy are given aid. Politics does not enter into the outdoor relief work. This is a great change from what it was fifteen or twenty years ago."[68] Cleveland presents another instance in which, in this case by its own account, a COS tried and failed to compel a city to abolish relief, and its failure was attributed to the effectiveness (or perceived effectiveness) of relief provision.[69] Ideas about policy, to state what seems obvious but often gets forgotten, affect policy change (the truth of those ideas is not necessarily important).

Boston, which had one of the nation's largest COSs by 1892, also did not withdraw relief. Attempts were made in 1888 and 1901, and both failed. Like other cities, ethnic-based relief societies appeared early in Boston's history: the Scots Charitable Society was established in 1657, and Irish, German, and other societies soon followed. Boston's first almshouse was erected in 1660. A Society for the Prevention of Pauperism was established in 1835, and in 1851 came the Boston Provident Society, patterned after the New York Association for Improving the Condition of the Poor.[70] By 1868, free soup was widely distributed, typically by the police; as in so many other cities, this practice was condemned by charity reformers, and was discontinued in the winter of 1873–74. But unlike New York and elsewhere, where the depression marked the beginning of a long period of relief withdrawal, the following winter Boston resumed distributing free soup and appropriated $5,000 for this; from the onset of the depression, the Boston Provident Association spent even from its reserve funds until 1877, when, fearing bankruptcy, it finally cut back on relief-giving. But when it did so, it hired another visitor to help better distribute the funds remaining.[71] The Provident Society would remain a consistent advocate for effective, limited relief.

Then, in 1875, influenced by both Octavia Hill and the Scottish Elberfield system, in Boston's North End Annie Adams Fields and Mrs. James Lodge established the Cooperative Society for Volunteer Visitors Among the Poor, which soon spread to other parts of the city. Boston established its COS, the Associated Charities, in 1879. Germantown, Pennsylvania, may have established the first COS in 1873, and Buffalo the first city-wide COS in 1877, but Boston may well have been the first city to begin a comprehensive rationalization of its relief efforts.[72] But this early organization would have its effects, for when anti-relief reformers sought to establish the Associated Charities, they were "bitterly opposed" by most every established charity in the city, especially the Provident Association, and had to win their favor "inch by inch." They succeeded only by allowing delegates from other Boston charities to comprise much of their central and district leadership. Despite (or perhaps because of) an apparent Associated Charities–orchestrated campaign to impugn it in the press, the Provident Society remained a fierce and public opponent.[73] Like Chicago, institutional competition limited the Boston Associated Charity's ability to act freely, to undertake reforms without opposition. Instead of New York's relations between public and private relief, where, for example, Lowell served as head of the State Board of Charities while she was director of the COS, or the very close cooperation between the city and the COS in Indianapolis, where the township trustee was a member of the executive committee of the COS, in Boston institutions were more liable to be in competition with each other over the policy of poor relief and the money that went with it.[74] This institutionalized resistance is one way to explain Boston's failure to abolish relief.

By the late 1880s, reports circulated among charity reformers and public officials throughout the nation about the successes of Brooklyn, New York, Baltimore, the District of Columbia, and Philadelphia, which had, the conventional wisdom said, abolished public out-relief and yet the poor had suffered no ill effects. The experiment had been made, they proclaimed, the results were in, and the findings were indisputable. In 1888, a committee consisting largely of Boston Overseers of the Poor visited each city to evaluate those claims and to consider changes to their own city's relief policy. They decided that any change "would be a change for the worse." They were particularly concerned about how the city would respond in the event of a depression and, citing Brooklyn, worried that large sums were given to private agencies that gave little aid to the poor. Moreover, they offered a little-noticed critique that goes to the heart of nineteenth- and twentieth-century reformers' claims about the effects of public relief upon private giving, upon the cost savings of relief cutbacks, and upon the potential labor-market effects of relief withdrawal: if Brooklyn was able to discontinue its public relief without any effects upon the poor, they mused, why should it not also discontinue its subsidies to private agencies now offering relief in its stead?[75] The *Boston Herald,* among others, disputed the report, insisting that an analysis of individual cases revealed the evils of outdoor relief.[76]

But that, it seems, was that. "If the report of the Boston overseers did not fully convince the residents of Brooklyn, Philadelphia and other cities that they had made a mistake in abolishing outdoor relief," wrote Devine, "it seems to have had a quieting effect on any agitation toward the same end at home, and in the period since the report was published there appears not to have developed any very general sentiment against outdoor relief. Several of the active workers of the Associated Charities, if not converted from their earlier faith, have at least come to acquiesce in the present system as not likely soon to be radically changed. Some have gone further, and doubt whether Dr. F.H. Wines may not be right in pronouncing opposition to outdoor relief a 'fad' and insisting that the whole question is one of administration."[77] One of the overseers' central claims was that no good case had been made that private relief functioned differently in its effects upon recipients than public relief, that public relief was more "adequate and uniform, and that its burdens are fairly distributed, while private relief is spasmodic, rests entirely upon charitably disposed persons, and may fail entirely because of shrinking income at the very time when destitution is greatest and the need of relief most pressing." The overseers also argued, contrary to anti-relief doctrine, that private relief might in fact pauperize more easily than public because private relief could carry less stigma. Public officials investigated relief and proclaimed it not so harmful as others claimed; they seemed to have resigned themselves to out-relief and, as a result, did not seek to whip up public opposition to it. Boston did not abolish its public outdoor relief, despite having given the proposition serious consideration.[78] This elite and rhetorical resistance seems another factor in Boston's failure to end its out-relief programs.

Finally, Boston divided responsibility for outdoor and indoor relief among different overseers, enabling, Watson suspected, each program to be better administered; that "better administration," in turn, "weakened opposition to it." Devine similarly pointed to some decreases in relief and "stricter administration" as reasons that western cities were home to "fewer *successful* attempts" to abolish relief.[79] The corruption of relief, as we have seen, was a central theme of charity reformers. It may follow, then, that cities such as Boston, which had managed to create public relief systems that were perceived to be better administered, and directed apart from political considerations by "honest and capable" and "public-spirited men and women," as one overseer put it, were less susceptible to this strain of the reformers' indictment.[80]

Devine, trying at the turn of the century to generalize about why certain Gilded Age cities did or did not abolish public outdoor relief, threw up his hands. He said that in each city that abolished relief the change must be "attributed to special and local causes."[81] There is something to be said for this approach, for there are few clear patterns across cities.[82] The COSs, whether we interpret their activism as having failed or succeeded, were clearly central players, and surely helped make the possibility of relief repeal a topic of serious debate in cities throughout the nation, but one of the key differences between the nineteenth- and twentieth-century campaigns against relief was that the COSs, unlike their think-tank counterparts, failed to achieve some of their most ambitious goals. The COS was a strong force, but it could be overcome, and occasionally it was.

PROTEST AND RELIEF

While their activism does not seem to have prevented massive relief repeals, we should note the fact that the poor and unemployed were not passive during the Gilded Age. Throughout the country there were large-scale demonstrations "accompanied by extravagant demands."[83] In the 1870s, as the *Workingman's Advocate* described it, a "short-lived but quite vocal 'movement' demanding public aid for the unemployed spread" and "struck terror into the hearts of the many."[84] With each new economic downturn, industry lowered already-modest wages, precipitating yet more strikes, riots, boycotts, and protests. "Symptoms of danger, premonitions of violence, are appearing all over the civilized world. Creeds are dying, beliefs are changing. . . . Political institutions are failing. . . . There is a growing unrest and bitterness among the masses . . . a blind groping for escape from conditions becoming intolerable," warned Henry George.[85] Battles raged in the streets. During the railroad strikes of 1877, Philadelphians destroyed 104 locomotives and more than two thousand railroad cars; over five thousand local militia and federal troops were brought in to quash the mobs.[86] In Chicago between 1881 and 1900 some 593,000 workers struck 17,176 businesses in 1,737 strikes; over one million struck in New York City over the same period.[87] One Chicago newspaper spoke of "a real threat of anarchy," and a cartoon of the period pictured marchers carrying a banner that proclaimed "Unemployed . . . We are starving . . . Work or War."[88] Fear was tangible, if not a bit overwrought. Wrote Ernest Crosby in 1883, "We have seen in our country what a power for evil these debased classes are, in the riots of

1877. . . . History will ever point . . . to the Reign of Terror in bleeding France."[89] The upper classes were fearful for their very heads, perhaps with good reason.

Given this tumult, historian Raymond Mohl has suggested that "if the Piven and Cloward model is correct, we should be able to find clear evidence of substantial expansion of public relief to temper the disorder among the unemployed and the poor, and then an effort to reinforce work norms when economic conditions improved and social turmoil subsided."[90] As they wrote in *Regulating the Poor:*

> Relief arrangements are ancillary to economic arrangements. Their chief function is to regulate labor, and they do that in two general ways. First, when mass unemployment leads to outbreaks of turmoil, relief programs are ordinarily initiated or expanded to absorb and control enough of the unemployed to restore order; then, as turbulence subsides, the relief system contracts, expelling those who are needed to populate the labor market.[91]

Yet, as we have seen, quite the opposite seems to have happened—with some exceptions, public relief was reduced or eliminated in most large cities, even in cities where some of the worst turmoil occurred. Piven and Cloward have responded to Mohl and this seeming refutation of their claims: "We never said, 'if mass disorder then mass relief.' What we did say is, 'if mass relief, then mass disorder preceded.' "[92] They have not argued that the unruly poor always get concessions from government, only that without disruption they are unlikely to get anything at all. The Rev. C.G. Trusdell understood this: "Charity has a twofold character. It is the practical expression of sympathy with the afflicted, and the price that society pays for its own safety."[93] The question becomes why, in this period of great unrest, were the poor not only not able to get new benefits, but lost what little relief they had previously won? In another book, *Poor People's Movements,* Piven and Cloward offer us a guide to confronting that question. Government will respond to insurgents in one of three ways, they posit: if the disruption is contained and unlikely to have larger impact, governments will ignore it. If, on the other hand, central institutions are threatened, the state is more likely to punish and repress protest. Only in times of great change, when those in power enjoy uncertain electoral support and the use of force poses risks, will they seek to placate, co-opt or undermine protesters by granting them concessions. Only then is protest likely to elicit relief.[94] That is how Piven and Cloward explained the New Deal and Great Society expansions of aid.

By contrast, in most cities of the Gilded Age the mobilized poor had their claims ignored or repressed. Kellogg said that the "trivial socialistic bread riots and hunger parades of last autumn failed as demonstrations and promptly ceased,"[95] and Gutman reported that protests in New York, Philadelphia, Chicago, Detroit, Cincinnati, Newark, Pittsburgh, Indianapolis, and Boston were largely ignored by city governments and ridiculed by the press as a hopeless, futile cry of ignorant immigrants.[96] Take this typical commentary from the November 10, 1873, *New York Graphic:* "There is no point in railing at the rich nor in scowling at the capitalists nor in condemning corporations simply because one's stomach is empty and he happens to be dinnerless. . . . Whining and whimpering are as useless as they are disgusting."[97] When relief was "temporarily" suspended in New York in 1874 many businesses simultaneously lengthened the working day and lowered the wages of their workers, this only six months after police were called in to quell large demonstrations in Tompkins Square Park.[98] When Paterson, New Jersey, tried to institute a public work-relief program, it was protest by opponents of relief that caused it to end.[99] The COSs were themselves efforts to control disorder not by expanding relief but by restricting and rationing it. As

Gurteen asked, "Are we to stand idly by while the State or the Municipality levies a tax upon our subsistence for officialdom to distribute—a tax demanded by Mendicity as the price of our safety in life and property?"[100] Lowell repeatedly spoke of public charity as extortion by the masses for the safety of the better classes, and said that COSs could offer a cheaper and more effective form of social insurance. As she said in an address to Sunday-school children in Harlem, "The money raised by taxation for the support of those in want is simply a public fund, paid from self-interest in the same spirit and for the same purpose as the far larger amounts spent for the police. It is for the public protection, and there is no element of charity in it."[101] For the COS, restricting relief could contain and control the poor just as extending it could.

Evidence of direct actions in support of relief is rare. Katz noted that "outdoor relief had no passionate, articulate champions, and the wealthy professionals who led the attack against it encountered little ideological opposition."[102] It is an important part of explaining relief withdrawal if there was no coordinated, strong opposition to it, and indeed the record shows little opposition in many cities. That may have much to do with whether what was being withdrawn was considered worth fighting for: by the end of the century, public relief in many cities had grown more paltry, harder to get, undependable, and demeaning. Buffalo, Syracuse, Detroit, and Milwaukee, which offered no cash out-relief, are among the cities with the highest total per-capita out-relief expenses by 1900: thus even cities with very "generous" relief may have offered very little money to poor people.[103] Alameda County, California, reportedly used its poor funds to buy lobster, salmon, and tobacco for the overseers.[104] Before it was abolished, aid in Brooklyn consisted of "pitiful" quantities of food or coal provided on alternate weeks, as it did in Massachusetts.[105]

Relief, for many, was a poor substitute for what they really wanted: a job. Among the placards carried by some of the ten thousand marchers in an 1886 rally in support of Henry George was this: "No Charity: We Want Fair and Square Justice."[106] During the depression of the 1870s, labor organizations did not usually include poor support among their demands;[107] said one mason in Newark, "Workers don't want charity but work," and marchers in Chicago carried signs that proclaimed "War Against Idleness" and "We Want Labor and Not Beggary."[108] Peter Mandler argued that during this transformative period, as people constructed "new work-centered-identit[ies]" in an effort to distinguish themselves from the undeserving Other, they "became more hostile to old-fashioned charity."[109] "Working classes hold charitable enterprises in detestation and scorn," confirms Kellogg. "The feeling does not arise simply from self-respect,—but from an economic and class conviction that charitable relief stands in the way of a juster distribution of profits, and is an aristocratic concession to poverty, in order to content it with an unequal and debasing social system. Labor demands justice, and not charity."[110] Even the Populist platform of 1892 proclaimed solidarity with St. Paul, declaring, "If any will not work, neither will he eat" (while still lamenting that "from the same prolific womb of government injustice we breed the two great classes—tramps and millionaires"). Gilded Age insurgents did not typically issue calls for relief.

Yet there is evidence that protest did help stave off some out-relief cutbacks. Chicago, which did not repeal relief, perhaps for the reasons offered above, was also arguably the scene of more violent and more widespread labor unrest than any other city during the late nineteenth century.[111] Perhaps the sheer disruptive force of poor and unemployed people presented a greater threat or perceived threat than it did in other cities, even though their appeals were not usually for poor relief. But when they were, they succeeded. As in many other cities, the depression of 1873 led to new demands for work and relief, including from some twenty thousand protesters at a single event; claiming that there was insufficient city funding available, the mayor asked the guardians of the Great Fire fund to borrow from it ($700,000 still remained by 1873). They refused. More protests followed, and when a thousand people applied for relief simultaneously, then two thousand on another day, the city renewed its pleas and began imposing new restrictions to try to stem the tide, such as requiring vaccinations before accepting relief applications. Though they would turn away 60 percent as undeserving, the city was forced to spend $149,196 in that year for relief to 5,984 families; by 1875, they had implemented more restrictive rules to prevent such expenditures again, but expenses continued to rise.[112]

Buffalo, with the first city-wide COS, could not boast the most successful anti-relief campaign, though Gurteen certainly tried. Early in the life of the Buffalo COS, Gurteen noted, "Wherever Organization has been started, it has, without a single exception, either abolished out-door city relief altogether or has reduced the amount hitherto annually expended, within comparatively reasonable limits," and then claimed that Buffalo's savings were about $50,000 annually.[113] Yet the elected overseer of the poor seems to have thwarted Gurteen and his agency successfully over the long term, inspiring bitter complaints from reformers about the agitation of an ignorant and unruly public whose rioting for bread and relief in the winter of 1893 caused relief rolls to rise, combined with unwise officials and the failure of private organizations to demonstrate an ability to take over from public overseers.[114] "In Buffalo," reported Almy, "the city alms are given by a single overseer of the poor, elected by popular vote, who is at present honest, but not over-intelligent; and this overseer of the poor is responsible to no one"—except, of course, to those who elected him, who seem to have demanded relief.[115] Relief expenditures fluctuated wildly, from $112,054 in 1876 to $32,360 in 1882, $52,700 in 1885, and

$118,803 in 1898, but relief per family remained relatively constant at around $35. In Buffalo, as elsewhere, a determined COS tried to abolish relief and ultimately failed despite very strong support from the city's business and professional men.[116] As late as 1900, reports of the NCCC still noted Buffalo's continuing attempts to reduce or abolish its high levels of relief, which were higher even than those of "lavish" Boston.

But such events were uncommon. Poor and working people believed, like their would-be benefactors, that self-sufficiency and work were their salvation, not charity, whether it came from private organizations or from the state. There were few relief protests in the late century, and Keyssar reports that those that did occur were "theatrical rather than coercive" and "aimed at audiences rather than targets."[117] That is, they did not threaten central institutions and could therefore be safely shut down or ignored. That so many trade unionists and workers, especially in the depression of 1873, condemned charity and demanded work instead is a measure of how well ingrained the anti-charity and work ethics are in American working-class culture. "I am a workingman, therefore an honest one, and would refuse a dollar I did not earn, for I am neither a beggar to accept charity nor a thief to take what belongs to another, however he came by it."[118] Indeed, it is this pride in work that makes reformers' claims about the moral causes of poverty so hard to fathom. As the Rev. S.S. Craig of Canada told the NCCC, "The poverty of today is not the result of a lack of industry on the part of those who are suffering. Labor is not refusing to go to work. It is clamoring, beseeching, praying God and man for an opportunity to work."[119]

THE RETURN TO RELIEF

One last set of observations is in order. By the depression of 1893, we can see many cities responding to turmoil by greatly expanding their relief programs. Relief *was* used to quiet the throbbing mob, *pace* Raymond Mohl. As John Brooks described the changing scene in 1894:

> Discontent never got so sharp and varied expression. Class hatreds never showed themselves in more sinister form. Socialistic opinions were never before so widely uttered, nor have they ever at any time received in the press such universal attention. . . . This new feeling comes from a democracy that has become conscious of definite political power. It at last believes that laws may be made and so directed that a broader and higher standard of living can be assured to the masses . . . [and with provocation from Socialists, men who used to accept seasonal unemployment] become restless and bitter against conditions which they have hitherto taken as a matter of course.[120]

Charities Review reported in 1894, "Some communities when the hard times came this winter, and the army of the unemployed swept through the streets, were panic-stricken, the inhabitants fortified themselves behind soup-houses, and threw loaves of bread out upon the besiegers; naturally the siege continued."[121] Ironically, the places where relief cutbacks did occur were least prepared for the widespread dislocations of the 1893 (and 1907 and 1914) depressions and were sites of some of the greatest agitation for renewed public intervention and great increases in relief. Some district committees in New York even established "secret slush funds" for relief as early as 1891.[122] By 1895, perhaps as many as half of all COSs had established their own relief funds.[123] Many cities created what today we would call public-works projects, and millions were appropriated for parks improvement in New York as a seemingly direct result of labor agitation. Beginning in 1893, in the wake of widespread new demands, numerous cities that had previously abolished or reduced aid reinstated or increased it, by 300 percent in Pittsburgh and Omaha, 200 percent in Milwaukee, and 43 percent in Detroit and Minneapolis.[124] Put another way, ending relief helped foster the conditions for expanding it, just as expansions of relief engendered calls for its reduction or abolition.[125] And, as we have already seen in New York and Philadelphia and shall see further, cutbacks in public relief often were followed by expansions in private relief and public subsidies to private providers that, in the case of Indiana, for example, replaced the public cuts 70 cents on the dollar.[126]

By the end of the century, anti-relief reformers had succeeded in dominating public and political debate about relief. But when there was elite resistance, as in Boston, it had impact. Relief, though vital to many of its beneficiaries, was, by design, stingy; in a political culture that valued work, any work, over welfare, and in which citizens had not learned to make demands of the federal government and were only beginning to make demands of their states, the Gilded Age unemployed did not often turn to government for relief. Instead, work was the focus of their agitation. But when there was more direct public resistance or disruption directed at relief offices or officials, as in Chicago or Buffalo, or more broadly after 1893, the poor achieved victories. We can now turn to how elite consensus and the failure of resistance enabled late-twentieth-century reform.

4

Reform Redux:

Dethroning the Welfare Queen

The lobbies are empty. There is no outcry against what we are doing.

—Daniel Patrick Moynihan,
from the Senate floor, July 18, 1996

The passage of the Personal Responsibility and Work Opportunity Reconciliation Act of 1996 marked the second great American relief retrenchment. Just as the COSs were central actors in the nineteenth century, though not the only ones, so too were anti-welfare think tanks important players in the twentieth century; their impact, though mediated by partisan political struggles, budget pressures, and interest-group wrangling, was profound. It is not that relief was reformed simply because a cabal led by the think tanks wished it so, and it is more than some "vast right-wing conspiracy," but there *was* a conspiracy, a sometimes loosely organized but always well-funded network of conservatives whose successful long-term mobilization, though in evidence since the Reagan presidency, was fully revealed by the 1990s. Its signal achievement, along with great new representation in elected office, was to attain dominance over public debate and policy-making agendas, turning discourse away from twentieth-century liberalism toward the laissez-faire of the Gilded Age. Relief antagonists and the multifaceted institutions they inhabited achieved what Italian radical Antonio Gramsci would call hegemony: in three decades of activism they redefined the problem to be solved from the injustice of poverty to the dangers of welfare, and as E.E. Schattschneider reminds us, *"the definition of the alternatives is the supreme instrument of power."* [1] Consider the main provisions of the PRA—time limits on benefits, the abolition of the (limited) right to relief, marriage incentives, work requirements, antipregnancy programs—and ask what problems they sought to solve: dependence, laziness, profligacy. These problems existed in the political world, but they were not, by all available evidence, widespread social conditions.

Without the successful remoralization of policy discourse and the institutionalization of the anti-relief movement, the PRA could not have come to pass. This renewed prominence of old ideas and policy prescriptions was no accident of fate, nor the product of some cycle of history, nor was it evidence of some culturally embedded antipathy to poor relief; rather, it was the culmination of a sophisticated public relations campaign about labor policy, market regulation, taxation, and the very size and role of government that began more than twenty years before the passage of the PRA (and continues still), and for which welfare was one among a host of targets, albeit one of the most symbolically potent and politically vulnerable ones. These New Victorians sought reductions in programs that, like the outdoor relief of the late nineteenth century, had come to be seen as taking sides in the battle between capital and labor, acting on behalf of workers and interfering with the "natural" operations of the "free" market.[2] It is a measure of how far reformers have taken us that an American Enterprise Institute work cautioned in 1976 that, "partisan rhetoric aside, few people seriously envisage dismantling the welfare state."[3] Twenty years later the Speaker of the House of Representatives, Newt Gingrich, would envisage just that. With the help of a Democratic president and substantial Democratic support in Congress, AFDC was repealed. And today Democrats and Republicans alike contemplate the "privatization" of Social Security and regressive "reforms" to Medicare, Medicaid, food stamps, public housing, Head Start, the school-lunch program, and the Women, Infants, and Children Supplemental Nutrition Program (WIC). These newer campaigns build much of their logic upon the rhetoric of anti-welfare efforts; the near-universal unpopularity of AFDC and its limited reach made it a relatively easy first target for rollback. But, as has become clear, it was only a first target. We might thus think of welfare as a canary in the coal mine. A deceased canary.

A SUMMARY OF RELIEF AND RELIEF RETRENCHMENT

To understand recent welfare reforms we do not need to devote as much effort as we did with Gilded Age policy making to documenting what happened, where it happened, and when. In this case of national repeal (albeit one that consolidated some prior state-level changes), we have only one *why* to confront, not the multitudinous *whys* of local variation discussed in the previous chapter.[4] Aid to Families with Dependent Children (created in the Social Security Act of 1935 as Aid to Dependent Children) was, thanks to the relentless drumbeat of its opponents, despised. It was believed to be exorbitantly expensive and too generous: in a 1994 survey, 20 percent thought that welfare spending was higher than military spending.[5] In truth, welfare never reached more than 5.5 percent of the population, never even half of the poor,[6] and even with food stamps included, no state's AFDC benefits were ever enough to lift a family above the poverty line.[7] Nonetheless, cash benefits (along with Medicaid) were often higher than the return from the employment available to recipients, especially if expenses such as child care and transportation are included; this created a disincentive to accept low-wage work, as relief opponents have claimed. For much of its life, AFDC offered benefits only to children and (later) to their mothers; men and couples were ineligible until 1963. So-called man-in-the-house rules also in effect until the 1960s forced women to live alone with their children (or pretend to): this may well have discouraged marriage and two-parent households, and a household with a single wage earner, all else being equal, is likely to be poorer than a household with two wage earners, so single-parent families are generally poorer than families with two parents present.[8] Through these and other formal rules and informal but common practices, welfare intruded into and attempted to control the lives of poor women.[9] In a society unreconciled to its racial past and often in denial of its racist present, black women (who were often half of all those on the rolls and always used the rolls in greater proportion than their white counterparts) were identified as the beneficiaries of the program,[10] and as large numbers of middle-class women entered the workforce in the 1970s, some were taught to resent those poorer women who, thanks to welfare, were able to remain home and care for their children, although survival on welfare alone was impossible.[11] While myths persisted of a dependent class of long-term welfare users, from the 1820s to the 1990s the average "spell" on welfare fluctuated little, between eight and thirteen months.[12] Public antipathy nonetheless showed up often in opinion surveys. In a 1995 Public Agenda poll, 65 percent of respondents said that "welfare encourages the wrong lifestyle and values." In a 1997 *Newsweek* survey, 51 percent said that welfare cuts represented government "ending a system that keeps people poor."[13] These are some of the reasons that opposition to AFDC, though differently rooted kinds of opposition, was widespread. Complaints from the left were nearly as common as complaints from the right. As Harvard professor and onetime Clinton policy advisor David Ellwood wrote with only slight exaggeration, *"Everyone hates welfare."*[14]

The Personal Responsibility Act repealed Title IV-A of the Social Security Act; in place of Title IV's AFDC, which was granted to all who qualified no matter how many qualified, now stands Temporary Assistance to Needy Families (TANF), "block grants" of fixed amounts (i.e., no matter how many people qualify for benefits, the money available to each state remains the same). As Section 401(b) of the PRA emphasized, "This part shall not be interpreted to entitle any individual or family to assistance under any State program funded under this part." There were no federal criteria set for determining need: states were given broad latitude for setting benefit levels, with only the requirement that their program "serve all political subdivisions in the State (not necessarily in a uniform manner)," that eligibility be determined with "objective criteria," and that all recipients receive "fair and equitable treatment." The PRA decreed that no one may receive benefits for more than five years during his or her life, exempting 20 percent of each state's caseload. TANF recipients were required to work in exchange for any benefits after two years of assistance, earlier if states chose; Medicaid could be terminated if a recipient refused work. Because the PRA eliminated the automatic provision of Medicaid to welfare recipients, the PRA further "encouraged" poor women to move into the workforce by eliminating one of the most powerful "perverse incentives" of AFDC—health care for them and their children. The PRA changed the method of calculating food-stamp eligibility, reducing the average benefit from 80 cents per person per meal to 66 cents per person per meal. Childless unemployed Americans ages eighteen to fifty were permitted to receive food stamps for no more than three months per year. Even with subsequent revisions to the PRA, most legal immigrants were denied almost any federal cash assistance. The PRA permitted states to reduce benefits if recipients' children did not attend school ("learnfare"), to deny increased aid for children born while their mother was receiving benefits (the "family cap"), and to reduce benefits by as much as 25 percent if a recipient did not identify the biological father of her children ("spermfare," we might call this provision). Some $500 million was set aside for abstinence education programs, and cash bonuses were made available for the states that most reduced out-of-wedlock birth rates without increasing abortion rates.[15]

EARLY SUCCESSES

That the think tanks I have described achieved influence over a broad range of policies and decision-making processes is little disputed. Mobilization succeeded. More than thirty American Enterprise Institute–affiliated people occupied senior-level positions in the Reagan administration,[16] and twelve Heritage Foundation fellows had secured administration jobs by 1984.[17] The Hoover Institution, established "to demonstrate the evils of the doctrines of Karl Marx," was nearly bankrupt in the 1960s, but after an influx of corporate donations in the 1970s rose to such heights that it provided even more appointments to the Reagan administration than either Heritage or the American Enterprise Institute, a total of forty.[18] Brookings (which in its early history opposed the New Deal) may have served as a "Democratic government-in-exile during the Nixon-Ford years" but later shifted its focus rightward toward monetary policy, deregulation, and the USSR, in part to compete with the American Enterprise Institute for financial support.[19] Heritage "claimed that more than 60 percent of its proposals had been adopted by the [Reagan] administration,"[20] and the structure and the rationale for the tax cuts of Reagan's 1981 budget owe much to economists from Hoover.[21] The American Enterprise Institute provided the incoming Reagan administration with a briefing book, *Mandate for Leadership,* that was well regarded and much used by the administration, and even landed on the *Washington Post* best-seller list.[22]

Earlier, President Jimmy Carter had presided over large cuts in social programs in a failed attempt to combat inflation. Perhaps "the most conservative Democrat since Grover Cleveland," as one wag said, Carter believed that the federal government had grown too big and too expensive and that its programs served far too many. Although he did attempt, like Nixon, to pass a negative income tax (and 1975, under Gerald Ford, did see the implementation of the Earned Income Tax Credit), the postwar retreat on American welfare began under Carter, not Reagan.[23] But it was under Reagan that the assault was launched in full measure. Although overall social welfare spending increased throughout the 1980s, mostly due to rises in Social Security and Medicare, programs benefiting those most in need suffered as the Reagan administration and a complicit Congress carried out policies much in line with Heritage's recommendations. Procedural changes for determining AFDC eligibility enacted in Reagan's first budget alone "saved" $93 million per month and rendered ineligible some 493,000 families.[24] By 1983, food stamp spending was down 17 percent, school lunch programs were reduced by one-third, the job-training program CETA was eliminated, and housing spending was down by one-third from what it had been during the Carter administration. From 1972 to 1984, the combined real value of AFDC and food stamp benefits for a woman with three children declined by 22 percent. From 1982 to 1985, expenditures for unemployment insurance declined by nearly 7 percent, for AFDC by 12.7 percent, and for food stamps by 12.6 percent; child nutrition programs were reduced by over 27 percent (though WIC increased by more than 4 percent), and assistance to help pay heating bills declined over 8 percent.[25] From 1980 to 1984, a family with income below $10,000 a year paid $95 more in taxes, while those with income over $200,000 a year saw their tax burden decline by more than $17,000.[26] By 1985, the official national poverty rate had risen to 14 percent; it was 28.4 percent for Hispanic Americans and 31.3 percent for African Americans. More than 20 percent of all children, 39.6 percent of Hispanic children, and 43.1 percent of African American children were poor.

Nonetheless, by 1986 the Great Society concern for poverty had become increasingly a concern for welfare, thanks in no small measure to Charles A. Murray's *Losing Ground*.[27] In this climate, amid the rhetorical assault on the welfare queen, the National Governors Association, led by Arkansan Bill Clinton, presented a plan for welfare reform. It proclaimed that "the principal responsibility of government in the welfare contract is to provide education, job training and/or job placement services to all employable recipients."[28] That plan would become part of the 1988 Family Support Act (FSA), another Moynihan work-centered approach, which expanded his 1967 Work Incentive Program (WIN). The FSA required workfare for 15 percent of all adult AFDC recipients (20 percent by 1995) while providing matching funds for job training (through the state-run JOBS program); it required that states offer transitional child care and Medicaid benefits, extend benefits to some two-parent families under the AFDC-UP program, and enact child-support collection measures. The federal government was following the lead of the states: by 1987, forty already had some small workfare program operating under provisions of WIN, the 1972 Talmadge Amendments (which required recipients to register for work), and similar amendments in 1981.[29] Also in 1981, the Reagan administration issued the first grant of "waivers" of AFDC regulations to allow states to "experiment" with their welfare programs using a provision contained in a 1962 amendment to the Social Security Act.[30] Wisconsin received the first, allowing it to implement a "learnfare" program.[31] Other early "innovators," such as New Jersey and California, were soon followed by Michigan and Massachusetts, adopting learnfare, workfare, time limits, and family cap provisions consistent with proposals put forth by Heritage and the American Enterprise Institute; some were implemented and evaluated by Hudson.[32] (By the time of the PRA's passage, forty-three states had been granted waivers.)[33] The FSA was a very different kind of policy from those proposed and enacted in the 1990s, however; there was no sharp cutoff or strict sanctions, the entitlement status of AFDC was preserved (and never seriously in jeopardy), women with young children were exempt, and work requirements were modest and targeted at small numbers of recipients. The fact that the program was poorly funded and poorly implemented further limited its impact. The ideological intransigence and the harsh moralizing rhetoric that would come to dominate debate over the PRA were there, but only dimly, still on the fringes in the 1980s.[34] It took time to relegitimize Gilded Age ideas, and even these reforms met with some formidable resistance.

By 1990, fully one-seventh of all census tracts in the nation's one hundred largest cities had poverty rates of 40 percent or higher. The federal contribution to city budgets had declined from 18 percent in 1980 to 6.4 percent in 1990.[35] Between 1970 and 1990 New York City's per capita expenses for poor people dropped from $537 to $285.[36] From the 1970s to the 1990s, the real value of AFDC benefits had declined by 30 percent; the real value of AFDC and food stamps combined declined by 25 percent. By 1992, both programs brought a typical family of three only to 72 percent of the federal poverty line.[37] The value of the minimum wage declined by nearly one-third from 1979 to 1989. From 1979 to 1991 the ability of federal means-tested programs to lift families from poverty had declined 29 percent. During the same period, official poverty rates rose 23.9 percent.[38] Meanwhile, notions of dependency notwithstanding, by

1992 over 40 percent of welfare mothers had worked while receiving relief.[39] Eighteen percent of all poor families had a full-time worker in them.[40] By 1995, 29.7 percent of all workers earned poverty-level wages.[41] Despite the confluence of events, economic, demographic, and political, that had served to increase and deepen poverty (by 1994, nearly 40 percent of those in poverty had incomes below 50 percent of the poverty level)[42] and to weaken the ability of AFDC to reduce it, Clinton in 1992 and the Contract with America in 1994 "promised to end welfare *first* and end poverty *later.*"[43]

ENTER CLINTON

In 1991 Bruce Reed, a campaign volunteer who would later become a senior domestic policy advisor, wrote a speech that Clinton delivered on October 23 at Georgetown University. "In a Clinton administration," the candidate said, "we're going to put an end to welfare as we know it. We'll give them all the help they need for up to two years. But after that, if they're able to work, they'll have to take a job in the private sector, or start earning their way through community service."[44] That pledge would take on a political life of its own—"a guiding star," Reed called it. "You let loose a lot of forces when you say 'end welfare as we know it,' " warned Moynihan. Ellwood would later call the pledge "vacuous and incendiary."[45] Yet, as Wisconsin governor Tommy Thompson put it, "it's a fantastic campaign issue."[46] (The Contract with America made that clear, for 1994 was proclaimed to be "a campaign in which voters rewarded a barrage of anti-welfare attacks.")[47] The 1992 Clinton campaign built its advertising in close states around the welfare/workfare pledge:[48] as he said in one, "For so long, government has failed us, and one of its worst failures has been welfare. I have a plan to end welfare as we know it—to break the cycle of welfare dependency."[49]

Clinton's claim reveals that government relief had become so debased by the 1990s that even such gains as had been attributed to the War on Poverty were dismissed, and by a Democrat no less. As Lawrence Mead wrote in *Beyond Entitlement,* "Poverty did not really disappear; it was overwhelmed by cash. . . . Policymakers have not really solved poverty, only exchanged it for the problem of large-scale dependency."[50] Gingrich took this further, describing the downfall of civilization itself as "precisely where three generations of Washington-dominated, centralized government, welfare-state policies have carried us." Indeed, the failure of the Great Society ("a disaster more harmful to more Americans than the Vietnam War," said Gingrich), forms a key thread in late-twentieth-century anti-relief narratives.[51] Rector argued that there was little *material* poverty in the United States and that the problem was, instead, *behavioral* poverty, the core of which was welfare itself: "public spending in the past, intended to alleviate material poverty, led to dramatic increases in behavioral poverty. The welfare system established in the War on Poverty heavily subsidized illegitimacy, divorce, and non-work. . . . The War on Poverty may have raised the material standard of living for a few Americans, but it has done so at the cost of creating whole communities in which traditional two-parent families have vanished, work is rare or nonexistent, and multiple generations have grown up dependent on the government."[52] Gilder was less measured: "What actually happened since 1964 was a vast expansion of the welfare rolls that halted in its tracks an ongoing improvement in the lives of the poor, particularly blacks, and left behind—and here I choose my words as carefully as I can—a wreckage of broken lives and families worse than the aftermath of slavery."[53] "It is now broadly accepted," wrote Murray "that the social programs of the 1960s broadly failed; that the government is clumsy and ineffectual when it intervenes in local life; and that the principles of personal responsibility, penalties for bad behavior, and rewards for good behavior have to be reintroduced into social policy."[54]

The "failure" of the Great Society was rooted in a rhetorical sleight of hand that Rector and the Heritage Foundation used in 1995 with their "America's Failed $5.4 Trillion War on Poverty" (a trick Murray used earlier in *Losing Ground*). The report was used to fuel public and political indignation and the legislative and executive campaigns against relief (and Rector's figure was repeated like a mantra during congressional welfare reform debate in 1996). It was a simple enough game; he included in his figures expenditures such as the Earned Income Tax Credit (which only goes to working people), Medicaid (half of which goes to blind, elderly, and disabled people), and other programs that are not restricted to poor people (student loans, for example) or which Americans do not typically identify as welfare. The Center on Budget and Policy Priorities estimated that 70 percent of what Rector and others described as "welfare" programs went to households that did not receive AFDC.[55] But a war on poverty was never really even fought. Lyndon Johnson requested $500 million in new money from Congress for a "war" one Council of Economic Advisers economist estimated would cost $11 billion per year.[56] No matter. Facts are rarely useful in such debates. As Stefancic and Delgado observed, "Such stories grab attention more effectively than do the endless lists of statistics recited by liberals."[57] Piven concurred: "This sort of argument is not won or lost with facts, and certainly not with facts alone."[58] Whatever the actual evidence, the rhetorical failure of the War on Poverty was important. By arguing, as Reagan famously did, that we waged a war on poverty and poverty won, the case was made for the claim that state action cannot improve social conditions.

While Clinton's first bill built upon the Family Support Act and established measures to make easier the transition from "welfare to work," as the rhetorical flourishes of dependency and failed welfare programs merged with election-year politics and a bold new Republican majority in Congress, the legislation that would ultimately get enacted contained fewer and fewer provisions for support and assistance and a greater and greater focus on punitive measures to force women into the workforce, whatever the availability of decent-paying jobs, health care, and child care. These political circumstances were important, but inexplicable without this transformative shift in policy discourse, especially given the lack of empirical support for reformers' claims.

Three proposals were made public while Clinton's first plan was in formulation: one fairly moderate bill with 160 Republican co-sponsors, H.R. 3500; a more conservative bill sponsored by Representative James Talent and Senator Launch Faircloth drafted with the help of Robert Rector; and a third introduced by Democratic Senator Joseph Lieberman of Connecticut. All took the Clinton/Reed pledge to its logical conclusion and proposed to end welfare entirely for younger women with children, as Murray had been proposing for so long. That they understood the consequences seems clear, since they included in their bills increased funding for homeless shelters and new funding to establish orphanages, another idea that Murray had long championed. Lieberman defended one such bill by noting that his father had been in an orphanage and had said that it was "a wonderful place."[59] Each of those alternative proposals cost more than the plan Clinton would submit.[60] Charles Murray, William Bennett, and Bill Kristol decided that the leading bill, H.R. 3500, was "too timid" and jointly urged a move toward a more conservative strategy. Bennett's Empower America repeatedly condemned the Republican bill and urged Murray's abolitionist approach,[61] first in a public memo by Bennett, Jack Kemp, and Vin Weber[62] and then in op-eds that appeared in some twenty-five newspapers.[63] Gary Bauer of the Family Research Council lambasted conservatives for emphasizing the economic over the social, co-wrote family-focused op-ed articles about welfare reform with Texas senator Phil Gramm, and pushed for "family cap" provisions that allowed states to deny additional support to children born to any woman already receiving welfare benefits.[64]

Clinton's bill was unveiled on June 14, 1994. Among its other provisions were the strictest time limits ever proposed by an American president. It was dismissed by Republicans as too liberal. This is one measure of the success with which the problem had been redefined and the political terrain had been reconfigured. Kristol condemned it even before its official release as "merely a rhetorical diversionary tactic" and urged in the pages of the *Wall Street Journal* that conservatives focus more intensely on preventing illegitimacy by shaping a program that would better frighten women, one that enshrined as policy the belief that "if it is your own behavior that could land you on welfare, then you don't get it, or you get very little of it." Welfare reform legislation thereafter degenerated into something like an inverted arms race, with each player proposing stricter and cheaper measures than the last. While it seems undeniable that the Republicans, having gained majority congressional control in 1994, pushed Clinton to the right, it seems equally clear that Clinton pushed Republicans to the right, too; they ultimately set aside H.R. 3500 for a more conservative bill based upon the Talent/Faircloth/Rector proposal that had informed the Contract with America. More critically, Clinton's cavalier rhetoric, whatever his actual policy goals, made politically palatable even the more regressive proposals of Gingrich and other Republicans. As the *Weekly Standard* observed just prior to the PRA's ultimate passage, "Ideas like limiting welfare benefits to five years and abolishing the federal guarantee of cash payments to single mothers were not even contemplated by congressional Republicans as recently as three years ago."[65] The Chamber of Commerce had reported only in August 1994 that "most welfare reformers, even conservative ones, generally dismiss Murray's approach."

This was a battle between Democrats and Republicans, to be sure. Clinton's decision to veto the first two reform bills, which also included significant and politically unpalatable "reforms" to Medicare, attests to that. But it was as critically a battle among Republicans.[66] The family-focused arguments of the right gained increasing prominence and influence, even while a 1995 report from the Cato Institute, *The Work Versus Welfare Trade-Off*, offered widely circulated analysis arguing that "in 40 states welfare pays more than an $8.00 an hour job. In 17 states the welfare package is more generous than a $10.00 an hour job."[67] Such divisions among conservatives help explain the success of reform: Clinton's bill was economically conservative and consistent with many Republican suggestions for reform, and the marriage-focused reform plans offered Republicans who wanted to oppose Clinton for political (as opposed to policy) purposes a reason to reject his conservative reform as too tepid.

WELFARE AND THE THINK TANK

From the start of the late-twentieth-century mobilization of business, welfare was a target of the think tanks, Heritage especially. In the 1970s, articles in conservative journals like *The Public Interest* began forcefully reconstructing perverse incentives arguments, explaining to readers how welfare discouraged work and so caused poverty; Heritage's *Policy Review* explored the ways in which the War on Poverty had supposedly expanded the black and Latino underclass; and Hoover, among others, fought the suggestion of a guaranteed income by arguing that it would discourage work effort.[68] Among the very first projects of Heritage's predecessor organization was a campaign, with research conducted by Hoover and presented to the

Senate Finance Committee by California governor Ronald
Reagan, against the Family Assistance Plan.[69] Mead's *New Politics of Poverty* was funded by the Bradley, Olin, and Scaife
Foundations; Schwartz later wrote *Fighting Poverty with Virtue*
while at Hudson, whose Welfare Policy Center was established
with a $175,000 grant from Bradley. Olasky's *The Tragedy of
American Compassion* was funded by the Heritage Foundation,
where he worked from 1989 to 1991, and by the Bradley Foundation; *Tragedy* was reissued in 1995 with a preface by Charles
Murray. Gingrich, given the book by William Bennett, made it
required reading for all new Republican members of the 104th
Congress. Olasky was later invited by Karl Rove to lead the
policy team on welfare issues during Bush's 1993 Texas guber-
natorial campaign, and *Tragedy,* along with *The Demoralization
of Society* by Himmelfarb, a member of the American Enterprise Institute's Council of Academic Advisors since 1987, and
James Q. Wilson's *The Moral Sense,* were among the books
Rove gave candidate Bush to read. Olasky would become an
advisor to Bush's presidential campaign and a leader of "faith-
based" advocates who urged that greater government funding
for social services be granted to churches (even to those "perva-
sively sectarian" religious organizations precluded by courts
from receiving state aid) because they would be, by their very
nature, he said, more effective than any public program.)[70] The
Manhattan Institute can take much credit for *Wealth and
Poverty* and *Losing Ground,* two of the most influential anti-
welfare tracts. Murray, since 1990 a Bradley Fellow at the
American Enterprise Institute, may be the single most influential twentieth-century proponent of anti-relief policies, and
Sidney Blumenthal reported that *Losing Ground* was "the crucial text" of Reagan's second term—Gilder's *Wealth and Poverty*
was the crucial text of the first—and that Murray's book could
be found "on virtually every other desk" in the Office of Management and Budget.[71] It remained influential during debate

over the PRA: many of its provisions found their way into the legislation, congressional staffers and legislators cited it as a powerful guide, and Clinton himself found occasions to agree with the parts of Murray's (and Moynihan's) diagnosis that placed out-of-wedlock births at the center of the "welfare crisis" and the concomitant breakdown of traditional values.

Writing about the PRA, reporter Barbara DeLollis, like others, identified Heritage's Robert Rector as "one of the law's authors,"[72] and former House Ways and Means Committee staffer (now Brookings Fellow) Ron Haskins observed that while Murray may have been the "intellectual leader" of the pro-family reformers, it was Rector who plotted and pushed the successful political strategies.[73] Heritage helped draft the Contract with America, which included the Personal Responsibility Act among its provisions, a plan consistent with Gingrich's insistence that a conservative "opportunity society" should replace the "failed" welfare state. Gingrich was an ardent, vocal, and belligerent proselytizer for a "renewed American civilization," one built on Victorian-style values, and he regularly condemned individual politicians, and American society generally, for their immoral ways. Thomas Ferguson has written that foundation head Richard Mellon Scaife, a former CIA propagandist and longtime supporter of Heritage, "had as much to do with the Gingrich Revolution as Gingrich himself."[74] During the first one hundred days of Gingrich's 104th Congress, Heritage testified more than a hundred times and held over a hundred briefings for members, helping them compile data and marshal arguments to support their proposals.[75] Speaker Gingrich called Heritage "without question the most far-reaching conservative organization in the country in the war of ideas."[76] The Manhattan Institute was a key source of policy ideas for New York mayor Rudolph Giuliani and helped design elements of New York's workfare program.[77] The Bradley Foundation was a large funder of Hudson's Wisconsin welfare reform advocacy, and had a formal role in implementing its Wisconsin Works (W-2) program.[78] It even helped secure a spot for Charles Murray on Wisconsin's welfare reform "task force."[79] Decades of activism had paid off.

DISSENTING VOICES

Nonetheless, groups we might expect to oppose the PRA were amply represented in congressional testimony, and liberal think tanks and child and recipient advocacy groups testified about as often as conservative think tanks and social conservatives. According to Kent Weaver's analysis of those who testified between 1993 and 1996 before the House Ways and Means Committee or Senate Finance Committee on welfare issues, no other single type of group testified more than conservative think tanks, who provided 12.9 percent of all testimony. Social conservative groups offered another 4.84 percent. That's 18 percent of all testimony from conservative anti-welfare reformers, not including "centrist" think tanks (4.84 percent), and the conservatives who were among the governors, nongovernmental service providers, university experts, and those in other categories. Nonetheless, liberal think tanks offered 4.84 percent of all testimony, and "liberal/child/recipient advocacy" groups delivered another 8.06 percent, bringing this total also to 12.9 percent. By this crude measure, it seems an even match.[80] Opponents even achieved some successes, preventing policy from taking an even harsher turn, and congressional staffers credited the Center on Budget and Policy Priorities with preserving the food-stamp entitlement and including a "maintenance-of-effort" provision in the PRA, which prevented states from cutting their contributions to welfare-related programs below certain levels.[81]

Anti-reform forces ultimately failed, however, for several reasons. First, their influence was only superficial. Data on congressional testimony can be misleading, since some of those we might expect to have offered defenses of relief supported reform. Catholic Charities, for example, one of the "advocacy" groups, had influence in the reform debate mostly by virtue of its support for efforts to increase marriage and reduce pregnancy among the poor. R. Allen Hays counted the American Public Welfare Association among the most influential "public interest groups" that testified on welfare issues;[82] its name might lead one to expect anti-reform testimony, but it is the organization of state welfare bureaucrats, officials who served at the pleasure of their (often Republican) governors.[83] Michigan's welfare director, for example, who would come to take a job leading Lockheed Martin's welfare contracting department, spearheaded Governor Engler's anti-relief efforts: clearly, one to be counted among reform's proponents.[84] Labor unions were virtually absent (1.61 percent of testimony), while "private-sector citizens" and "everyday citizens," among whom we would presumably find recipients themselves, were entirely absent from the proceedings. Groups claiming to represent poor people were to be found, but poor people themselves were typically not.

That said, congressional testimony is not a particularly good measure of influence anyway, since, like speechmaking on the floor, it is often an act of theater more than an effort at persuasion, and the real locus of lawmaking power and the crafting of legislation takes place behind the scenes, in subcommittee meeting with a small handful of the most interested parties.[85] Some influential actors, like Jason Turner, did not testify.[86] Charles Murray did not testify either, yet even in the mid-1990s *Losing Ground* was repeatedly cited by those involved in the process as influential in their thinking.

Still, Robert Rector tied with the General Accounting Office for testifying more than any other group or individual.[87] Committee staff involved in the PRA interviewed by Pamela

Winston cited Rector as the most or among the most influential actors involved in reform, whereas the most prominent anti-reform groups, such as the Children's Defense Fund, "alienated" legislators with their "purist" positions and were of little or no influence in the process. Michael Laracy of the Annie E. Casey Foundation also noted the weakness of anti-reform advocates during the process of drafting and passing the PRA (noting instead the influence of Heritage, the Christian Coalition, and the Family Research Council).[88] Part of this failure of influence is a matter of partisan politics: once Republicans took over Congress in 1994, the Children's Defense Fund and other anti-reform advocacy groups that had affiliated themselves with Democrats and Democratic leaders had no ties to Republican representatives and their new committee leaders.[89] To varying degrees, and with some exceptions, "liberal" groups, whether they testified or not, had minimal influence on the shape of the legislation. The U.S. Conference of Mayors was "out of it," as one staffer told Winston. Governors were influential, but through the Republican Governors Association rather than the National Governors Association, and none was more influential or involved in the process than Michigan's John Engler and Wisconsin's Tommy Thompson, both of whom even edited drafts of the bill. Both, importantly, also had close ties with Representative Clay Shaw, the Ways and Means Human Resources Subcommittee chairman who was one of the principal architects of the PRA. Rector, on the other hand, magnified his influence because of the close ties he maintained with the marriage-focused "foot soldiers" of the Christian right, who had the ability to quickly generate mail, phone calls, and press. The director of legislative affairs of the Christian Coalition reveals his dependence upon Rector's advice: "I know that I can just pick up the phone and call Robert. It's like calling your mechanic or doctor."[90] Winston reported that staffers credited Rector with the illegitimacy bonuses and abstinence-education provisions of the PRA, and the Progressive Policy Institute (the Democratic Leadership Council's centrist think tank) with the performance bonus provisions. Cato and the American Enterprise Institute (especially Douglas Besharov, their welfare "specialist") were "somewhat influential."[91]

Another cause for failure was that anti-reform (let alone pro-welfare) arguments did not infiltrate media coverage of the events leading up to the PRA. With the exception of Jason De-Parle of the *New York Times,* most mainstream reporting on welfare was ill-informed by credible social-science research and based upon the presumptions and stereotypes that the right had been working for so long to bring to light, which is unsurprising given the dependence of the elite press on conservative think tanks. Myths about the liberal media notwithstanding, there is a growing body of research documenting the greater presence of conservative policy organizations as sources for major media; this need not reflect ideological bias, however, nor is that my claim. Much of the higher presence of conservative versus liberal think tanks in national newspapers (*New York Times, Wall Street Journal, Washington Post, Washington Times, USA Today, Christian Science Monitor*) can be explained by their larger advocacy budgets (and therefore their greater ability to be available to journalists on deadline and provide them with useful, concise information) and their greater presence (and therefore accessibility) in Washington, D.C.[92] As Rich and Weaver summarize:

Newspapers tend to rely on the same think tanks as sources. The Brookings Institution is the most commonly cited in all except the identifiably conservative Washington Times, where it is the fifth most commonly cited. The Heritage Foundation and the American Enterprise Institute (AEI) are ranked in the top three in all but the Washington Times, where AEI is fourth. Think-tank citations in all of the national newspapers show a striking concentration in just a few organizations, with the frequency of mention of the top three think tanks cited ranging from 32.3 percent (*New York Times*) to more than 41 percent (*USA Today*) of total think tank citations.[93]

Liberal media watchdog Fairness and Accuracy in Reporting (FAIR) produced studies that confirm Rich and Weaver's findings: in 1995 conservative institutions received 51 percent of all think-tank citations in major newspapers and broadcast media, "centrist" organizations received 41 percent (Brookings falls into this category in their study), and progressive think tanks (for example, the Economic Policy Institute and the Center on Budget and Policy Priorities) received 8 percent of all citations.[94] This "conservative advantage" was as pronounced in 1996, the year of reform: 54 percent of all major news media citations were of conservative organizations, although citations of progressive institutions rose to 13 percent.[95] In 1995, Heritage was cited more than any other; in 1996 it came in second to Brookings. In that year, Brookings, Heritage, the American Enterprise Institute, and Cato received more than a thousand citations each, more almost than the next twenty institutions combined.[96] And as Paget noted of another study, "Corporate funders were rarely identified, even when they made up more than a quarter of the [conservative] institute's budget. By contrast, when the Economic Policy Institute was quoted, both its ideological predisposition (liberal) and its funding source (roughly one-quarter of its budget is from labor) usually were identified."[97]

There was a similarly distorted spectrum of opinion in major media during welfare debate. A FAIR study of the *New York Times, Washington Post, Time, Newsweek,* ABC News, and the *MacNeil/Lehrer Newshour* from December 1, 1994, to February 24, 1995, found that in reporting on welfare, which affects mostly women, men constituted 71 percent of all sources. Almost 60 percent of all sources were current or former government officials, with Representative Clay Shaw the most quoted source and Newt Gingrich close behind, followed by Bill Clinton. Of state and local officials, anti-welfare governors Engler and Thompson dominated, while their states' programs went largely unexamined, much less critiqued. Welfare recipients were about 10 percent of all sources, but they usually appeared as "embodiments" of "pathology," or to reaffirm "expert" opinion, and teenagers, although a small percentage of mothers on welfare, were grossly overrepresented. Similarly, when welfare advocacy organizations were called upon (9 percent of all citations) it was typically to disagree at the margins, not to offer a critique of the whole enterprise or to refute the assertions of welfare opponents. As the authors of the study put it, "Critics of the Republican plan sometimes seemed to span the spectrum from A to B." Organized labor was rarely present, and a representative of a women's rights organization appeared once. The stories were about the deviant behavior of poor women, the ire of taxpayers, and the partisan gamesmanship taking place within a broad Washington consensus that welfare had failed. Reporters made little effort to critically evaluate the claims of reformers.[98]

This dominance of pro-reform voices constrained not only elite political debate and policy itself but seems to have influenced polled public opinion.[99] From 1991 to 1995, while the value of welfare benefits declined, the number of those responding that too much was being spent on welfare increased from 40 percent to over 60 percent. Eighty percent responded in 1995 that welfare required "fundamental" reform. Public support for increased spending on "welfare," "the poor," and even "poor children" all declined. Support for each of the PRA's major provisions (time limits, work requirements, and the family cap) increased throughout the early to mid-1990s.

From 1982 to 1995 the percentage of those who attributed poverty to "insufficient effort" on behalf of the poor nearly doubled. A poll in 2001 by National Public Radio, the Kaiser Family Foundation, and the Kennedy School of Government found that half of all respondents with incomes at least twice the poverty line thought that the "welfare system," a "decline in moral values," and "poor people lacking motivation" were all "major" causes of poverty; about half as many (27 percent) thought a "shortage of jobs" was a major cause. Most striking, perhaps, is that respondents with incomes below twice the poverty line responded similarly across most issues, and even *more* of them thought a "decline in moral values" was a major cause of poverty.[100] Over 80 percent of those polled supported the final reform bill.[101]

Yet most respondents cannot accurately describe policies they say they support.[102] They didn't support the PRA per se: they supported the idea of reform and they supported what they were told that reform meant, and those meanings were defined in the public mind by opponents, not supporters, of poor relief. The larger shift in discourse (perhaps even political culture) that evolved over thirty years, coupled with the dominance of anti-welfare rhetoric in major media during the period of reform debate, enabled reformers to point to all-but-meaningless opinion data and proclaim public support for their efforts. As Fried and Harris have shown, "elites not only react to the public's distrustful mood, but also seek to shape it, frame it, and employ it."[103] Once the full-scale reform campaign ended, opinion returned to its prior level.[104] Had a different story dominated, one that highlighted the industrial causes of poverty, that deconstructed and disproved the myth of the welfare queen, or that showed low-income working people their own financial stake in welfare, the PRA would not have been enacted.

Reformers were able to succeed because there was no mobilization of pro-relief rhetoric to counter this assault, as there had been in some Gilded Age cities, and as there had been, importantly, during Reagan's efforts to scale back the welfare state; this in part helps account for the timing of the PRA. It is a Nixon-in-China effect, that only a president who identified himself as a Democrat could so frontally assault welfare without a massive response from the left. That it was an election year proved important, too. Former Clinton official Peter Edelman described the lack of protest over the PRA from Democrats who wanted Clinton reelected as a "de facto conspiracy of silence."[105] More than once on the Senate floor Moynihan bemoaned the dearth of outrage from advocates for poor people, except for pressure from some religious organizations. National women's groups were unable or unwilling to mobilize their membership against welfare reform, perhaps, as Gwendolyn Mink argued, because "welfare reform did not directly bear on the lives of most [i.e., white, middle-class] feminists" or perhaps because middle-class women who were increasingly compelled to enter the workforce (in the wake of declining family wages since the 1970s) felt little solidarity with women who did not work.[106] This failure of resistance is all the more important given the role it played in many nineteenth-century cities that successfully resisted reform efforts.

BUSINESS REVEALED

Concurrent with the activity of think-tank reformers, the U.S. Chamber of Commerce worked to mobilize businesspeople to support Republican welfare proposals, and was so effective that the National Association of Manufacturers set aside its own plans to lobby for reform since it was so much in agreement with the Chamber's positions.[107] One Lockheed Martin lobbyist was reported to have been at all hearings on the PRA, "presumably for a reason," observed Winston, and, as some Capitol Hill

players revealed to her, business interests generally and potential contractors more specifically "had more influence behind
closed doors than conservative policymakers were willing to
admit."[108]

As sociologist Charles Post reported, "A [1994] *National
Business Agenda* survey of approximately 5,000 of the
Chamber's 210,000 members identified welfare reform as the
fifth highest priority because it 'discourages marriage, under-
writes out-of-wedlock births and creates an expectation of dependence rather than self-sufficiency."[109] A Chamber survey
the following year found that 75 percent of its members
thought a five-year lifetime limit on benefits was too long (20
percent thought it "about right") and 77 percent agreed that all
aid should be denied to children of an unmarried teenager "except in cases of rape or incest."[110] Only 2 percent thought a requirement that all "able-bodied" food-stamp recipients be
required to work for benefits within ninety days "too tough."
Forty-six percent thought tax credits should be offered to businesses as incentives for them to hire relief recipients, 21 percent
preferred training grants or wage subsidies, 19 percent chose
"flexible wage scales" that presumably would exempt them
from minimum-wage laws, and 14 percent thought that no incentives were needed or warranted.

The Chamber's anti-welfare position emphasized issues of
dependency and work over illegitimacy and marriage. In 1995,
its president made clear the purpose of pushing women off the
rolls: "Well, there are lots of jobs. Anytime there's high unemployment, there's also [nonetheless] the long list of jobs that go
a-begging. The fact of the matter is everyone wants to start in
the middle or upper middle, and now you're going to be driven
to start at the bottom and begin to work your way up."[111] They
approvingly cited HHS Secretary Donna Shalala, who noted
the inherent "unfairness" between "those who get up in the
morning and go to work at entry-level jobs and those who stay

on the welfare system."[112] *Business Week* made a similar observation, explaining to its readers that the "economic incentives for redesigning welfare" derived not just from the fact that "welfare wastes tax dollars" and causes crime and illegitimacy, but that the "cost to businesses of such wasted [human] potential is high, resulting in a dearth of qualified applicants for even low-skilled jobs such as running a cash register."[113] Much of the Chamber's attention to welfare-to-work programs focused upon the importance of changing welfare recipients' "attitudes" toward work—especially toward low-status, low-wage work. It lauded programs that offered small businesses subsidies for employing recipients; encouraged policy makers to follow the lead of Oregon, whose program, said one of the Chamber's members, allowed him "to essentially get a good solid employee at a minimal cost";[114] and agreed with Shaw, who earlier introduced his welfare bill at a Chamber event and noted the ways in which welfare reform could "improve the quality and availability of people looking for work."[115] The Chamber urged that small businesses be "centrally involved in all phases of the new welfare system's design, development, operation, and evaluation," that reforms "lower the cost of hiring a low-skilled worker," that employees hired off welfare rolls be subject to a probationary period, and that "during that period they couldn't sue under federal employment regulations pertaining to laws such as the Fair Labor Standards Act, the Americans with Disabilities Act, and the Occupational Safety and Health Act."[116] *The Economist* avoided such self-serving claims, arguing instead that "for the sake of the poor themselves, welfare has to change."[117] In September of 1996, after the final passage of the PRA, the Chamber of Commerce reported succinctly to its members in a headline from its *Nation's Business* journal: "Welfare Overhaul Likely to Please Business Readers."

The Hudson Institute, an advisor to welfare-to-work pro-

grams in Wisconsin, Indiana, and Florida, made the connection between labor-market needs and welfare reform explicit.
While in advance of the PRA it conceded that wages for other
low-skilled workers might be driven down if a sufficient number of former recipients were pushed off the rolls into the labor
force,[118] the real advantage was that "replacing" welfare "is a
boon for low-income citizens who want a career rather than a
welfare check, and for business managers seeking quality employees in a tight labor market."[119] Moreover, training programs for recipients could help employers reduce their training
costs and minimize employee turnover without having to retain workers by raising wages.[120] With Hudson's leadership
and the cooperation of the Chamber of Commerce, Orlando
instituted a "business-driven reform effort." Hudson research
fellow Donald Jonas wrote:

> Leaders in Florida's statewide welfare and workforce agencies
> took the enlightened step to recruit the business community in
> the search for solutions to this seemingly ever-shrinking labor
> market. Beyond heightening the business community's inter-
> est in welfare reform, Florida officials wanted a local business
> community to take ownership in smoothing the process of
> connecting workers who need jobs with employers who need
> workers. . . . Welfare reform opened a window for the busi-
> ness community's return to its necessary seat at the policy
> making table.

He added,

> With welfare reform, Florida and other states are pre-
> sented with a golden opportunity to upgrade their pool of
> available workers to compete for the best jobs in the global
> economy.[121]

American businesses, especially those that needed low-wage, low-skilled workers, clearly understood the economic benefits of welfare-reform just as their counterparts had over a century earlier. While their activism appears below the radar, the Chamber and other business organizations sought to influence the shape of welfare-reform legislation.[122] Their unwillingness to engage more publicly in support of reform might be attributed to a number of factors. First, to make arguments during a period of record inequality and growing corporate power that ending welfare for very poor women would benefit business could do more harm than good. Second, business organizations did not need to act in such explicit fashion: a range of policy organizations (which they had funded) made arguments for them, in language that celebrated the opportunities for upward mobility and the freedom from dependence that reform would offer. Third, their most important activism and key successes had already occurred before the debate over the PRA. The terms of debate had been so well shifted and the range of appropriate solutions so clearly focused upon work that whatever the details of the final legislation, it was likely to be to their benefit. By the time public policy making reaches the visible stage of lawmaking, many of the important decisions have already been made, including decisions on what not to propose (the ability of business to keep certain kinds of proposals off the policy agenda can also be a measure of their strength). Business does not even need to exert direct influence, for given political leaders' dependence upon them for campaign contributions and their desire to appear to support job creation and economic growth, they may act in business's interest without direct pleas to do so.[123] Finally, with established ties to the new Republican leadership, business did not need to take the public stage in order to affect policy because it had other means of influence, including lobbying and contributions through their PACs.[124] More visible, direct efforts to effect change might be an indicator of weakness, not of strength, and would risk expanding the scope of political conflict beyond their ability to control it.[125]

RELIEF REPEALED

The American Spectator saw the dearth of protest discussed above as evidence that reform proposals couldn't possibly be real. "Believe me," wrote its Washington correspondent in 1994, "if a proposal to throw people off welfare after two years was anywhere near the drawing boards there would be the most unbelievable uproar you ever heard in your life. . . . If there is no uproar [in the mainstream press], the 'end of welfare as we know it' is nowhere in sight." [126] But it was. And by the time the Children's Defense Fund held a cautious Stand for Children rally in June of 1996, the game was over.

As Weaver so well described, a confluence of events pushed reform ever more rightward and ever more toward law. The new 1994 Republican majority, with its Contract with America promise to reform welfare in hand, and many in the Democratic minority tried to outbid each other for the status as reform leaders: Democrats did not want to take positions to the left of Clinton on welfare, who was moving ever rightward, and Clinton and some of his advisors feared that vetoing welfare legislation for the third time during the 1996 presidential campaign against Bob Dole would harm the campaign.[127] The outcome in this light makes some sense. But there is more to the story, as I have argued. Only by acknowledging the ways in which welfare debate had been pushed so far to the right that a Democratic president would repeal AFDC without electoral consequences (indeed, perhaps there were electoral benefits) does the PRA become comprehensible. It was not, as the U.S. Chamber of Commerce would have us believe, that "lawmakers at all levels of government [were] responding to public demands that welfare recipients be required to take more responsibility for ending, or at least easing, their dependence on public support." [128] But dependence on public support was "eased" nonetheless, with a Democratic president's signature and the votes of ninety-eight Democratic representatives and twenty-five Democratic senators.

5

Results of Reforms

Experience leads me to think that an earnest reformer, were he also wise, would wish to die immediately after the practical adoption of his favorite reform; thus only will he be spared disappointment in its fruits.

—Charles Bonaparte, chairman of the board
of directors of the Baltimore COS, 1892

Late-nineteenth-century reformers promised that cuts in out-relief would reduce dependency, lower costs, produce more effective and efficient forms of aid, improve the lot of poor people, even reduce class conflict and create an improved moral climate. Instead, costs rose, need rose, suffering rose, and unrest grew. Reformers failed. The only one of their explicit goals that succeeded was to reduce relief rolls. We should not minimize the import of that. While few people in the nineteenth (or twentieth) century got much in the way of relief, and those who did rarely received cash, to those who could secure such benefits they were important, even literally vital. When public relief was made unavailable to poor women, their lives were made more difficult. They sought private relief, they established credit accounts with merchants, they borrowed money, they worked more hours or took another job, they gave up their children in hopes of getting them back when they could better afford to keep them, they moved in with friends or family or a mate, they cut back their already threadbare budgets, they sold their furniture, they moved, and they usually managed to survive and to care for their children.[1] They were made not less "dependent" but more dependent upon sources of support other than out-relief. In many cases, the abolition and reduction of aid drove poor people into workhouses and into prisons, where they could be made more compliant and forced to labor at low wages for the profit of their jailers, or they were driven into the labor market, forced to compete for low wages that would only be lowered more by their presence.

Late-twentieth-century reforms failed, too, and in a similar fashion. Welfare reform, its advocates promised, would lower costs, reduce dependency, increase self-sufficiency, decrease poverty, decrease out-of-wedlock births, increase marriage, and improve the lives of poor families and their communities. Yet, as before, need rose, costs rose, suffering rose. Despite the conventional wisdom, reform failed. Supporters of the PRA (and much of the press) pointed to a body of evidence they said showed that reform had achieved "astounding" success, and at first glance, the evidence seems compelling. By September 2002, rolls were down 65 percent from their 1994 peak, from 14.2 million to 4.9 million. Since the passage of the PRA, the number of welfare recipients had declined in some states by much more.[2] At the same time, official national poverty rates declined to near-record lows, and did so even for children, including African American children, whose poverty rate did reach a historic low in 1999.[3] Many women, once on welfare, were working, some earning wages well above the legal minimum.[4] By those measures alone, fewer "dependent" women and fewer poor children, we might call the reforms of 1996 a success, as their advocates did. But it is more complicated than this.

OFF THE ROLLS

Relief rolls did decline, and in both eras it was this reduction in pauperism or dependence that was the common measure of success. The tautology of this was lost even on reform's critics. What was dependence but use of welfare? What was pauperism but receipt of relief? Of course pauperism and dependence declined: laws designed to push people off the rolls were passed and then enforced. Reformers err in arguing that the decline in relief rolls is a measure of anything other than this: fewer people were able to receive aid. It does not reveal changes in the need for assistance or in the desire for it. To report that substantially fewer people received relief does not help us evaluate the import of that. It is the blind spot nineteenth-century observers had after abolition in New York, Brooklyn, Baltimore, Philadelphia, and elsewhere. By misreading the meaning of declines in relief receipt—by presuming that they constituted evidence that prior relief had been unnecessary or overgenerous—they were unwilling or unable to identify the immiseration and growing discontent among the poor and hidden classes as a product of reform. So too for contemporary policy makers.

Some critics of the Personal Responsibility Act have resisted the conclusion that it should be credited with these historic declines in the welfare rolls, arguing that it was the "booming" economy. This seems to me not only incorrect but equally blind, for it denies the very real impact these policy changes have had and fails to account for why during other periods of economic growth and low unemployment similar declines did not occur. Understanding the reasons women have left welfare is very much an investigation in progress. Data available in 2003 suggested that only 15–30 percent of the caseload drop could be attributed to economic growth, 30–45 percent to the incentives or sanctions of the PRA, and 30–45 percent to effects of the Earned Income Tax Credit and other subsidies that increased the value of low-paying jobs.[5] It was not the economy alone that pulled people off the rolls, it was governors, legislators, mayors, city commissioners, and ultimately welfare workers themselves who pushed (or did not push) people out of the system, using the latitude the new law gave them.[6] New York Mayor Rudolph Giuliani and his Human Resources Administration were repeatedly sued (and consistently lost) for illegally discouraging poor people from even applying for relief and for illegally dropping people from the rolls; others were effectively denied relief by being refused a translator.[7] Many other states engaged in similar actions to inhibit food-stamp applications.[8] Up to one-third of the declines in Arkansas, Florida, Missouri, South Carolina, Idaho, Iowa, and Missouri could be attributed to sanctions alone.[9]

Attention only to national caseload trends also serves to obscure variation among the states, and sanctions and work requirements have differed in troubling ways. States with higher percentages of African Americans and Latinos were, all else being equal, more likely to impose strict time limits and a "family cap" provision. States with more African Americans on their AFDC caseloads were most likely to impose tough TANF sanctions.[10] States with higher incarceration rates and tighter labor markets were most likely to impose strict work requirements.[11] The "experimentation" that the PRA permitted created new opportunities for local and regional biases, racial biases particularly, that belie the notion that devolution is an unmitigated good.[12]

Pointing to national declines obscures more. In the late twentieth century national rolls did drop sharply; they had already fallen 32 percent by 1998. From then on, however, declines began to level off and even reverse in some states.[13] Of those who did leave the rolls, some 20 percent returned.[14] Declines varied geographically, too, and were more likely in nonurban areas: the states with the sharpest drops from August 1996 to September 2001, for example, were Wyoming (92 percent) and Idaho (89 percent). The result is that welfare recipients were increasingly concentrated in major cities: by 1999, ten urban counties contained nearly one-third of all TANF recipients.[15] Those remaining on the rolls were also disproportionately older, less educated, black, and Hispanic.[16] There are potentially significant political consequences to these developments, for if welfare becomes perceived even more to be a black, urban problem, the national support for the program, such as it is, erodes further; the political imperative to intervene is thereby diminished given the generally Democratic majorities in urban centers and the Republican majorities in suburbs and rural areas, who in turn control a majority of statehouses and the Congress.

RISING NEED

Nineteenth-century reformers said that in cities that abolished relief there were no ill effects. Lowell reported, "The poor have not suffered by the entire cessation of public relief; but there is less idleness."[17] "Diligent inquiry showed," noted Kellogg, "that no suffering ensued in consequence of the withdrawal, while the admissions to almshouses and infirmaries in the cities named contemporaneously decreased."[18] Warner argued: "There is no well-authenticated instance where outdoor relief has been stopped and any considerable increase either of private charity has been required, or any marked increase of the inmates of institutions has occurred."[19] Dissenting voices were exceedingly rare in the charity journals and during the proceedings of the NCCC, yet reformers were wrong—need and costs rose after reform.

We do not have reliable poverty statistics for the period, and unemployment measures were new and even less meaningful than those of the late twentieth century, so it is difficult to look to such data for effects.[20] We do have some reports from contemporaneous observers that belie the conventional wisdom. Rev. C.G. Trusdell, for example, reported to the NCCC that "on a visit to the city of Brooklyn a few years after this marvellous reformation [of abolishing relief], we were surprised to learn from the officers of the Association for the Improvement of the Condition of the Poor and from other private charities that they were pressed to their utmost ability to relieve distress."[21] And the Boston overseers failed to repeal relief in their city in part because they judged the results in cities that did to have been poor, as we have seen.

Nineteenth-century relief antagonists built their case for the success of reform by noting the failure of poorhouse populations to rise in cities that abolished or cut back aid to the poor. The number of people inhabiting public poorhouses did remain relatively constant in the wake of reform. After the city of New York's repeal in 1873–74, the poorhouse population fluctuated only modestly throughout the 1870s. In Brooklyn, almshouse paupers consistently numbered about ten thousand from the late 1870s to the mid-1880s and had even declined slightly by 1890.[22] The number of Indiana state paupers remained relatively constant throughout the postrepeal 1890s,[23] and in the years after Philadelphia abolished relief, Pennsylvania's poorhouse population changed little, even while total population grew.[24] In wondering where poor people went after repeal in Brooklyn, two contemporary economists agreed that it was not the poorhouse, "which leaves the options of either entering the labor market, relying on private charity, or relying on familial support."[25] This gets us partway there, reminding us that the poorhouse is only one place to look for the postreform poor.

There is another possibility, however: while the total number of poorhouse residents in most cities remained relatively constant, poorhouses were in fact flooded with new inhabitants as others—children, the insane, and able-bodied men—were expelled or segregated into orphanages, asylums, penitentiaries, and labor colonies.[26] Gilded Age reformers ended (as

early-nineteenth-century reformers had tried to do) the universal institution in which the poor, the insane, young children,
the old, criminals, men, women, the sick, and the healthy were
all confined together. By 1891 there were in New York, for example, separate state-run institutions for the blind, deaf, dumb,
idiots, feeble-minded youth, juvenile offenders, criminals,
men, women, epileptics, the insane, and state paupers (those
with no local settlement).[27] (The creation of new institutions
served another purpose beyond the resegregation and reclassi-
fication designed to improve treatment and control: by removing the sick, the insane, the very old, and the very young from
the home, as the COS often fought to do, women were freed
from caregiving and could thus enter the workforce.)[28] It is not
that these classes of people were no longer poor, but that they
were to be found in places other than the poorhouse or the
home. The overall total of "indoor" poor actually exploded in
the wake of relief repeals.

Look at what happened to children. From 1870 through the
1880s they were moved from poorhouses into orphanages, foster homes, and group homes in New York because of the passage of an 1875 law that mandated that anyone between the
ages of three and sixteen be removed from the poorhouse.
(Michigan, Wisconsin, Massachusetts, Indiana, Ohio, Pennsylvania, Minnesota, Rhode Island, and Kansas soon passed similar bills.)[29] Half were removed within a year, and by 1883 most
were gone.[30] Children may no longer have been in the poorhouse, but by 1875 there were already 123 orphanages with
17,791 inmates. Homer Folks later complained that "New
York city in 1897 was supporting, by public or private charity,
in round numbers one thirty-fifth of all the child population of
the city in charitable institutions."[31] Between 1877 and 1880
alone the number of children placed in the Catholic orphan
asylum doubled to 1,640, and other Catholic agencies received a
large share of children from the poorhouses. Others were sent

west to work on farms or be adopted by local families; Brace's Children's Aid Society alone would send off some ninety thousand children over the last half of the century (by 1929, some quarter of a million children had been so dispatched by Brace's CAS and other local agencies inspired by its example).[32] For some families it was one strategy of coping with constant scarcity, while other children were taken by force. Lowell was succinct: "If parents do not want to give up their children they must support them or put them in private charity to maintain."[33] In the wake of relief abolition, the number of "dependent" children in New York climbed from 14,773 in 1875 to 35,404 in 1898,[34] in part no doubt because adults who did enter the poorhouse often had to surrender their children.[35]

Just as in the aftermath of Gilded Age reform poor children were to be found in greater numbers but not to be found in the poorhouse, so too do we find greater numbers of poor men in the late nineteenth century, but we find them not in the almshouse but tramping the country searching for work or paying the penalty for that search by "working" in a jail or penitentiary. Pennsylvania's Diller Luther noticed with some satisfaction this shift from housing vagrants in poorhouses to housing them in jails.[36] By 1890 there were some one hundred thousand men in jails or penitentiaries nationwide at any given time, most of whom performed labor for outside contractors.[37] A majority were often poor, uneducated, foreign-born, unskilled laborers.[38] How many of these men might formerly have been found in poorhouses or workhouses I cannot say, but their numbers suggest that we might look beyond the poorhouse to the prison to find evidence of the scope of poverty, just as we might do so in future examinations of contemporary poverty, given our current prison population of poor, less educated men of color (see also Chapter 6).[39]

Similarly, it is difficult to know how many moved from the poorhouse to the asylum, but it is likely that a non-trivial number did. The Herkimer, New York, superintendent to the poor John Crowley observed in a puzzled letter to Lowell that "the number of our insane is increasing; while pauperism is slightly decreasing, insanity is increasing with us."[40] Such accounts can be found throughout the late-century proceedings of the NCCC. The population of asylums was similar to that of the prison and the poorhouse. They served as a "dumping ground for social undesirables."[41] Thomas Ebert reports that *all* of the inmates in the Wisconsin asylums he studied were "poor or very poor"; 71 percent of the men and 57 percent of the women (who could be as much as half the population) were foreign-born; 39 percent of inmates had no education or had a very poor one.[42] Those confined were not necessarily mentally ill by any definition we might recognize today; standards were impre-cise, and one typical statute defined the insane as anyone "un-able to function in society."[43] Tobacco and alcohol use, masturbation, grief, overwork, and heartbreak were all consid-ered causes or symptoms of insanity. Poverty itself was seen by some as a form of insanity or a cause of it. One asylum director noted:

> The insufficiency of wages, the uncertainty of employment, the cares of a family whose wants harass him from day to day, the thought that next year and succeeding year will find him engaged in the same hard struggle for subsistence; all these prey upon the health and vigor of his mind, to an extent that few, perhaps, appreciate.[44]

The recovery of patients in one Worcester facility was judged by whether they were "able and willing to work" and "able to act like normal" versus those who were still "lazy and shiftless," "too proud of own ideas," or "not very cooperative."[45] An 1880 Wisconsin law made it possible for "any respectable citizen" to commit someone to an asylum, and Wisconsin and other states were well aware that some families in deep poverty would commit one or more of their members to shift the cost for their care onto the state or county: "before 1910 voluntary patients were extremely rare." As many as 15 percent may have been alcoholics.[46] "Undoubtedly," wrote Scull, "one of the attractions of the asylum as a method of dealing with the insane was its promise of instilling the virtues of bourgeois rationality into that segment of the population least amenable to them."[47]

It is not just that poorhouses, prisons, workhouses, and asylums were populated by similarly marginalized people, but they functioned in similar ways: 70 percent of late-century Wisconsin asylum inmates worked, as did roughly the same percentage of state hospital inmates. They labored in the laundry and kitchen, made boots and slippers, linens and towels, or worked on outdoor projects building roads or farming. The Outagamie asylum, like many others, was a profitable enterprise as a result, earning some $8,000 in the mid-1890s and $20,000 by 1905. That throughout the late nineteenth century they emphasized work while limiting medical staff and maintaining high inmate-to-staff ratios helped such institutions profit through methods similar to those pursued by late-twentieth-century institutions. At the turn of the century, by one estimate, New York asylum labor produced over $1 million worth of goods.[48]

There is one final reason to be skeptical of the argument that the abolition of relief caused no harm if it offers as evidence statistics on steady or declining poorhouse populations. Strict less-eligibility principles were enforced; indoor relief was therefore very undesirable, by design. If a woman lost her benefits from the city or county, it was likely—indeed, it was encouraged as a matter of policy—that she would seek every other remedy before admitting herself to the poorhouse, since admittance would typically be considered evidence of her "unfitness" and result in losing her children. That people did not choose to enter the poorhouse can offer no evidence to support the proposition that they were therefore not in need, even dire need. And yet more people probably did enter the poorhouse. The admittedly suggestive evidence above shows that during the period when reformers claimed that suffering did not increase because poorhouse populations remained steady, large (if here unquantified) numbers of poor children, the poor insane, and the unemployed moved out of the poorhouse into orphanages, asylums, jails, and workhouses. The implication is that if so many groups of people were transferred from the poorhouse to other institutions while at the same time the population of the poorhouse remained relatively constant, then paupers moved into the poorhouse in numbers roughly equivalent to those who moved out. Reformers were wrong—poverty and need did increase in the wake of reform, just as they would a century later.[49]

Official poverty rates declined after the passage of the PRA, it is true, but to credit reform with that violates a fundamental scientific principle: correlation is not causation. Reform proponents presumed that there was a connection between relief repeal and poverty declines, and there probably was, but the relationship was more likely the reverse of what they assumed. The declines in poverty so casually attributed to welfare reform were a reflection of the combined effects of slowed growth in income inequality, modestly higher wages at the low end of the labor market, an increase in the average number of hours worked, and the Earned Income Tax Credit. These forces in the late 1990s drove official poverty rates down perhaps 3.3 percentage points; simultaneously, the reduced effectiveness of transfer payments, thanks to welfare reform, added some 1.6 points back to the rate. In the absence of reform, official American poverty would likely have reached unprecedented lows. Reform, as predicted, increased poverty. That will become clearer, alas, since the macroeconomic trends of the mid- to late-1990s that obscured this rise in poverty are in retreat.[50] Indeed, national poverty in 2001 grew by 1.3 million people from 2000, the poverty of African American families rose from 19.3 to 20.7 percent, and those in poverty were poorer than at any other time on record, as were poor children.[51] The number of Americans in poverty grew again by 1.7 million in 2002, and the official poverty rate rose to 12.1 percent.[52] Further, at best 60 percent of those who left or were pushed off the welfare rolls were working at any given time.[53] Perhaps 70 percent of those who did find work earned wages at or below the official poverty line in jobs without benefits; many were poorer after leaving the rolls than they had been before.[54] Between 2000 and 2002 the unemployment rate for low-income single mothers was again rising, and faster than overall rates.[55]

The contemporary results for children seemed to bode ill, too, some changes in official poverty rates notwithstanding. From 1993 to 1999, child support payments to welfare recipients increased by 44 percent, less impressive when one notes that the increase is over a "somewhat paltry base of $253" annually.[56] After the PRA, not only were women forced to endure yet another level of state intrusion into their most personal decision making, thanks to new child support enforcement provisions, but they were thereby compelled to make contact with men who may have been a danger to them. Worse, women and their children benefited little from such intrusion, since most (and in some states all) of the money collected was retained by the state to "reimburse it" for welfare expenditures. Some women were made worse off, since the fathers of their children had supported their children with what they could when they could; some of those men, angered when faced with government intervention, ended support entirely.[57] A lower percentage of poor children received food stamps (total food stamp participation declined 38 percent from 1994 to 2000), fewer eligible families received Medicaid,[58] and 400,000 more poor children lived in deep poverty in 1997 than in 1995.[59] The average poor person was poorer in 1999 than in 1993,[60] and 700,000 families were "significantly worse off in 1999 than their counterparts" had been in 1995.[61] The number of children in foster care climbed to 588,000 in 2000, from 547,000 in 1999 and 483,000 in 1995,[62] while only 12 percent of eligible women received subsidies for child care.[63] The number of children living with relatives other than a parent more than doubled in the 1990s.[64] Some Head Start providers reported increased signs of anxiety, abuse, and neglect among children of "workfare" participants; increased child abuse or neglect may have been in evidence more generally, one analysis showed, and another study found increased behavioral problems and lower academic achievement among children of workfare participants.[65] According to the Children's Defense Fund, by 2001 more African American children were in deep poverty that at any time since such data had begun to be collected, and the percentage of such very poor children was at a near-record high.[66]

Yet, just as crude poorhouse population data cannot tell the whole story of late-nineteenth-century need, official poverty statistics alone do not reveal the scope of need today, and there are other growing indications of reform's failures.[67] In 2001 alone national demand for emergency shelter increased by 15 percent.[68] By August 2001, the New York City homeless population reached a then all-time high, and the number of children living in homeless shelters rose 29 percent between 2000 and 2001. Washington, D.C., Chicago, and Oakland, reported similar increases.[69] The New York City Coalition for the Homeless reported the number of nightly shelter residents at over 31,000 by February 2002 and an average of 38,463 per night by January 2003, an increase of 82 percent from 1998.[70] In Milwaukee, emergency shelter referrals rose 88 percent between 1997 and 2000, city and county disbursements for emergency housing doubled from 1995 to 2000, and evictions climbed 13 percent from 1995 to 2001.[71] The number of people seeking food at soup kitchens and food pantries rose nationally some 17 percent in 2000, 23 percent in 2001, 19 percent in 2002, and yet another 17 percent in 2003.[72] In late 2003, the U.S. Department of Agriculture confirmed that in 2002 hunger and "food insecurity" had increased for the third consecutive year.[73] One Urban Institute study reported that one-third to one-half of all those who left welfare had difficulty buying enough food for their families.[74] Catholic Charities reported in 2001 that since 1996 their affiliates' emergency food programs served 20 percent more working people each year.[75] In Wisconsin, home of innovative reforms pioneered by Governor Thompson (who would later become George W. Bush's secretary of health and human services) and Jason Turner (who became commissioner of the New York City Human Resources Administration and then in 2002 a fellow at the Heritage Foundation), emergency food referrals climbed 136 percent between 1996 and 2000, while food stamp enrollment declined 30 percent from 1995 to 2000.[76] Boston Medical Center reported a 45 percent increase from 1999 to 2001 in the number of hungry or malnourished children they treated.[77] And many of these data mark trends that were in evidence before the recession of 2001 and obscure significant variation among the states. In both eras, when relief was cut, need rose.

THE RISING COSTS OF PUBLIC RELIEF AND PRIVATE SUBSIDIES

The burden on public coffers rose too, in part because indoor relief has always cost more than outdoor relief.[78] Noted Massachusetts's F.B. Sanborn, "Here we see one reason why outdoor relief is everywhere and always more common than indoor relief,—for the same sum of money a much greater number of poor can be aided."[79] As Davis reported at the very first meeting of the NCCC in 1874, "There is not a State nor a city wherein the cost of public out-door relief exceeds that of in-door relief."[80] To provide institutional aid, after all, one must build, maintain, staff, and operate an institution. Outdoor aid is comparatively cheap—one distributes money or supplies. As a result, what are touted as "cutbacks" in relief may in fact increase municipal spending. For the city of New York, while the number of poor relief recipients as a percentage of the population steadily declined,[81] real per capita expenditures on relief *doubled*,[82] and the percentage of all recipients relieved in the poorhouse *quadrupled*.[83] The pattern for the rest of the state, though not as pronounced, was similar. A report from the president of the New York State Board of Charities showed that all "expenditures for charitable and reformatory purposes" more than doubled to $17,605,661 from 1880 to 1891.[84] Public indoor relief expenses from the mid-1880s to the mid-1890s nearly tripled in Pennsylvania, doubled in Michigan, and rose fivefold in Wisconsin.[85]

Costs rose also because private institutions could assist those abandoned by the city only by turning to it for funding; not only did public expenditures for public institutions grow, so too did public expenditures for private institutions. New York subsidies to private institutions grew from a mere $9,863 in 1850 to $128,850 in 1860, $334,828 in 1870, $1,414,257 in 1880, and $1,845,870 in 1890. In 1900 total subsidies were $3,079,259, none of which was distributed to organizations for direct cash relief to the poor.[86] In 1889, of a similar total amount ($3.2 million) only $19,251 went to agencies that delivered relief.[87] In Philadelphia, subsidies rose from $201,250 in 1870 to $506,254 in 1893.[88] In 1889 fully one-third of all of Pennsylvania's expenditures for charities and corrections was paid to private institutions, and from 1850 to 1905 Pennsylvania consistently divided its high indoor relief expenditures about equally between public and private institutions.[89] Even as early as 1870, one-half of the New York Children's Aid Society budget was paid by the city.[90] Frank Fetter here comments on the 1899 comptroller's report: "In the period 1850 to 1898 the population of New York city was multiplied by 6.66, the cost of prisoners and public paupers was multiplied by 5.53, and the cost of subsidizing private institutions was multiplied by 317.51." His data make the shift clear: the percentage of total city indoor relief appropriations that were devoted to caring for prisoners and paupers in private institutions rose from 2.3 percent in 1850 to 14.7 percent in 1860, 19.8 percent in 1870, 51.2 percent in 1880, 48.6 percent in 1890, and 57.3 percent in 1898, when such support totaled over $3.13 million of $5.47 million expended.[91]

While this phenomenon was most pronounced in New York and Pennsylvania—leaders in relief abolition, we should note—subsidies were identified as a problem throughout the country. Of the thirty-four states surveyed by Fetter, only Arizona, Nebraska, Nevada, Washington, and Wyoming reported offering no state or local subsidies to private charities—only in these few (western) states did private charities raise all funds from private sources. This would not have surprised members of the NCCC. "As almost everyone knows, the private charities are supported largely by public funds," reported *Charities Review*.[92] Of the twenty-nine other states supplying data, total state subsides were $6,668,600 and total local subsidies to private charities were $4,316,115.[93] Opposition in New Orleans to subsidies proffered in response to the 1873 depression led to a campaign against them, culminating in 1897 in legislation forbidding Louisiana to fund them.[94] In New York, reported Barbour, "public sentiment in every case appears to be growing in opposition to the practice."[95] One result was an 1896 constitutional amendment prohibiting the legislature from requiring counties or cities to contribute to any private charity. Another law was passed in 1899 amending the New York charter to limit the power of the Board of Estimate to grant subsidies, and

Brooklyn ended over one-fourth of its subsidies.[96] Gilded Age private charity was none too cheap and none too private.

Reforms in the 1990s were expensive, too, although the Contract with America predicted that welfare reform would save some $40 billion.[97] In 1997 alone states received $4.7 billion more under TANF than they would have under AFDC.[98] Nonetheless, by 2001 and 2002, all states combined spent more than $2 billion per year over and above the basic TANF block grant.[99] Funding increased, and states received substantially wider discretion in its use: some increased expenses for work-support services such as child care or job training (federal child care expenditures rose $4.5 billion from 1997 to 2002, and states used $3 billion of their TANF funds to purchase child care), but others used such funds to replace general revenues or to help finance tax cuts.[100] In fact, all states but three were spending less on anti-poverty programs in 2001 than they were in 1994.[101] Some spent money on monitoring and punishing recipients in lieu of offering relief—in 1999 Wisconsin and New York, for example, spent $9 million and $4 million respectively on operating their "learnfare" programs, which sanctioned recipients for their children's failures to meet school attendance requirements.[102] Not only did total expenditures rise, but by 1997 federal resources per recipient were 38 percent higher than they had been the year before.[103] However, the percentage of welfare spending that was distributed as cash aid to recipients *declined* from 76 percent in 1996, to 41 percent in 2000, 38 percent in 2001, and 33 percent in 2002; in nine states it was less than 25 percent by 2000.[104] Median monthly benefits had declined from $399 in 1996 to $381 by 2000.[105]

Less cash was received by poor people in the wake of reform, but private companies and not-for-profit organizations saw large increases in their revenues from government welfare contracts. This is one of the great as-yet-untold stories of welfare reform. In 2001, state and local governments spent more than $1.5

billion on contracts for basic TANF services and administration, and in every state but South Dakota some welfare services had been privatized.[106] New York City alone awarded $400 million in welfare contracts from 1998 to 2001, many to for-profit corporations.[107] Randstad, an Amsterdam company that owned a New York TempForce franchise, received a $578 million, three-year contract ($75 million of it in federal monies) to employ former recipients.[108] Five companies saw combined profits of over $27.5 million for W-2 services in Milwaukee from 1997 to 1999. Maximus, one of the five, had welfare contracts in 2001 of over $350 million[109] and saw its stock price rise 63 percent from 2000 to 2001 and profits increase 15 percent to $9.9 million.[110] Maximus won its first welfare contract in 1985, when hired to rout out fraud in New York City's programs, and in 1988 was hired to operate welfare-to-work programs in Los Angeles. By 1999, it had secured contracts for social service provision in all fifty states,[111] despite charges of fraud, corruption, and mismanagement in Los Angeles,[112] Milwaukee,[113] and New York.[114] In 2002 alone it received a $1 million contract to provide "smart cards" for the U.S. Treasury and a three-year, $19.9 million contract for welfare-to-work case management in Orange County, California; in late 2001, it had received another Wisconsin contract for $19 million, despite problems with prior arrangements.[115] By 1997, Lockheed Martin IMS already had TANF contracts in thirteen states; its parent company, Affiliated Computer Services, had 2002 revenues of $3 billion, about one-third of which was derived from contracts with state and local governments.[116] Citigroup was awarded the lone contract to provide electronic food stamp and welfare benefits services in Maine, New Hampshire, Vermont, Massachusetts, Rhode Island, Connecticut, and New York;[117] complaints from recipients and officials were abundant.[118] In 2000, Electronic Data Services, the company founded by former independent presidential candidate Ross Perot, earned some $3 billion through government contracts to administer federal and state welfare and health care programs, a 34 percent increase over 1999. This despite settling charges of overbilling in Texas, having a $45 million contract canceled by Virginia for failure to fulfill it, and losing a Connecticut contract for being unable to implement programs.[119] Accenture (formerly Andersen Consulting, of Enron infamy), despite seemingly credible charges of corruption, political cronyism, and poor management in their Ohio welfare contracts, received a thirteen-year, four-county California contract in 2001 to administer welfare systems; its bill for developing a child welfare monitoring system in New York came in at $362 million, triple their estimate and three years late. Similar problems were documented in its contracts with Florida, Texas, Nebraska, Virginia, Canada, and the United Kingdom.[120]

Whether it's the subsides of the late nineteenth century or the more recent welfare contracts, reform has not saved money, as many of its proponents promised. But it has redistributed it.

RETRENCHMENT REVEALED

In the 1990s, AFDC was abolished, but the Earned Income Tax Credit (EITC) was expanded. Between 1993 and 1999, federal spending on the EITC, which subsidized the wages of low-paid workers with children, increased from $15.5 billion to $30 billion, and the number of families receiving the credit climbed from 15.1 million to more than 20 million. By 1995 the federal EITC cost more than the combined national and state share of AFDC had.[121] Its effects were not trivial: the federal EITC turned a $6 per hour job into one worth $8.40 per hour; when combined with the additional EITCs operating in many states it rose to as much as $9 per hour.[122] Ron Haskins here makes the crucial caveat, however:

Despite the effectiveness of the EITC and other [changes in personal income] taxes, the overall impact of government programs in 1999 reduced the poverty gap by only 56.3 percent, less than in any previous year except 1983 and well below the 62.4 percent reduction of 1979. . . . The major reason for the reduced effectiveness of government programs in reducing the poverty gap is a decline in the impact of means-tested cash benefits.[123]

Relief reduced the poverty gap by 14.9 percent in 1999 compared to 28.8 percent in 1979: half as many poor people were lifted to or above the poverty line by welfare and food stamps in 1999 as had been in 1979. And the EITC could not be depended upon to make up the difference, nor could it benefit any former recipient who was not working. Yet without it, many families would have been even worse off. While the percentage of income of female-headed families in the bottom fifth of the income distribution derived from cash welfare benefits declined 42 percent from 1993 to 1999 and the percentage from food stamps dropped 23 percent, the percentage of their total income derived from the EITC jumped 243 percent, from earnings 82 percent, and from child support 44 percent. For similarly situated families in the second fifth of the income distribution, the portion of their income derived from the EITC rose 191 percent.[124] This move from relief to tax credits shifts public monies away from those not working (not working above the table, at any rate) to those in the low-wage labor market, acting as a reward and incentive to the prospective employee and as a wage subsidy to his or her employer.[125] As Nobel prize–winning economist Robert Solow reported, "Employers should understand that they benefit from the EITC too, because, like any subsidy, it puts a little downward pressure on the market wage."[126]

Twentieth-century welfare "cutbacks," as Piven observed,

were no such thing,[127] but rather a shift from "decommodify-ing" programs to more expensive ones that rewarded or com-pelled work and shifted funding from poor people to private and not-for-profit contractors: "Welfare state spending has not been slashed; it has been increased, much as academic theories would have predicted. What theories did not predict is the on-going reorganization of the American welfare state . . . [to] re-inforce labor market participation."[128] As Joel Potts of the Ohio Department of Job and Family Services candidly put it: "For the first time in Ohio's history we are spending more welfare dollars to support work than to support dependency."[129]

Josephine Shaw Lowell argued that poor relief depresses wages for the laboring classes.[130] But poor relief does quite the opposite: it sets a floor for wages.[131] Lowell often discussed the ways in which whatever injuries may be done to the poor man by pauperizing him, and they were many, those who ultimately suffered most were those who "work all night in cellars to give us our daily bread . . . who carry us safely on thundering rail-way trains . . . who cook for us and wait upon us and clothe us; all those men and women without whom we could not live in comfort for one day."[132] There are the workers and the idlers, and offering aid to the idlers harms the workers, whom we should celebrate, as Lowell does above. But she overlooks that these are not distinct classes, not then and not now—the line between working and idle, between just getting by and not get-ting by at all, is a thin one, a permeable membrane through which people pass back and forth and back and forth again. Class *is* fluid in America—but not in the way that Alexis de Tocqueville or Horatio Alger or Newt Gingrich would have you believe.[133] It is most fluid at the margins, where the benefits of relief are most fully felt.

And it is there where an influx of new workers into the labor force has its greatest effects: job displacements, wage reduc-tions (especially at the lower end), or both.[134] Even ardent pro-work reformers such as Mead acknowledged this: "I think there is enough increase in the labor supply due to welfare reform that there might be some tendency for real wages to fall slightly," he said.[135] Economist Timothy Bartik estimated that welfare reform added four hundred thousand low-wage workers to the labor force from 1993 to 1997 and one million by 2002, and he predicted that waivers and the PRA could be responsible for two million additional workers by 2008 (assuming recession in 2001 and recovery in 2005). While Solow predicted a 3 to 5 percent decline in the average real wage as a result of reform, Bartik expected little overall effect (perhaps one-half of 1 percent), but about a 3 percent increase in the number of less-educated women in the labor market—which would lower the wages of a female high school dropout by between 5 and 15 percent (Jared Bernstein estimated 13.2 percent, and even more for black women). Moreover, reform will have spillover effects, increasing unemployment among male high school dropouts and reducing their wages as well. Without the PRA, Bartik concluded, the rise in real wages in the late 1990s would have begun earlier and the distance between overall wages and those of male dropouts would have been narrower.[136]

There were other, more easily discernible labor-market effects of reform. New York mayor Rudolph Giuliani cut twenty-two thousand municipal jobs between 1995 and 2000, and most were replaced by "workfare" workers. At its peak, the welfare-recipient Work Experience Program numbered over thirty-five thousand, a New York City workforce second in size only to the police department. Part-time welfare workers constituted 75 percent of the labor force of the Parks Department and one-third of sanitation workers. The average city clerical salary was $12.32 per hour, while it was $1.80 per hour for Work Experience Program workers, who received no benefits.[137] The city's Department of Homeless Services replaced unionized workers with welfare recipients fulfilling workfare obligations.[138] Many welfare recipients, contrary to most assumptions, replaced moderately skilled workers and assumed key responsibilities from managing case files, conducting safety checks, and opening and closing public facilities to providing care to children and the elderly.[139] One Salt Lake City official told the *New York Times,* "Without the welfare people . . . we would have had to raise the wage . . . maybe 5 percent."[140] In 2000, New York City welfare offices even distributed fliers from a security company seeking five hundred replacement workers in anticipation of a possible strike.[141]

What's more, much of the job training offered recipients was not in the "hard" skills needed for particular careers but "soft" skills such as dressing appropriately, being on time, and maintaining the appropriate attitude in the workplace, helping to ensure a compliant, docile, and dependent workforce for private companies with public funds.[142] Jamie Peck summarized it succinctly: "Workfare is not about creating jobs for people that don't have them; it is about creating workers for jobs that nobody wants."[143] In an analysis of case files of the late-nineteenth-century COS in Indianapolis, economist Stephen Ziliak found that visiting the poor and educating them to reformers' ideas of virtuous behavior had no statistically significant impact on their success in finding employment.[144] This will not surprise those who have operated work-readiness programs for people on welfare to help make them more "employable." There is no contemporary evidence that such efforts at "life skills" or moral reeducation achieve more than, at best, short-term, temporary employment successes.[145]

Seen in this light, the PRA's sharp limitations on the aid available to legal immigrants was part of a comprehensive retooling of relief to drastically reduce the number of people able to refuse low-wage work. As economist Rebecca Blank wrote, "The changes in welfare program design have almost surely made less skilled women—and particularly single mothers—

more vulnerable to the economy." [146] And those pushed into the labor market did seem more vulnerable: The Manhattan Institute noted (approvingly) that after reform the sharpest declines in welfare receipt and the largest gains in employment were among "young (18–29) mothers, mothers with children under seven years of age, high school dropouts, black and Hispanic single mothers, and [for welfare receipt only] those who have never been married." [147] Blank observed, "As these women rely on earnings for an increased share of their income, and as they face tighter restrictions on their access to public assistance, they will be more subject to the vagaries of the labor market." [148] That was the key outcome of reform.

PRIVATE CHARITY OVERWHELMED

The success of reform must also be judged in light of the demands placed upon private charities during the depression of 1893–98, and the measures they undertook to confront destitution so severe as to "break hearts of oak," as the director of New York's United Hebrew Charities put it.[149] Again, reform failed. By the depression, the inability of private institutions to either ration relief or meet the need was apparent. Closson reported that in New York between February 1893 and February 1894 "a careful estimate places the value of private, family, and office giving in New York City during the year ending with February at $7,300,000, as against $1,300,000 in a normal year." [150] By 1897 in New York, over a hundred thousand people (one in seventy) were incarcerated in public or private charitable or correctional institutions at a cost of over $25 million, and that does not include the expenditures of churches, newspapers, and other relief funds.[151] After the two relatively stable decades we've discussed, New York poorhouse populations climbed sharply in the early 1890s, hitting 67,828 by 1895.[152] In 1899, Philadelphia Society for Organizing Charity Secretary James

Walk said, "We feel that there is no need whatever in this city for the restoration of municipal outdoor relief and that the private benevolence of our citizens is sufficient to supply the need,"[153] but after relief abolition women were simply confined in private asylums instead of public almshouses, and private charity expenses exploded, especially for the heavily subsidized private indoor institutions.[154] Private charities were still not up to the task, and by 1901 the society had "lost a grip on the situation." There were by then twenty-four hundred relief agencies and eleven soup houses feeding eighty thousand people and spending $25,000. "The city was, moreover, competing with Chicago as to which sheltered the larger number of vagrants."[155] The New York Charities Directory of 1896 listed 89 public charities, 343 agencies for temporary relief, 111 for permanent relief, 73 for "special" relief, 35 for relief for foreigners, 220 for medical care, 72 mutual aid societies, and 263 "miscellaneous" agencies—and this does not include the hundreds of churches providing aid. The Society of St. Vincent de Paul reported a 300 percent increase in their expenditures; AICP expenditures more than tripled; COS expenditures were up 20 percent over the previous year, as their caseload tripled.[156] And still reports of widespread suffering and the clamor for aid abounded as "the columns of the newspapers were given up during a large part of the winter to long accounts of suffering and exaggerated reports of sore distress. These were coupled by frantic appeals for the establishment of new agencies for aid and relief."[157] Such events were repeated throughout the country, and most emphatically in those cities that had substantially reformed their relief provision. Many moved quickly to resume outdoor relief.[158] By 1896 national relief expenses were estimated variously at $50 million to $75 million,[159] yet still by the turn of the century some ten million Americans and more than one-fifth of the populations of New York, Massachusetts, Connecticut, New Jersey, Pennsylvania, Ohio, Illinois, Indiana, and Michigan lived in deep poverty.[160]

Today, much of the relief burden has been shifted to not-for-profit emergency service providers, who are struggling, not always successfully, to meet new needs just as foundation, corporate, and individual giving declines in the wake of drops in their respective investment portfolios. As an October 8, 2001, headline in the *New York Times* read, "A Mass of Newly Laid-Off Workers Will Put Social Safety Net to the Test." The *Chronicle of Philanthropy* ran an article on August 9 of that year with the headline "Welfare Law Puts Strain on Urban Charities That Serve the Poor." More poor Americans were receiving emergency food from soup kitchens and food pantries than were receiving food stamps—this at the same time that many food providers reported a decrease in private donations.[161] In Milwaukee, as elsewhere, private providers, especially churches, were overwhelmed and unable to adequately meet the new demand thrust upon them in the wake of retrenchment.[162]

Whether reform failed or not is a matter of perspective, as such evaluations often are. The conventional wisdom offers one kind of success narrative (one that has been ably deconstructed by Schram and Soss).[163] In its crude form, it states that since rolls declined and during the same period poverty rates declined, welfare reform succeeded; some claim that cutting the welfare rolls caused the reductions in official poverty measures. I have above outlined a kind of counternarrative that tells the story of relief and welfare reforms as failures—failures to reduce poverty or need, failures to reduce costs, failures to ensure that public obligations do not become avenues for private gain. But there is another narrative here: reform did not fail, it succeeded quite remarkably, for these policy changes, as intended, drove women from relief, leaving them to the vicissitudes of the labor market or the discretionary aid of overburdened private charity providers. But nineteenth-century "successes" left reformed cities unprepared for the depression of 1893, and their inability to placate and control new masses of the poor and unemployed helped fuel calls for renewed relief efforts. Abolishing out-relief helped create the conditions for expanding it and laid the foundations for broader Progressive Era reforms. Whether we will see similar outcomes today remains to be seen.

6

The Squeegee Guy
and the Tramp

Labor is the life of society, and the beggar who will not work is a social cannibal feeding on that life—a social highwayman with his
hand upon the throat of that society, asking for both its money and its
life, and just in proportion as society is greater than the individual, so
in proportion is a beggar the highest of all criminals.

—John Glenn, *Charities Review,* 1891

Discussions of welfare have traditionally focused on
women, while men have been present mostly as the
unemployed and therefore undesirable potential husbands of poor women, or as "deadbeat dads."[1] But men were
important players in Gilded Age relief dramas—perhaps as
vigorous as the COSs' movement against outdoor relief were
anti-begging campaigns, battles to combat "tramps," and a massive incarceration of poor, immigrant men. What these efforts
had in common with anti-relief agitation was mandatory work
for all those who would receive any aid and the incarceration,
forced labor, or expulsion from the community of any who
would not accept the bargain; they were thus but another piece
of a struggle to mold a workforce better suited to the new needs
of industrial capitalism. Much of that struggle is familiar: the
business-backed flood of immigrants as cheap, dependent, and
expendable workers; the use of private Pinkertons and public

police forces to quash strikes or kill strikers; the use of courts to prohibit strikes through injunction or to control workers by applying feudal-era legal standards to their claims.[2] Similarly, during the more recent war on welfare, whose symbolic target was the black woman, concurrent campaigns were waged against the poor black man: a so-called war on crime and a crusade against the homeless. These campaigns pushed some men into the low-wage labor market, or some other means of survival, and threw others into prison, where many were compelled to work (although this practice was not as widespread as it was in the Gilded Age). These assaults served to drain poor neighborhoods of the men who might most constitute a threat to order, the same threat that was posed by late-nineteenth-century unemployed men who grew increasingly insistent that they be afforded the opportunity to provide for their families.

There are differences between these campaigns against the female relief recipient and the unemployed man: the surveillance and stigmatization of poor women on welfare seemed an effort to make their poverty visible, whether it was by marking their need with workfare assignments that required them to wear a bright orange vest as they picked up trash in New York City (we might instead brand a scarlet *W* across their chests) or by the public denunciations of their dependence by politicians and think-tank experts who brandished their status as warnings to other women who would seek refuge from the labor market. By contrast, the assault on poor men seemed to make their poverty *in*visible, whether it was by pushing encampments of the homeless further and further toward the edges of the respectably occupied city or by incarcerating them. Part of the difference may reside in our lingering national fear of black men and our contrary impulse to scorn black women—we continue to inhabit a society in which race and gender affect policy and politics, and those practices are nowhere more clearly inscribed than in issues of welfare and criminal justice.

But at heart they are not so different: assaults on the squeegee guy and the tramp, the panhandler and the sturdy beggar, sounded a clarion call that public displays of need would be dealt with harshly and that the search for public relief or private charity was as much a question for the police as for any department of social services, just as the more visible supplication of women sent a similar message about the connection between punishment and poverty. That this criminalization of need "sets a moral tone," as Gilded Age reformers approvingly put it, has long been emphasized by Piven and Cloward.[3] For them it is the "ritual degradation of a pariah class," and it serves an essential political-economic function: remember that "to demean and punish those who do not work is to exalt by contrast even the meanest labor at the meanest wages."[4] With these late-century assaults on poor and homeless men, like the campaigns against relief, the COSs, the think tanks, and their allies fought to compel labor from those whom they perceived to be surviving by other means and to punish those who would refuse, all the while creating a class of deviants who might be blamed for the declining fortunes of so many in these Gilded Ages.

DANGEROUS MEN

The tramp was a stock character in late-nineteenth-century reform circles, a source of fear, scorn, and disgust (only early in the twentieth century would he become the benign tramp of Charlie Chaplin films). Yale College's Francis Wayland offered a fine summary at the 1877 National Conference on Charities and Corrections:

As we utter the word *Tramp,* there arises straightway before us the spectacle of a lazy, shiftless, sauntering or swaggering, ill-conditioned, irreclaimable, incorrigible, cowardly, utterly depraved savage. He fears not God, neither regards man. Indeed, he seems to have wholly lost all the better instincts and attributes of manhood. He will outrage an unprotected female, or rob a defenceless child, or burn an isolated barn, or girdle fruit trees, or wreck a railway train, or set fire to a railway bridge, or murder a cripple, or pilfer an umbrella. . . . Practically, he has come to consider himself at war with society and all social institutions. . . . He has only one aim,—to be supported in idleness. He has only one fear,—to be deprived of his liberty.[5]

Unlike most poor women or families, who even if deemed "undeserving" of aid were usually understood to be relief problems, the tramp was a police problem. "Nothing short of making street begging a crime," wrote Jacob Riis, "has availed to clear our city of this pest to an appreciable extent." Best known as a reporter and photographer of the slums of the Lower East Side, Riis worked closely with the police, which was his beat, and with the New York Charity Organization Society, for which he was a donor and volunteer.[6] Regarding these roaming beggars—these vagrants, vagabonds, hobos, pike bums, jumpers, or shovel-bums—Devine wrote that "there is no choice but to prosecute and deal with such offenders as criminals.[7] And in response to what reformers noted with alarm as a "tramp epidemic" (employing here again the "rhetoric of contagion"),[8] new laws, often called Tramp Acts, were passed throughout the nation in the last third of the century "to check or exterminate the tramp."[9] Many locales made it illegal to appear in public without a "visible means of support." In 1877 alone, a year of widespread labor unrest, the year of the Great Strike, a year historians Charles and Mary Beard said made the fearsome post–Revolutionary War tax revolt of Shays's Rebellion "appear like a mere argument at a garden party,"[10] there were more than one million vagrancy arrests in the United States, double the number of the previous year.[11]

There followed nearly three decades in which throughout the nation cities and towns enacted statutes that made begging illegal, loosened legal standards for arrest and conviction, demanded work in exchange for assistance, and made refusal to comply *"prima facie* evidence of tramping,"* which could in Massachusetts be punishable by one to three years in a state prison, labor colony, or reformatory. In Missouri, convicted beggars were auctioned off as workers to the highest bidder.[12] Other locales enacted mandatory minimum sentences as long as three years or fines of up to $50; those who couldn't pay such fines, and few could, were put to work, as were those who could not pay the fees often charged to cover the costs of their arrest, conviction, and transportation to public prison or private labor camp. This offered sheriffs a powerful incentive to make arrests, since those fees could be part or even all of their compensation.[13] In New Hampshire and Pennsylvania, anyone could arrest a beggar for a $10 reward; the prize was $5 in Connecticut and Rhode Island, and in Nevada $10 rewarded each conviction.[14] Some statutes placed the burden of proof upon the accused, and sanctioned summary judgments in juryless trials that could last less than one minute.[15] Baltimore removed judicial discretion over punishment, automatically condemning all those convicted to prison.[16]

By 1890 there may have been on any day 100,000 or more men in jails or penitentiaries nationwide and perhaps 1 million over the course of the year.[17] In 1882, New York police alone made between 70,000 and 75,000 arrests, fully one-fourth for intoxication or vagrancy. About 50,000 men every year were confined to the Tombs, the Gotham jail that held those serving short-term sentences, those awaiting trial, or those awaiting execution (local thieves called it City College); 35,000 were there on drunk and disorderly charges, of whom 12,000 were women.[18] Massachusetts vagrancy arrests doubled from 1892 to reach over 300,000 in 1895.[19] There was a distinct character to those imprisoned. Of the nearly 50,000 in the city of New York's prisons in 1879, 65 percent were foreign-born, as were perhaps one-third of those in Pennsylvania prisons, one-half at Auburn (New York), and six-sevenths at Sing Sing.[20] In the first three months of 1874, 78 percent of the 30,000 "lodgers" in New York police stations, which functioned as early homeless shelters, were foreign-born (and perhaps two-fifths were women).[21] Even as early as the late 1860s, prisons in New York, Pennsylvania, Massachusetts, Illinois, Ohio, Kentucky, and Tennessee were populated with poor, uneducated, immigrant men.[22]

MORE DANGEROUS MEN

Something similar happened a century later, after an interim in the twentieth century in which incarceration rates remained fairly steady.[23] The United States prison population increased more than 500 percent between 1972 and 1993, from 200,000 to 1.2 million in prison, with another 500,000 in local jails. By 2000, the total number had grown to over 2 million, with 621,000 in local jails, 60 percent of whom were under the influence of drugs or alcohol when arrested. The United States, with 5 percent of the world's population, held 25 percent of the world's prisoners. Over 100,000 were juveniles. The per-capita incarceration rate climbed from 160 per 100,000 in 1972 to 645 in 1997, 690 in 1998, and then 699 in 2000, finally beating out Russia to become the world's highest. It was 702 per 100,000 by 2002. (By comparison, it was perhaps 61 per 100,000 in 1880, but 170 per 100,000 for twenty- to forty-four-year-olds.) Half of all prisoners and 70 percent of state prisoners were incarcerated for nonviolent property or drug offenses. Federal public order offenses resulting in incarceration increased 99 percent from 1972 to 1998; drug offenses increased 446 percent, and they accounted for one-fourth of all inmates in 1996, up from one-tenth in 1983. Twelve percent of all state prisoners from 1985 to 1995 were incarcerated for public order offenses. Half of all prisons in 1999 had been built since 1979. And those incarcerated had much in common. Half of all those imprisoned were African American. Sixteen percent were Hispanic. In New York in 1990, blacks and Hispanics constituted 91 percent of all those imprisoned for drug possession. Nationwide, a black man now has a 29 percent chance of spending some portion of his life in jail or prison; it's 4 percent for a white man. While from 1985 to 1995 women's incarceration rate increased 204 percent, in 2001 93 percent of all inmates were still male. Sixty-eight percent of all state prisoners in 1997 had no high school diploma. In 1996, over one-third of those in jail had been unemployed prior to their arrest.[24] Once again the tramp was behind bars.

This wave of incarceration of poor black (instead of immigrant) men was, as with the earlier period, in part the result of a plethora of new laws increasing penalties for petty crimes or creating new kinds of crime. These attempts to control the poor have many roots; one is the urban riots of the mid-1960s, caused in part because a large migration of African Americans to northern cities occurred just as deindustrialization had begun in earnest and jobs were leaving those cities. (Labor-force participation for both black and white men ages sixteen to twenty-four in the 1950s was around 70 percent; by 1985 it had dropped to 65 percent for whites and under 45 percent for blacks.)[25] The threat posed to order was clear, if not a bit terrifying to those in power, and, as Christian Parenti has demonstrated, *crime control* became code for *race control, urban* became a code word for *black,* and drug enforcement became the means by which the federal government would impose order. As H.R. Haldeman confessed, "[President Nixon] emphasized that you have to face the fact that the whole problem is really the blacks. The key is to devise a system that recognizes this while not appearing to."[26] At the state level, New York's Rockefeller drug laws of 1973, which imposed long mandatory minimum sentences for minor offenses, set the standard, and were soon copied by other states. Congressional action followed in 1982 with the creation of regional drug task forces armed with $125 million in new funding. Subsequent bills in 1984, 1986, and 1988 enacted and expanded mandatory minimums, took sentencing discretion away from judges (just as some Gilded Age statutes did), and increased fines and asset forfeiture provisions, offering financial incentives for arrests and convictions (just as prior statutes had done), which simultaneously gave policing agencies some independence from municipal, democratic budgeting controls.[27] The Heritage Foundation and the American Legislative Exchange Council were among the many think tank sources of "scientific" studies demonstrating the cost savings that resulted from incarceration and urging a tough approach to "urban" crime. John Dilulio (of the Manhattan Institute and Brookings, he would later briefly head George W. Bush's Office of Faith-Based and Community Initiatives) and Heritage fellow William Bennett later helped stoke "lock-'em-up" rhetoric and policies with *Body Count,* warning of the danger posed by the "superpredators" who had been transformed by the culture of poverty ("crimonogenic communities," they called it) into "brutally remorseless youngsters, including ever more pre-teenage boys, who murder, assault, rape, rob, burglarize, deal deadly drugs, join gun-toting gangs, and create serious communal disorders . . . they are perfectly capable of committing the most heinous acts of physical violence for the most trivial reasons."[28] It's Wayland's indictment of the tramp. And before he helped end welfare, in 1996 Bill Clinton signed a $30 billion crime bill that funded new prisons, further toughened drug penalties, facilitated the incarceration of illegal aliens, expanded the death penalty, and sought to pay for a hundred thousand new local police officers.[29] Just as Gilded Age Tramp

Acts were an effort to control a society seemingly out of control thanks to industrialization, so too were these laws efforts at managing the worst effects of the postindustrial corporate assault on poor and working people: those mobilizations expanded the ranks of the potentially dangerous classes and thereby increased the need for their containment and their control.[30]

While this took on a national character in the latter period, local controls were just as evident. Since the late 1980s "cities from Portland, Maine, to Portland, Oregon"[31] enacted strict statutes against panhandling, harassed homeless men, criminalized begging on subways, enacted or enforced new loitering statutes, rousted those sleeping in public places, and passed and enforced an array of "quality-of-life" statutes while selectively enforcing curfews and laws prohibiting jaywalking, removing objects from trash cans, urinating in public, and spitting on sidewalks.[32] This phenomenon was not limited to conservative or southern cities—the Castro district of San Francisco, Minneapolis, Honolulu, Santa Cruz, and Santa Monica (once derided as *Soviet* Monica by some for its liberal politics) enacted some of the strictest laws and enforced them most severely. Even Berkeley tried to ban all panhandling. (There were few laws, it seems, that prohibited the *giving* of alms in either era, though many critics condemned those who were foolish enough to do so.) Of forty-nine large and midsized cities surveyed by the National Law Center on Homelessness and Poverty in 1999, 86 percent had laws that criminalized begging, and nearly one in five had either enacted new laws or toughened ones already on the books to restrict the use of parks, sidewalks, and other public spaces by those who appeared homeless; almost three-fourths also had enacted laws that prohibited camping or sleeping in public spaces. From 1992 to 1996, 31 percent of the fifty largest cities enacted more anti-begging laws or amended old ones. From 1997 to 1999, more than one-third launched new crackdowns on homelessness, and nearly half initiated sweeps to remove or relocate the visibly poor from targeted areas.

One Nevada law prohibited loitering with *intent* to beg. Santa Ana adopted an official policy that homeless people "are no longer welcome in the city." In Miami, where law provided that being "idle" constituted "disorderly conduct," police arrested homeless people, then confiscated and destroyed their belongings, including food stamps, eyeglasses, and prescription medication. Fort Lauderdale prohibited begging on its beaches. The Dallas City Council proposed offering vagrants bus tickets to any city of their choosing, and police in Huntsville, Long Beach, and Cleveland drove vagrants to the edge of town and deposited them there. Tulare County, California's MOVE program (More Opportunities for Viable Employment) paid poor residents an average of $2,300 each to move away ("I think this is splendid," Robert Rector told the *Washington Post*). South Carolina, Oregon, and Kentucky operated similar programs. This is the "warning off" that William Graham Sumner recommended, one of his preferred means of eliminating poverty, or, rather, paupers. Other cities sought to enact fines of up to $500 and jail terms as high as six months, as Atlanta did prior to the 1996 Olympics; loitering in Raleigh could bring a $500 fine and thirty days in jail; in Chester County, Pennsylvania, $1,000. Seattle law provided for a $100 fine for violation of an ordinance against sitting. In the first year of its Matrix program to coordinate anti-homeless policies, San Francisco issued perhaps as many as 22,500 citations and arrested 350 others for offering free food in public spaces.[33]

In 1989, the same year that Dade County, Florida, outlawed roadside windshield washers (statutes targeting these men, who became known as "squeegee guys," soon spread), the New York City Transit Authority implemented its new no-begging regulations, distributing pamphlets and posting warnings throughout the system that said: "Panhandling on the subway is illegal. No matter what you think. Give to the charity of your choice, but not on the subway." In affirming the legality of the program, a court noted that panhandling was "nothing less than a menace to the common good." Some years later, shortly after he took over from Giuliani, New York mayor (and billionaire businessman) Michael Bloomberg and police commissioner Raymond Kelly announced a renewed crackdown on "quality-of-life" crimes called Operation Clean Sweep. They established a hotline (888-677-LIFE) and urged the public to report low-level crimes—panhandling, prostitution, and squeegee ing, especially.[34] These renewed efforts coincided with record levels of homelessness and local television news reports that, for the first time in some years, focused on those who slept on the streets and why they did so.

The justifications for passing such statutes and enforcing these laws tended to be much the same—to protect the health of the public (from public urination and defecation) or its safety (from the dangers of mentally ill street persons or, as a Palo Alto law noted, from being distracted by or tripping over homeless people). Following the "broken windows" theory of crime control, many asserted that by controlling the minor offenses of "unconventional individuals," a message is sent to the public that no lawbreaking will be tolerated.[35] In fact, one Santa Monica police sergeant admitted that arrests were less important than the symbolic threat posed by stepped-up enforcement.[36]

CHARITY ORGANIZATION IMPLICATED

Charity organization societies and their benefactors were greatly involved in Gilded Age campaigns against tramps, and "many of these statutes," observed Amy Stanley, "were the direct accomplishment of charity reformers."[37] As the Boston COS's Robert Treat Paine told the Brooklyn Bureau of Chari-

ties, "even the tramps and paupers have organized a mighty assault against Christian benevolence; out of sheer protection it is
essential that the charities launch a counter-organization."[38] As
Paine also said, "What influence can be worse for all who see
that begging pays better than work?"[39] Businessman Alfred
Mason recommended establishing a "Charity Trust," a com-
bine modeled after Standard Oil, so that begging should "not
simply be lessened, but choked to death" with more effective
use of the police.[40] Many COSs included anti-begging campaigns as part of their advocacy work. Others went further. In
Louisville, the COS was granted formal police powers, while in
dozens of other cities the COS and police worked together to
arrest and convict beggars. The most "continuous," "systematic," "efficient," and "severe" efforts were made in St. Louis,
Boston, Detroit, Milwaukee, Jersey City, Newark, Cincinnati,
Minneapolis, Worcester, Kansas City, Denver, New Haven,
Hartford, and Springfield.[41] Lowell herself wrote New York's
1880 anti-vagrancy law.[42] The New York COS established its
own Mendicancy Squad, which, in cooperation with the police,
detained vagrants and brought them to the courthouse for
prosecution. It faithfully published its successes in each issue
of *Charities Review,* noting the number of cases, the total
"warned," the total committed, and the total number of
months of incarceration or enforced labor the convict would
serve; the average from 1891 and 1892 ranged from one to three
months.[43] When the squad was discontinued in 1906, vagrancy
arrests declined by 50 percent.[44] At the 1883 NCCC, a representative from Buffalo reporting on vagrants and tramps noted
that "the Charity Organization Society has been most successful in preventing this class of cases from any thing like a permanent abode with us and in no direction has exceeding vigilance
been more rewarded. The society has found it necessary to
prosecute these cases directly; and in each case unless its demand has been complied in, has had the persons arrested and

prosecuted in the police courts; the result is that our streets are entirely free from these eye no sores [*sic*]." Gurteen claimed that "the discontinuance of door-to-door begging [was] due to the Society *alone*."[45]

Charity organization societies were dogged adversaries. Representatives of COSs personally appeared at trials to urge conviction and harsh sentences, and expressed frustration at what they perceived to be the unwillingness of judges to convict enough of the accused (it was 20–50 percent).[46] They fought also to ensure that, once convicted, the tramp would be compelled to work. "At present," complained Warner, "a man who is sentenced for vagrancy is usually sent from ten to ninety days to a warm and pleasant jail, where he can play cards, chew tobacco, discuss crime, and tell indecent stories with his peers. To threaten a vagabond with arrest under such circumstances, is merely to promise to do him a favor."[47] Philip Ayers reported, "Memphis has long been a central station for tramps, and only when the United Charities turned this undesirable element over systematically to the police who put each vagrant at hard labor, has the city been rid of them."[48] Lowell fought to close police lodging houses, noting that in 1889 there were a total of 147,634 lodgings (69,111 of which were for women), averaging 189 women and 215 men each night. She noted more approvingly that the same year there were 82,200 arrests (including 19,926 women): those arrested, unlike lodgers, worked as part of their sentence.[49]

By 1896, police commissioner Theodore Roosevelt (his father was Lowell's colleague on the New York State Board of Charities) finally ended the practice of police lodgings, under pressure also from Riis.[50] Lowell fought against private lodgings, too, citing their dangers in an 1896 letter to the Salvation Army when trying to dissuade them from opening a shelter. Lodgings, she insisted, had the "1. Danger of physical contagion; 2. Certainty of moral degradation; 3. Encouragement of vagrancy." Instead, send would-be lodgers to the workhouse, she urged, and give them "moral and spiritual care," but don't offer poor men incentives to come to the city. "One of the great evils of cheap lodging houses, whether commercial or charitable, is that a man who gets good wages can earn by one or two days' work enough to pay his way for a week, and a man who works two days each week and idles four is not a desirable person, whether regarded as an individual or as a member of the community."[51] That is, the chief danger of cheap lodging was that it made it possible for workers to survive while working less.

ANOTHER PARIAH CLASS

By late in the century, strikers, rioters, marchers, soapbox speechmakers, and the various "armies" of unemployed men led in protest by "Generals" Coxey, Kelly, Frye, Browne, Fitzgerald, and Swift, were castigated and dismissed as idle beggars or tramps:[52]

> *Hark, Hark! Hear the dogs bark!*
> *Coxey is coming to town.*
> *In his ranks are scamps*
> *And growler fed tramps*
> *On all of whom working men frown.*[53]

Levi Barbour captured the fear of the tramp, and the connection between tramps and disorder: "Unless restrained from his nomadic course of life, the tramp and the beggar would ultimately threaten our very social existence. To-day we see them organized into what they are pleased to call 'industrial armies,' threatening the very heart of the nation with violence unless furnished with work which they never intend to do. What this gathering horde really demands is that the Nation adopt the system of 'outdoor relief,' and that all its members shall be the recipients of that living which they conceive the world owes them, regardless of any effort they may make, regardless of any demand for particular kinds of work and prices in payment, regardless of all rights of property, regardless of the right of their fellows to accept work, and regardless of the right of society to do without them."[54] Barbour stated specifically that state boards of charity could remedy this if they were staffed by men "who have been busy and successful in professional and other higher business walks of life."

Yet as John McCook discovered in an 1893 survey, of those tramps lodged at police stations, 57 percent had a skilled trade or a profession (41 percent were unskilled), half had jobs that *required* them to travel (sailors, railroad workers, etc.), 56 percent were born in the United States, and 90 percent were literate. Most if not all were men, and 90 percent were probably single, said McCook in an 1895 study, because single men were typically laid off before married men were. Most worked, when work was available. He estimated there to be just under 46,000 tramps in the United States in 1893. Tramp populations in large cities changed with the seasons.[55] In an 1877 letter to the NCCC Charles Loring Brace reported, "Nothing can ever prevent the annual inpouring of vagrants and tramps every winter into the large cities, to enjoy the benefit of city charities and the excitements of winter life in the city; nor their exodus in the spring, to obtain chance jobs in the country, pick up alms, and enjoy a gipsy life in the warm months." He recommended that they not be allowed to travel without instituting "some pass-system."[56] But at the same conference, another member noted that "the difficulty of deciding whether a man be a laborer in search of work, or a tramp trying to avoid it, is the difficulty which runs through the whole administration of the subject."[57]

Their number only grew, from 46,000 in 1893 to 86,000 in 1895 and 430,000 by 1905, many of whom "infested the railways."[58] McCook estimated that the cost for their care in 1895 exceeded $17 million, while Warner estimated $18.5 million by 1905.[59] Part of this "explosion" in tramping, which reflects a change in available employment, was likely a result of the deep depression of 1893–1898. Just as the crises of the late century helped transform reformers' thinking about poor relief and its recipients, so too might these large events have helped change common understandings of those men who traveled the country in search of work. "It was both ironic and telling," Keyssar reports, "that tramps received less public attention once it became apparent that they were victims rather than villains, that they were obeying, rather than flouting, the dictates of the economy."[60] Feder observed that "since the previous depression, thoughtful study and experimental treatment had clarified problems of the homeless. No longer merely a threatening mass, to be handled as cheaply as was consistent with community protection, homeless men had been revealed as persons with specific problems."[61] While it would still require even more severe depressions to engage the national government in response, this period was an important stepping-stone in the long transformation in thought about the connection between industrialization, boom and bust cycles, employment, and the capacity for individual self-sufficiency. By the mid-twentieth century, the tramp had almost disappeared. But he would return.

PRISONS AND PROFIT

Of the hundred thousand or so men in jails and prisons in 1890, most performed labor for outside contractors. This was a source of much debate. Even Josephine Shaw Lowell complained: "Do you know that when the stove men were on strike in Albany, the State penitentiary undertook the manufacture of stoves, and broke down the strike?"[62] Citing a special committee of the Ohio legislature, General Brinkerhoff reported that "the contract system carried on in our penal institutions is directly responsible for a large percentage of the reductions which have taken place in the wages of thousands of our mechanics during the past four years. Nearly every manufacturer who testified before your committee attributed a large percentage of the reduction in wages to the system which enabled manufacturers who have prison contracts at cheap rates to go into the market and undersell them."[63] Half of all total U.S. prisoners (54,495 in 1887) were employed in a mechanical industry; convicts made up 20 percent of all broom and brush workers, 31 percent of all chair makers, 19 percent of all saddlery hardware makers, and 12 percent of the whip industry, but, he noted in order to offer a defense of prison labor, only 2.5 percent of all mechanical labor in all industries was performed by prison labor. Just as specific trades were more adversely affected than others, state-by-state variation is obscured by low national effects. In Michigan, Indiana, Wisconsin, and Missouri, convicts produced 23 percent of all boots and shoes, for example.[64]

Mississippi recorded a net profit of $30,090 in prison agricultural labor for 1896; Texas prisoners took in $101,905 "over and above the cost of their keep" in 1895 and 1896; Virginia in 1897 netted $14,232.[65] In the late nineteenth century, prisoners in Alabama were "leased out" to "businesses hungry for hands to work in farm fields, lumber camps, railroad construction gangs and, especially in later years, mines."[66] The practice was hardly limited to the South, although there convict leasing took on a particular character as it supplanted slave labor with new forms of indentured servitude. The percentage of all inmates in Nashville who were black rose from 33 percent in 1865 to almost 68 percent in 1879, remaining near that level into the new century, while 70 percent of Louisiana's prisoners and 88 percent of North Carolina's were black.[67] Businesses paid the state an average of 48 cents per day for labor, while competitive wages might have been as high as $1.75 per day.[68] Boasted Rev. J.L. Milligan of Allegheny, Pennsylvania, in 1879, "All our prisoners are employed."[69] Blackmon observes, "Leasing prisoners to private individuals or companies provided revenue and eliminated the need to build prisons." But its effects extend beyond the direct and economic: "its ideological and psychological importance should not be underestimated. Prison labor was widely *perceived* by workers as a potential or immediate threat, and thus lurked in the background of the general conflict between labor and capital as an instrument of discipline."[70] (Asylum labor was as widespread, though less often decried.)[71]

Private interests profited from mass incarcerations in the late twentieth century just as they did in the late nineteenth century. By 1998, 7 percent of all U.S. prisoners were housed in private facilities; for-profit prison revenues exceeded $1 billion, almost all of which went to twelve firms, while over 77 percent of all contracts went to two firms, Corrections Corporation of America and Wackenhut Corrections Corporation.[72] By 2001, thanks largely to changes in Texas, the number of prisoners housed in private facilities had declined to 6.1 percent, although in five states more than 28 percent of their prisoners were privatized.[73] In 2003, one of the largest welfare contractors, Maximus, acquired National Misdemeanant Probations Operations, "one of the largest providers of community corrections services in the country," to "complement" its other contracting areas, according to the *Wall Street Journal*.[74] Lexus, Boeing, Microsoft, TWA, IBM, AT&T, and Victoria's Secret all used prison labor at some point in their production or sales process; most such laborers were paid between 20 cents and $1.20 per hour, often even cheaper than labor in a Mexican *maquiladora* or an Indonesian sweatshop.[75] Starbucks and Nintendo contractor Signature Packing Solutions paid their prison workers minimum wage, without incurring health or retirement insurance expenses. The Washington State Department of Corrections kept half its prisoners' wages. "The mission is," said a DOC representative, "to give offenders, if nothing else, a work ethic and experience."[76]

The use of prison labor began to decline in the late nineteenth century because the demands of efficient production were increasingly incompatible with the complexities of controlling inmates at work;[77] there are similar difficulties evident in late-twentieth-century production, perhaps accounting for why the market has grown only modestly.[78] Yet to confront the dilemma of profitable privatization, Wackenhut and Corrections Corporation of America have expanded their services to include other indoor relief such as mental institutions and drug-treatment facilities, with their eye on care for prisoners with AIDS, older prisoners, and Immigration and Naturalization Service lockups, the last of which has become something of a growth industry thanks to the "war on terror."[79] Taking another approach, a Corrections Corporation of America representative served on an American Legislative Exchange Council task force that drafted legislation to limit prisoners' eligibility for parole, thereby prolonging their incarceration. Forty state legislatures had passed such a law by the late 1990s.[80]

ECHOES OF THE TRAMP
AND THE CHAMBER, TOO

Robert Ellickson has also drawn parallels between these two crackdowns a century apart, although for a different reason. Commenting on the modern profusion of begging in Harvard Square, he wrote that it did not indicate a lack of adequate relief, but instead "suggests the generosity of local welfare efforts. In the 1990s, panhandling has been most common in Berkeley, New York, San Francisco, Washington, D.C., and other cities that have relatively expansive social-welfare programs. It appears that taxpayers willing to support relatively generous welfare programs are also relatively more inclined to give to panhandlers. Panhandlers have no trouble recognizing these realities. . . . The point was well understood in the late nineteenth century. 'Beggars increase in number in proportion to the means provided for their relief.' "[81] This 1885 observation that Ellickson quotes sounds much like Mayor Schmoke's 1995 plea to the citizens of Baltimore that they should "give to charities that provide for the truly needy, as giving to panhandlers merely worsens the problem,"[82] or the Maryville, California, police chief who observed, "Panhandling is a supply-and-demand business. . . . If there's no supply of spare change, then panhandling goes down immediately."[83] And they all sound much like Rev. Gurteen.

The comparison can go further, for just as the Chamber of Commerce worked with the COSs and local police departments to pass and enforce anti-tramping laws, so too were local businesses central players in the passage of these late-twentieth-century laws criminalizing and punishing public pleas for assistance and visible displays of need. District of Columbia and New York City business improvement districts formed "homeless task forces" to coordinate business community response and activism. Glendale, California, rousted day laborers after repeated complaints from local businesses, then provided a single site for them to offer themselves to prospective employers.[84] Charlotte cleared out selected parks and other public areas "to appease business owners,"[85] Seattle police and local businesses worked together to enforce no-trespassing laws,[86] and Baltimore passed redundant anti-panhandling laws "to prove to business that the city government is responding to the panhandling problem."[87] In other cities (Tulsa, Albuquerque, Long Beach, Las Vegas, Reno) business organizations funded campaigns to discourage the public from giving any money to beggars.[88] These efforts went well beyond what would have been required to merely remove homeless men from blocking access to businesses—they were broader efforts to cleanse the city itself of this plague of tramps, a plague that could only highlight the inequality of these Gilded Ages and raise troubling questions about its causes.

The business press followed developments with particular attention. *The Economist* reported that Sony banned people with "excessive packages" from its public spaces and that other shop owners ran water over their sidewalks to prevent sleeping and loitering.[89] *Crain's Cleveland Business* described with some awe the collaboration between the Salvation Army and the Cleveland [Business] Partnership to stop panhandling.[90] *Crain's Detroit Business* noted that local businesses were urging police to more aggressively enforce panhandling punishments of fines and jail time.[91] *Crain's Chicago Business* lauded a new program based upon those in Berkeley and Seattle that issued vouchers as an alternative to cash: "aggressive panhandling has decreased in areas covered by vouchers." Earlier it reported that "business owners who feel that the problem is spinning out of control" helped drive the "backlash" against panhandling.[92] *American Banker* praised a New York law prohibiting panhandling near automated teller machines that carried a $25 fine and ten days in jail.[93] The Disney Corporation, working with the Orlando City Council and the Chamber of Commerce, helped pass the licensing ordinance described above, which prescribed penalties of $500 and sixty days in jail for unlicensed begging. One Orlando sergeant admitted, "We're actually hoping we'll displace people to other cities."[94]

Other accounts confirm that local businesses were central players in many anti-begging campaigns of the late twentieth century, organizing an anti-panhandling campaign with the Chamber of Commerce and the police department in Lawrence, Kansas,[95] driving reforms for undercover police officers and establishing "community courts" without standard civil protections for accused beggars in Baltimore,[96] supporting (through the business organization the Downtown Phoenix Partnership) city regulations that imposed strict limitations on acceptable public behavior near businesses especially,[97] and, bringing things full circle, in Buffalo, home to one of the nation's most aggressive anti-tramping initiatives in the nineteenth century, helping to create that city's 1995 Downtown Initiative, a zero-tolerance policy that strictly enforced no-panhandling regulations in its business district. Said the deputy police commissioner, "The business community wasn't satisfied with the way things were. This is our response."[98] Throughout the 1990s, sweeps of the homeless especially intensified under pressure from businesses before sporting events, business or political conventions, board or trustees meetings, or any large, potentially profitable gathering in cities throughout the United States,[99] just as they did during the Winter Olympics in Salt Lake City, when some men were "deported" to other cities while some two thousand to three thousand others were herded into shelters and offered extra meals if they would remain in them, hidden from view.[100] One 1992 survey of law enforcement agencies found that 68.9 percent identified "street people" as a police problem.[101]

Like nineteenth-century lodgers, those arrested under anti-begging and other statutes were not all "idle"; 30 percent of all shelter residents, for instance, worked during any given week.[102] Up to 40 percent were veterans.[103] We should not (as many of the articles cited in this section do) assume that panhandlers and beggars were homeless. One Baltimore study concluded that a "very small percentage" of its street beggars were homeless; a Philadelphia study found that almost half of its panhandlers had a place to stay other than a shelter;[104] Chicago estimated that 60 percent of its beggars were not homeless;[105] and 65 percent of those arrested in one three-month period in 1993 in Atlanta were not homeless.[106] Many were men who, like their Gilded Age brethren, had little value in the labor market, and begging was a means, albeit an unconventional one, to supplement their meager, irregular earnings. Still, as before, their acts were seen as criminal and profitable. Said one Chicago police sergeant, "Panhandlers are thieves. . . . They make $40 to $90 a day. It's a darn good business." [107]

Nineteenth-century reformers understood the link between these policies almost intuitively—the national professional association that sought to maintain order in the tumultuous years of the Gilded Age was, after all, the National Conference on Charities and Corrections. The connection is rarely made so forthrightly today, although the PRA did permit states to deny TANF and food stamps to any applicant with a felony drug conviction and, in one grim and ironic instance in 2002, New York City, for a time, reopened a Bronx jail and used it as a shelter for homeless families. The message, though no doubt accidental, was once again clear, if perhaps more subtle than erecting the gallows next to the almshouse.[108] These elaborate dramas of welfare and criminal justice are about maintaining order, about creating controls over those who, with good reason, might seek to rebel against their marginalization and demand more. The "dangerous classes" had grown so great in number, thanks in large measure to changes in government policies, that the incarceration of many of them was needed to render them harmless and submissive. Repression helped secure redistribution. Indeed, Richard Fording's analysis suggests that there may well be a quantifiable relationship between welfare and incarceration—as relief benefits decline, prison populations rise, and one form of control, of pacification, is traded for another.[109] Katherine Beckett and Bruce Western came independently to the same conclusion, showing that since 1995, states with weaker welfare protections consistently had higher state prison populations, and vice versa. (And those states that spent less on welfare tended to have larger black populations.)[110] Incarceration makes for a brute form of control, to be sure, and it is one that by dint of its sheer expense and capriciousness may be losing its legitimacy, but it is a form of control that we must consider when examining the uses and meanings of relief in America's unequal, troubled Gilded Ages, given that it is the same population that is the object of both programs.

It is not just the threat of violence from the poorest among us that is notable, however, for they might pose an electoral threat as well. It is instructive to remember that in forty-eight states prisoners are denied the right to vote. Thirteen states permanently disenfranchise some or all ex-offenders. Thirty-three deny the right to vote to parolees. By 2002, one in fifty adults had lost the right to vote because of a felony conviction, while fully 13 percent of black men were disenfranchised. In seven states where ex-offenders cannot vote, 25 percent of all black men were *permanently* disenfranchised. If these trends persist, 30 percent of young African American men can expect to lose their right to vote at some point in their lives.[111] This is only the most easily discernible of many means by which poor Americans are dissuaded from voting.

Finally, prisoners, like welfare queens, serve as a degraded, immoral, and threatening class upon whom antipathy from the beleaguered middle and near-marginal classes might be directed. They are scapegoats. They constitute a wedge that might be driven between all of the poorer classes and the middling ones as part of a campaign to inhibit the majority from uniting to depose the propertied minority, which is old news indeed: early in our colonial history black slaves were segregated from white indentured servants because they had begun to identify common cause and unite against their oppressors, and the history of the American labor movement is rife with anti-labor activists sowing racial and ethnic divisions among workers for fear that they would join together. Perhaps it is only with "a revolt of the guards," in historian Howard Zinn's phrase, in which the poor and the middle classes find common cause against their mutual antagonists, that the corrupt bargain might be broken.[112]

7

Poverty and Propaganda

While for the present, charitable organization, both public and private, is perhaps necessarily dealing with the symptoms rather than going to the root of the disease, alleviating distress rather than taking measures to prevent its recurrence, the time is near at hand, I trust, when public charity will not consider more radical measures beyond its scope,—when it will recognize even more distinctly and comprehensively than it does to-day the intimate relation between the problems with which charity has to deal and those larger social, moral, and industrial problems which are beginning to perplex and oppress the world. . . . As we come to have a more correct conception of the causes which fill our charitable institutions with inmates and lead to a constant increase in the demands for outdoor relief, we shall, I think, come to realize that a great deal of the occasion for charity, public or private, can be avoided in the future, if not in the present, by a wise extension of political democracy into social and industrial democracy.

—Josiah Quincy, National Conference
on Charities and Corrections, 1898

The late-century campaigns against poor relief and public displays of need achieved two results: the policies they helped bring to fruition made poor men and women more vulnerable to the demands of the low-wage labor market, and the campaigns themselves sent a symbolic message to others that poverty was a mark of failure, of punishable failure at that, and that work alone was the means toward security or salvation. The Personal Responsibility Act's abolition of the (limited) right to relief was a profound transformation in modern relief policy and part of a movement to call into question the state intervention in the market that became the hallmark of the Progressive Era, and to which the New Deal and Great Society gave legal force and legitimacy.[1] It returned us to Gilded Age conceptions of social obligation.

This was not the explanation reformers offered the public as to what they were doing. Instead, they concealed their desires. Through the "experts" of charity organization societies or think tanks, which businessmen funded generously, anti-relief reformers argued that to take away welfare from poor people was to give them freedom and opportunity. They told lurid but familiar stories about the dangers of relief and the poor themselves. They repeated their tales over and again, telling them to politicians and the public alike with such consistency and frequency that they effectively drowned out alternative narratives, such as they were, of poverty and relief. Over time anti-relief reformers succeeded in insinuating these ideas, and with them the reforms they contained, into mainstream policy debate and public discussion. Instead of a public discussion about poverty—which might focus attention upon corporate power, economic inequality, the real value of wages, regressive taxation, or exclusionary politics—reformers launched a debate about welfare and cultivated antipathy not to poverty but to the pauper and the panhandler, to the welfare queen and the tramp. This debate, under the banner of reducing dependency and illegitimacy and rewarding work, supported by the logics of Thomas Malthus, Herbert Spencer, and Josephine Shaw Lowell in the nineteenth century or Charles Murray, Gertrude Himmelfarb, and Marvin Olasky in the twentieth, shaped and constrained the actions of policy makers and encouraged them to advocate and enact harsh new policies that would render poor men and women more vulnerable. These reconfigurations of relief and the meanings they conveyed pitted the poor and working classes against each other, inhibiting their ability to identify common cause in and therefore defend liberal relief, and shifted social expenditures away from people most in need to wage subsidies for their employers and contracts to non-profits and the private sector. Reformers simultaneously preached the virtues of work to the working poor, punished the idle, pushed welfare recipients into low-wage jobs, and further lowered the price and power of labor.

In the preceding pages I have sought to describe the means by which these class-dividing, ideology-enforcing, and labor-regulating functions were achieved in two periods, and how they affected men and women differently. Though it remains incomplete, I have painted a fuller picture of late-nineteenth-century relief policies and their variation from city to city. I have offered descriptions of the manner by which the suppos-edly "functionalist" explanations of relief offered by James O'Connor and Piven and Cloward were achieved, and in so doing have shone a spotlight on powerful forces that are largely absent in other accounts of reform. I have identified some of those who strove to withdraw relief and what they did to achieve their goals, revealing in the process the striking simi-larities between actors, institutions, ideas, and events a century apart. This book has sought to demonstrate that there is more to the story of relief withdrawal than what is told in accounts that depend upon the "normal" politics of electoral competi-tion, the partisan balance of congressional or municipal power, the structure of political institutions, the press of constituent opinion, the constraints of budget deficits, the politics of race, and the legacy of prior policy. In so doing, I have tried to bring attention to a neglected aspect of American social welfare pol-icy and history—the instances in which the state has with-drawn hard-won social benefits from its citizens with relative impunity—to offer a reminder that victories gained in one era may be withdrawn in another.

ONE RETURN TO RELIEF

The considerable successes of anti-relief campaigns were short-lived in the late nineteenth century, however. While many charity reformers in the 1870s and 1880s helped convince their cities to abolish or sharply restrict public poor relief and to shift the burden of care to the voluntary sector, in the wake of the depression of 1893 many cities found themselves overrun with the newly unemployed, a growing, angry, dangerous class desperate for food, fuel, and work. Despite innovative efforts and works programs that anticipated the larger-scale programs of the New Deal, most cities found that voluntary efforts were insufficient to confront the need they faced. In some cities people who had once been anti-relief reformers petitioned local governments to intervene and offer outdoor relief; chastened and afraid, many softened or abandoned their opposition to public aid and waged new campaigns to expand public relief and to increase government regulation of the economy through efforts we now identify with the Progressive Era.

Charity organization societies were engaged in a difficult task throughout the late 1800s, often ambivalent about their own effectiveness and struggling to maintain their idea of social order in the midst of radical transformations in the nature of work, social relations, and family ties. That reformers' ideas of pauperism (soon to be called *poverty*), and workers' ideas of relief, too, would be jumbled, shifting, contradictory, inconsistent, and oddly conjoined is to be expected—what we see when we examine charity reformers' attempts to understand the world is a people, albeit a privileged and educated one, trying to come to terms with a transformation in human society and to find a role in it. Only once reformers realized that restoring to city dwellers the social relations of the countryside was not possible in a new, urban, industrial world did they attend to those very industrial changes and seek to ameliorate their effects on those least suited to survival in a competitive market. Only once they realized that private charity could not hope to alleviate the distress this new world demanded of some for the advancement of others did they relinquish their ardent opposition to public relief.

Lee Frankel, manager of New York's United Hebrew Charities, noted the change in 1903:

> No more significant fact was developed at the last meeting of the National Conference of Charities and Correction than the changed attitude of its members to the use of relief, or more specifically, of material relief, in the care and treatment of needy families. The revulsion of feeling in favor of relief in the proper treatment of the family taken as a unit, was as marked as the stand taken against its indiscriminate use twenty-five or thirty years ago, when charity organization movements were brought into existence to counteract the evil influences of such indiscriminate and ill-advised giving.

He went on to offer a defense of outdoor relief:

> With all the good that has been accomplished throughout the long and incessant campaign for improved methods in relief giving, we have also done harm. So long and insistent has been the demand for "substitutes" for material relief that in many quarters the opinion is current that material relief of itself is evil. Let us once and for all get rid of this fallacy. Let us realize that material relief is as efficient an agent in the removal of certain forms of dependency as the substitutes which have been recommended in its place and that there are specific forms of poverty in which material relief, and material relief

only, can effect the desired result. The pauperism and the resulting evils arising from the giving of material relief have
been largely exaggerated.[2]

In the early 1930s, the New York COS looked back upon its
first fifteen years, from 1881 to 1896: "Fifty years ago civic
minded people who started the C.O.S. and other welfare agencies had much more of a puritanical outlook, feeling for the
most part that if clients did not respond to the C.O.S. efforts to
rehabilitate them, it was simply because they did not want to
and therefore relief was cut off for their 'lack of cooperation.'
Some years later, however, it began to be clearer that the situation was not as simple as all that."[3] As Watson wrote, "material
relief acquired a new dignity"[4] that "would have been heresy
twenty-five years ago," added deForest in 1908.[5] Frankel again:

We have divided and subdivided them [the poor] until today
we have a grand array of causes, objective and subjective, direct and indirect. We have classified our poor into categories
and groups until they appear as objects distinct from ourselves, possessed of different attributes, aims and ambitions.
We have the sluggard and the shiftless, the drunkard and the
criminal, the sick and the aged, the improvident and the de-
serter. In our treatment of needy families we have assumed
that the cause of distress and dependence which we find on the
surface are primal and basic and have lost sight of the fact that
the causes which are immediately apparent are in most instances but the resultant of causes more deep seated and occult.
Many of the subjective causes which are laid at the door of the
dependent family's condition are the product of anterior objective causes for which the Society itself is responsible.[6]

This is an important insight, that what are judged causes
may instead be effects, and it characterizes succinctly the

changing understandings of poverty and poor people in the late century. By 1896 even the charter of the New York COS had been amended to discontinue distinguishing between "deserving" and "undeserving" applicants,[7] and by the late 1890s reformers seemed to have resigned themselves to out-relief and abandoned their efforts to abolish it; papers on abolishing outdoor relief nearly disappeared from the proceedings of the National Conference on Charities and Corrections. That insight could be learned anew by contemporary anti-relief reformers. As I write, the long-delayed reauthorization of the Personal Responsibility Act is set to toughen its provisions, the American economy is in recession, unemployment has been climbing, hunger has risen, poverty has deepened, homeless populations are at record levels, and even the squeegee guy and the subway panhandler have reappeared in New York City. Some of the conditions, though still writ small, that led to a repudiation of relief retrenchment in the late nineteenth century seem in evidence again. Yet there is no indication that we shall soon repeal our recent reforms, absent a crisis comparable to the deep depression of the late Gilded Age, and even those members of Congress who decry the failures of the PRA do not propose fundamental changes to its most radical reforms.

RESISTANCE TO REFORM
AND THE RESILIENCE OF RELIEF

As I have emphasized, these periods of reform were about more than mere poor relief. In the wake of threats by the poor and working classes, the gilded classes of both eras launched countermobilizations to secure or restore their power and their profitability. Relief policy was one battleground of a larger war, a battle in which the relative power of poor and working people was contested by self-interested actors who fought under cover of their reform organizations, losing some battles, winning many others, meeting with varying degrees of resistance in different cities. The charity organization movement did not sweep across the country like a beneficent contagion, as some would have it (nor did the public in the late twentieth century rise up and demand welfare reform). These were long, complicated struggles, and they changed over time—their rhetoric, their diagnosis of the problem, the policy solutions proposed, the relative influence of one group over another, the political climate, and even the composition of the contestants themselves. Classes were never static, nor were class interests. That the COS's philosophy was not mere "social control" is testament, perhaps, to the enduring difficulty inherent in ameliorating misery without upending an industrial order that depends upon it for its advancement. While some business and professional men (and some women) were active, either visibly or behind the scenes, in anti-relief campaigns, others of the better-off classes were advocates of ample, relatively unrestricted charity, unconcerned or unaware of its potential effects upon business profitability, and were acting out a different set of more socially grounded class interests—the preservation of a less contentious social order.[8] Those pro-relief forces were minor players in most of these dramas, however, and when the dust settled, poor people in most cities were worse off than they had been before, having lost what few gains they had previously fought to win.

But not in nineteenth-century Boston, Cleveland, Chicago, and Buffalo. Some cities were able to fend off attempts to roll back their public protections, however inadequate, for their most vulnerable citizens. Chicago and Buffalo failed to repeal relief in part because the threats posed by a mobilized poor inhibited them from doing so. Josephine Shaw Lowell characterized such events as a kind of extortion. The resistance to relief withdrawal exemplified by Boston, on the other hand, seems to have been partly institutional. Institutions not only channel conflict in particular ways, as Schattschneider tells us,[9] they also are sticky, stubborn things; they *congeal preferences*.[10] The formal structures and rules of decision making affect the ability of even powerful actors to exert their will. The guardians and overseers of the poor in Boston, and as we have seen in other cities as well, fought to retain their prerogatives over what were in some places powerful pools of patronage. That was the source of some of the strength of outdoor relief, and is at the heart of Lui's interpretations of outdoor-relief battles in late-nineteenth-century New York.[11]

Many people's support for contemporary welfare programs is also rooted in the benefits they dispense or receive. This kind of support by the recipients of relief is not absolute, however—some of the harshest critiques of welfare and of its recipients could be heard from recipients themselves, as I have noted.[12] Why should this be so? Because, as we saw in Boston and in Cleveland, the resilience of relief to the assault against it was based both in the actual operations of those institutions, and thus the patronage-based support for them, and in the public perception of those institutions independent of knowledge of their performance. The Boston public was told a story about the effectiveness of relief and the efficiency of its administration that was little disputed by local actors; in fact, because Boston was the home to so many traditional relief-giving organizations, some dating from the 1600s, the dominant refrain appears to have been in favor of relief, not opposed to it, and anti-relief reformers met greater resistance from other organizations than they did in other locales when they tried to take over or withdraw aid. Public opinion of relief is rooted in people's experience of it but also in their understandings of it, its *meaning* to them. That meaning is conveyed in many ways, partly through people's own experiences, to be sure, and through those of family and friends, but also through the stories they are told by elites and experts (in newspapers and magazines or on television and radio), and through the "dram-aturgy" of the "public rituals of degradation" they witness—the workfare worker in an orange vest picking up trash from the ground, the arrest of vagrants and panhandlers—that so dramatically link poverty and punishment.[13] Different relief dramas convey different meanings; in Boston's drama, relief was not the antagonist. But in other late-nineteenth-century cities and throughout the nation in the late twentieth century, the story told by anti-relief reformers occupied almost the en-tire stage.

Public opinion polling typically measures attitudes or asks respondents to assess their awareness of, involvement in, and concerns about various policy questions. Less often does it seek to measure people's knowledge of facts. When it does, the pub-lic is found to be largely ignorant about welfare.[14] It is in such ignorance that their antipathy is usually rooted—people hate welfare for what they think it is, not for what it actually is. Or perhaps more accurately, they have been told only one story about welfare, and have rarely been told one that celebrates welfare as a force that allows men and women to lead their lives and care for their families in ways that are impossible when their very survival is tethered to the relentless demands of the low-wage labor market. They have never been told the story of how welfare can make them more independent, how it can make them more free.

The repeal of AFDC may have come about partly because this targeted, means-tested program had a smaller constituency than relief programs in some other Western nations and could not claim the concentrated local support outdoor relief enjoyed in some Gilded Age cities. A moribund and legally circum-scribed labor movement limits opportunities for organizing resistance among working people, as does an electoral system that systematically inhibits the access and the formal influence of dissenting voices. The demise of the Democratic South and the rise of a Republican congressional majority defined a new political landscape. Race, as so many have documented and so many have experienced, has hindered American welfare state development and relief provision in profound ways. The movement of so many women into the workforce in the 1960s affected support for AFDC because it allowed some poor women to remain at home with their children when other, less-poor women could not. And welfare can conflict with some widely held tenets of American political culture. These and other explanations are important, and while I have given them little attention, I do not minimize them. My claim is that the significant successes of the anti-relief efforts discussed here must also be attributed to the greater vigor of coordinated, well-funded American anti-relief efforts and the pervasive ideological assaults against relief waged through sophisticated, state-of-the-art propaganda campaigns, and the absence of large-scale counteroffensives by welfare recipients and advocates.

Institutional resilience alone is likely insufficient to protect what powers poor and working people still retain, normal politics affords them little influence, and a social movement is a difficult thing to plan. What must therefore be included as part of any project to advance the reach of American poor relief, absent more radical transformations, is the kind of ideological offensive against neo-liberal hegemony that Susan George has called for. The left must better understand, as Powell and Weyrich and Scaife and Coors and others on the right have since the 1970s, the Gramscian insight that, as George puts it, "if you can occupy peoples' heads, their hearts and hands will follow." [15]

THE CAMPAIGN CONTINUES

Paul Pierson and Piven and Cloward, despite the apparent accuracy of their predictions (so far) that democratic support for distributive benefits will prevent outright cutbacks in the key protections of the American welfare state, might nonetheless put too much faith in the institutional resiliency of such programs and give too little credit to those who wish to dismantle them.[16] In a lecture for the American Enterprise Institute, William Kristol, son of Gertrude Himmelfarb and Irving Kristol and perhaps their most enduring legacy, demonstrates that he too understands the ways in which the welfare state has become entrenched by extending its reach, and how it might be quietly uprooted:

> We now have a public opinion that could support a broad attack on unlimited government. But because particular policies have beneficiaries who will fight to keep them, while the opposition to these policies is often diffuse, the best strategy for containing and rolling back the liberal welfare state may be to look for ways to cut the Gordian knot, rather than trying to unwind it one string at a time. Thus the attraction of proposals such as the balanced budget amendment, term limits, tax and spending limitations at several levels of government, the devolution of power to states and localities, and the privatization of government functions. Such policies are radical in the sense that they do not seek simply to contain some of the damage done by the welfare state, or to address its particular pathologies one by one. Rather, they seek to change the patterns of behavior of the political system as a whole and to make it more supportive of relimiting government.[17]

This is a "politics of liberty," he says, that would open new avenues for and be "softened" by a "sociology of virtue," that is, the transfer of government functions to the private for-profit or voluntary sphere. In this way, we can see how the moral goals of the religious countermovement coincide with the political and economic goals of the corporate countermovement—to simul-

taneously limit government interventions on behalf of its economically marginal citizens and to channel its support to private and religious agencies. George W. Bush's Office of
Faith-Based and Community Initiatives thereby takes on a new
character—to view its agenda as most perniciously a threat to
religious liberty is to be run over by a Trojan horse.[18] We have
seen this rhetoric successfully wielded in the campaigns against
relief; we see it again in the campaign for the privatization of
Social Security and Medicare, and in new assaults upon WIC
and food stamps. These battles are being built upon the rhetorical foundation that made possible welfare reform. This is not
unanticipated. Eighteen days prior to the enactment of the Personal Responsibility and Work Opportunity Reconciliation Act
of 1996, Senator Daniel Patrick Moynihan wrote "The conference report before us is not 'welfare reform,' it is 'welfare repeal.' It is the first step in dismantling the social contract that has
been in place in the United States since at least the 1930s. Do not
doubt that Social Security itself, which is to say insured retirement benefits, will be next. The bill will be called 'The Individual Retirement Account Insurance Act.' Something such . . .
[T]his legislation breaks the Social Contract of the 1930s [which
promised that] we would care for the elderly, the unemployed,
the dependent children. Drop the latter; watch the others
fall."[19] He was wrong only in that it was Medicare that came
next.

   People can resist ideas just as they resist other forms of control, of course. As a result, advocates of harsh reforms that
harm poor and working people have had to confront the fact
that Americans have consistently reported that they do not
wish to see policies enacted that leave poor people, and children
especially, to the vicissitudes of the marketplace if that means
that they will suffer.[20] Any successful reform is best portrayed
as beneficial to poor families, and the dilemma has been cir-
cumvented in two ways. First, reformers returned to old dis-

tinctions between worthy and unworthy, to segregate those who are truly in need of relief from those who are capable of work (always with the presumption that they are unwilling and that work is available), which serves to recategorize need as laziness, unfitness, or dependence and to stoke resentment among overworked, underpaid wage earners.[21] The second method has been to denigrate the value of relief itself—to demonstrate that it causes poverty, rather than reducing it, and that the most charitable gift to poor men or women is to deny them relief because relief will sap them of their industry, instruct them in the wrong lessons, and speed them toward their own pauperization while breeding a potentially dangerous class of dependents. What may seem compassionate is, in truth, doing great harm. Victorians and their revivalists have urged us to avoid the "lazy benevolence" of giving alms[22] and to "resist the temptation of cheap virtue."[23] Charity, we have learned, is injury. Suffering is compassion. Liberty is responsibility. As Josephine Shaw Lowell or Marvin Olasky might argue, what the poor need is "not alms, but a friend."

Such ideas, whatever their power, do not themselves make policy, and culture and propaganda are not causes of welfare reform; rather, they have created the context within which relief contests have been fought and constituted tools wielded to advance one kind of policy over another. It is not that American cities abolished outdoor relief because the nation is classically liberal or individualistic, and it is not that we repealed AFDC because we have a Puritan work ethic, but, rather, it is that the shrewdly crafted rhetoric that tapped into deep-seated American myths of self-sufficiency and work was repeated so endlessly and reinforced so often in an environment in which alternative messages were so rare that the public followed the lead of elites and repeated their political arguments back to them as if they were carefully considered and deeply held beliefs.[24] As Piven wrote, the right "launched an *argument*" in the

1970s.[25] Charity reformers of the 1870s did the same. Whether by emphasizing the laissez-faire of Spencer or the moral education of Malthus, or with both, like Lowell or Rector, late-nineteenth- and late-twentieth-century reformers used such ideas to convince policy makers and the public that relief caused poverty and that government intervention harmed not only the poor but working people, too. This despite the fact that, quite to the contrary, relief, however inadequately, protects its recipients from poverty-wage work, and government intervention offers workers some little leverage against the market and their employers.

The challenge for poor and working people and their allies is thus great indeed, for they must not only make their own arguments, craft their own rhetoric, and find their own stories to tell that are as compelling as those of our Old and New Victorian friends, but they must then find the financial and institutional resources with which they can insinuate them into the discourses of policy makers and the public as effectively as those on the right have done with their stories over the last three decades, just as they did in the last three decades of the nineteenth century. But poor and working people, unlike the barons of capital and the burghers of finance, have little political power and little to offer the state in exchange for enacting their policies. Little, that is, except for their willingness to remain passive in the face of degradation and immiseration.

AFTERWORD

There's a standard litany of recommendations that, by tradition, ends books of this sort. Many of you could write that chapter yourselves, for you know the wish list. To truly address the problems of modern American poverty, hunger, homelessness, inequality, despair, we must increase the minimum wage to a living wage, one that rises with inflation. We must provide health care to our citizens, as do all of our Western European industrialized counterparts. We must ensure the availability of ample and adequate child care for those who work, and we should alter the legal definition of "work" to include child rearing, or providing care for another, and extend the protections we now offer to traditional work to those no less productive activities. For workers to form a union should be easy, and companies who act to impede their formation or undermine their autonomy should suffer for it. We must find the means to end the system of legalized bribery that sustains American elections, and make voting simple, accessible, and more resistant to the corruption of parties and candidates. We must undo the racial and economic apartheid that is public education, and reinvest in it; we might start by systematically disinvesting in the manufacture and sales of war-making machinery while recommitting to behaving like a citizen of the globe instead of its belligerent master (and it would cost less to protect ourselves if we devoted less effort to making our own future enemies). We must return the public airwaves to public control, affording broader access to divergent and unprofitable opinions on television and radio. We must enact sweeping criminal justice reforms, in no small measure to restore to their communities the black men who have been incarcerated for petty offenses, and then commit to offering them real opportunities once they are home. The problem of the color line will be the problem of this century, as it was of the last, without change. You may add your own preferred reform here.

But to make a list is not to make change, or to move us from utopian thinking toward practicable and democratically enacted reform. The impediments to reforms even more modest than these are formidable. Where to begin? Worse, though it is a cliché, it is true that we live in a deeply cynical age, and it is especially cynical about politics. Half the electorate, maybe more, will not vote come the next election. But the reason so many people don't vote is not because they're too lazy or apathetic, and it's not because they don't care, as the common refrain goes. The majority don't vote because they have accurately concluded that politics doesn't want or need them. But it need not continue to be so. As political scientist E.E. Schattschneider wrote in 1960, once someone finds a way to reengage the majority of Americans who abstain from electoral politics, they will hold power for at least a generation. One means by which we may do so is by appealing, as Lincoln urged us so long ago, to the better angels of our nature. To live in a society, to live in a polity, necessitates, just as living in a family does, that we periodically place the well-being of others, or of the nation as a whole, above our narrow self-interest. How quaint, how naive, how *juvenile* that sounds. And that it does is a measure of how dire the state of our political culture, how corrupted our politics has become by the entirely rational cynicism of citizens who believe that ours is a government constituted among the few for the few, against the interests of the majority. We have abandoned, and become ashamed of, noble aspirations.

Some of this complaint, of course, could have been made at pretty much any point in our history. Much of it was in the first Gilded Age. But as all people trapped in their own time seem to do, I argue that there is something different here and now, something dire and dangerous. The United States has become resoundingly callous, elitist, selfish, arrogant, and smug. Smugness ill befits a nation that can be counted among the OECD nations with the highest rates of poverty, infant mortality, and murder, and the lowest rates of voter participation and high school graduation.

Thomas Paine argued eloquently in "Common Sense," the small, sharp pamphlet that helped kick-start the American Revolution, that ours was the cause of all mankind, that we could begin the world anew. That enigmatic other Tom, some few months later, argued in the still stirring and still radical words of the Declaration of Independence that when any government did not derive its just powers from the consent of those it governed, and when it did not use that borrowed power to preserve for all its citizens the basic human rights of life and liberty, then it was the absolute right of that people, and their solemn obligation, to replace that government with another. It is that time, and time to begin to think as ambitiously and boldly as the right has, understanding that large-scale reform will take time, patience, evolving strategy, a positive, affirmative agenda, and money. The last seems the hardest part, but it need not be. The assets of putatively liberal foundations dwarf those of the right's Four Sisters. The difference is that liberal foundations have sought to be apolitical and have preferred to fund "objective" social research. But as Sanford Schram wrote, "Research that explicitly avoids confronting politics too often gets co-opted by it." Ask Mary Jo Bane, the Harvard professor who resigned from the Clinton administration when confronted with the crude uses that had been made of her objective, nuanced, scientific work. Foundations and universities both might rethink the all-too-prevalent idea that valid research must be value neutral.

Leaders of the larger mainstream foundations need to simultaneously help build an explicitly political, progressive movement, and with a comparatively modest allocation of targeted, dependable resources, they could dwarf the financing of the right. We can see the stirrings of such a movement from, mostly, our friends in the private sector: some Chicago venture capitalists have been working with satirist Al Franken to create a liberal radio network, which by the time you read this might already be a reality, and a Silicon Valley venture capitalist provided seed money for the American Majority Institute (now the Center for American Progress), a think tank explicitly designed to counter the Heritage Foundation. The American Constitutional Society can now counter the Federalist Society, and the National Caucus of Environmental Legislators serves as something of an alternative to the American Legislative Exchange Council. Other institutions, like the Center for Budget and Policy Priorities, Center for Law and Social Policy, MoveOn.org, and more, could together form the foundation of a counterweight to the institutional power of the right. And surely progressives need not cede the political power of the church to the radical right, so that institutional resource could again be as central to widespread change as it was in the late twentieth century. But leaders of the right knew that building a real movement meant achieving political power from outside the system (by building institutions to pressure and influence it, and by changing the very political culture itself) as well as from within (by electing its members to state and national positions of power). Given the structural impediments to third-party formation in the United States, the left must therefore also take back the Democratic party from those who use it to seek power instead of progress. The right knew that regaining power would take time. So too will a progressive countermovement.

Among its goals must be a strong, stirring, unapologetic defense of welfare. This would seem a minor issue, given the much broader assaults undertaken by George W. Bush and his administration on Social Security and Medicare; their efforts to further undo the progressive tax code; the repeal of a host of regulations protecting public safety, workers, and the environment; the new and newly unleashed police powers of the federal state; and the virtual declaration of endless, needless war. But the battle for the poorest among us, beyond questions of simple moral right, has important consequences. As people study the effects of "globalization" and evaluate whether advanced welfare states must cut back along the American model in order to be competitive, for example, the American case can show the world that it was not the inexorable force of globalization that caused welfare-state retrenchment, though that was one excuse, but actors pursuing their own narrow class interests, hiding behind these and other rationales. Relief repeal in the United States was a solution in search of a problem; the "explosions" in relief in the post–Civil War period and the 1960s provided the problem. The public never supported reform, they supported what they were told that reform would mean, and by not realizing the stake that they had in welfare (and the welfare state more generally), most people failed to resist change, which made the political price to be paid for supporting harsh reforms very low indeed. The repeal of AFDC was thus more seminal an event than most believe: through entirely legal subterfuge it legitimized a more narrowed role for the state, and the assault on it helped lay the ideological groundwork for much broader assaults on other state protections already unfolding. The public must relearn the stake they have in broad, generous social protections, unite, and resist.

There remains an institutionalized disadvantage to those who would fashion an American politics less respectful of economic power. Perhaps it is time, therefore, that we think more boldly and consider a second Constitutional Convention, fraught with dangers though that may be. We should do it as much to alter the government itself as to debate the questions that have been excluded from our politics by those powerful few who would not profit by them. We could ask what world we might now help create anew given our wealth, our power, our influence. We might begin by acknowledging our universal dependence, our need for each other, and proclaim that, the Iron Lady's famous, foolish dictum notwithstanding, there *is* such a thing as society, and none of us exists apart from it. For a long time now we haven't really consented to be governed. We must consent anew, or withdraw our consent entirely.

ACKNOWLEDGMENTS

I owe a debt to those who have read all or parts of this book, in various stages, and lent me their insight and their expertise. My thanks to Fred Block, Jocelyn Boryczka, Thomas Cornell, Herbert Gans, Thomas Kessner, John Mollenkopf, Carol Myers, Frances Fox Piven, Alexandra Poe, Andrew Polsky, and Sanford Schram. I am also grateful for the many thoughtful critiques I have received from those who responded to bits and pieces of this work presented at various professional conferences. I am indebted to Kyle Kauffman, who generously shared laboriously gathered data on Gilded Age Kings County (that's Brooklyn to the rest of you), and send my thanks to the staff of the Hunter College School of Social Work Library. The usual caveat applies—none of them should be held responsible for the failings of this book. Well, maybe some of them should be. . . .

One early inspiration for this inquiry was Andy Polsky, a fine teacher and a sharp critic, who pointed me toward events in nineteenth-century poor relief he thought I might find intriguing. He was right, it would appear. Why did so many American cities abolish relief at the end of that century? Why did other cities not do so? I began that investigation in hopes of simultaneously addressing Michael Katz's complaint in *In the Shadow of the Poorhouse* that "all discussions about the reasons for variation in [late-nineteenth-century poor] relief must remain speculative until historians do research on the topic. Virtually none exists at the moment."[1] But to fully answer that challenge was, I soon realized, a fool's errand, not least because of the scarcity of reliable data. I am hardly the first to note the problem. F.B. Sanborn quipped at the 1877 National Conference of Charities and Corrections that "Mr. Canning once said in parliament, 'I can prove anything by figures, except the truth.' This is eminently the case with the figures which relate to pauperism." The 1891 president's address to the NCCC noted that "no state keeps complete statistical records." Someone else complained in 1892, "It is impossible to obtain statistics of value from the majority of the States." Amos Warner wrote in 1894, "There are absolutely no reliable statistics of outdoor relief in the United States as a whole." As late as 1922, an exasperated Katherine Howland of Smith College wrote, "Not only is there no central body of our federal government which collects statistics on poor relief, but in a large number of states not even figures are available for all the counties." You get the idea. Suffice it to say I have not here offered the kind of rich analysis of poor relief patterns city by city that I suspect Katz would have liked to have seen. Instead, I gathered what data I could, given the usual constraints of time, money, and energy, and have, I hope, offered the next person to tackle the problem a few more pieces of the weird puzzle that is nineteenth-century out-relief, and tried to show how many of the same forces have more recently been at work once again.

I have also picked up a gauntlet tossed down by Frances Fox Piven and Richard A. Cloward, who lamented that "much of the history of popular political struggles over poor relief in the United States before the Great Depression remains to be written."[2] True enough. Most people, I daresay, didn't even know that there were heated battles over outdoor relief in the late 1800s or that many cities abruptly cut off assistance, imposed work requirements, tightened eligibility standards, and enacted other "reforms" that eerily echo the "reforms" made in the late twentieth century. This remains a faint response to their fair challenge, alas (and one that owes much to their work together and to Frances's guidance, friendship and wisdom), but it has helped, I hope, solve another puzzle: given that Americans have always been ambivalent about welfare (whatever we have called it), why only at the ends of the nineteenth and twentieth centuries did we so give up on offering aid to poor people, and in so much the same way? Why *then* and why *now*?

But more than anything, these pages were, as is no doubt painfully clear, my reaction to those Gilded Age charity reformers and some contemporary would-be Victorian revivalists who argued that it was a decline in values (virtues, Gertrude Himmelfarb would insist we say) that was the real problem, and that public efforts to reduce poverty by offering material aid, however well-intentioned they were, only made matters worse, encouraging dependency, breeding illegitimacy, and leading generally to the demise of all things noble, decent, and good. Then and now, such understandings permeated public debate and private discussion about welfare, about poverty, about poor people, and about the proper role of government itself. These are myths. They are lies. But however wrong they may be, they helped revolutionize American welfare policy, twice. We should understand more about where these stories came from and why they became so universally accepted. Again. I hope that *The New Victorians* has aided that cause. It is to those myths then, to the tall tales of the Jukes and the welfare queen, the squeegee guy and the sturdy beggar, to

Josephine Shaw Lowell, Stephen Humphreys Gurteen, and Charles Loring Brace, and to Charles Murray, Marvin Olasky, and Gertrude Himmelfarb that I have most responded here and to whom I, albeit reluctantly, dedicate this book. Sorry, Mom—the next one's for you.

N O T E S

Preface

1. There is an extensive body of quantitative, qualitative, and theoretical literature rebutting such claims about the pernicious nature of welfare and its recipients; for a concise review for a general audience, see Albelda, Folbre, and the
Center for Popular Economics 1996.

2. This argument and much of the theoretical framework of the book adopts
Piven and Cloward's (see esp. 1971) understandings of the multiple functions
of welfare: regulating the labor market, suppressing unrest, and exalting low-
wage work.

3. Hernes 1987; Piven and Cloward 1989; Esping-Andersen 1990; Sainsbury
1996.

4. Fraser and Gordon 1994; K⋯⋯⋯⋯ nd Tronto 2002.

5. ⋯⋯⋯⋯⋯⋯⋯⋯⋯⋯ *tion* 7/31/1996; *Milwaukee Jour-*
⋯⋯⋯⋯⋯⋯⋯⋯ /1996; *Newsweek* 8/5/1996; *St.*
⋯⋯⋯⋯⋯⋯ *st* 11/12/1996; *New York Times*

6. ⋯

7. ⋯⋯⋯⋯⋯⋯⋯⋯⋯⋯⋯⋯ 'Connor (1973, 1981), al-
⋯⋯⋯⋯⋯⋯⋯⋯⋯⋯ a reduction in total social
⋯⋯⋯⋯⋯⋯⋯⋯ *etrenchment,* a shifting of
⋯⋯⋯⋯⋯⋯ to help maintain political
⋯⋯⋯⋯⋯ shifts might take place, he
⋯⋯⋯⋯ , Pierson (2000a, 2001) also
⋯⋯⋯ sits a theory of resilience to
⋯⋯ repeal itself. And Harold
W⋯⋯⋯⋯⋯ cited than read, describes a
m⋯⋯⋯ n it is often given credit for.

8. T⋯⋯⋯⋯⋯ social welfare rights of the

twentieth century have inexorably followed upon the extension of civil rights granted in the eighteenth century and the political rights gained in the nineteenth century. Subsequent analysis also described the expansion and elaboration of welfare state programs: with few exceptions, theories of the welfare state explain progress and differ chiefly by what their authors cite as its most important causes. Some argue that it is industrialism itself, as economic growth provides the fiscal means for the state to offer assistance to a growing population of older, less productive workers and remove them from the labor force (Wilensky and Lebeaux 1958; Wilensky 1975). For others, the key mechanisms driving expanding benefits are pressures from the working class and labor parties (Korpi 1983; Shalev 1983; Esping-Andersen 1990), heightened electoral competition, which encourages political parties to offer benefits to certain voters in exchange for their support (Burnham 1970; Key 1968; Schattschneider 1960), or the corporate sector's desire to enlist the state in helping it sustain and reproduce a healthy work force (Quadagno 1984). Others suggest that relief expands because bureaucrats and progressive-minded reformers press the state for changes (Heclo 1974; Patterson 1994; Trattner 1994), their opportunities and successes conditioned by the institutional exigencies they face at any given time (Skocpol 1992), or the political culture of the polity they inhabit (see Lipset 1996). Which of these evolutionary theories best describes welfare-state expansion is not at issue (see instead Skocpol 1992, 1–62; Piven and Cloward 1971/[1993], Ch. 12), since none of them helps explain the events under consideration.

9. Thus the title of historian Walter Trattner's book, *From Poor Law to Welfare State* (Trattner 1994).

1. Same As It Ever Was

1. Edelman 1997, 45.
2. As the Chairman of the Senate Finance Committee, the Congressional Budget Office, and others conceded at the time of its passage. See Moynihan, *Congressional Record,* July 18, 1996 (S8074-5). While it no longer contained proposals to block-grant Medicaid and food stamps, the final bill had tougher work requirements and greater limitations on relief to legal immigrants.
3. *Congressional Record,* July 18, 1996 (S8075).
4. Katha Pollitt, *New Republic* 8/1996, "What We Know."
5. House Ways and Means Committee, press release, 2/4/2003.
6. Mead 1998. See also *New York Times* 3/3/2002, "Welfare in the Post-Welfare Era," for the Washington consensus on reform's success.
7. Quigley 1998; Goldberg and Collins 2001; Block 2003; see also historian James Patterson in *St. Louis Post-Dispatch* 8/18/1996; *Foreign Affairs* Sep./Oct. 1997, "The Social Question Redivivus"; *New Statesman* 1/22/2001, "Back to the Workhouse for America."
8. In Nill et al. 1891, 42–43.
9. There were other European influences on Gilded Age relief policies. Brace traveled abroad (in Ireland, England, Hungary, and Germany), as did most re-

formers (and other well-bred men and women of the age), and the Children's Aid Society, created with the help of some "concerned bankers, lawyers and ministers," was inspired in part by his visits to the *Ruche Haus,* German homes for vagrant children (S. O'Connor 2001); Gurteen's COS was built specifically on the London model. For Progressive Era European influences on other policies, see Rodgers 1998.

10. This is not to say that these are the only instances in which American poor relief was reduced from a prior level. That these eras marked *sustained* and *successful* campaigns against relief is the point, for there were short-lived local reductions in relief in a few cities in the early 1800s, and the emergency relief measures of the early New Deal were also quickly ended, but neither was a coordinated campaign against relief or a major policy reconfiguration.

11. Trattner (1988) argued that there was significant federal involvement in social welfare in the nineteenth century, but his evidence rests mainly with federal land grants to states (some of whom used such land for establishing charitable and medical institutions), ad hoc disaster relief, and grants-in-aid for veterans' care in institutions. As with Skocpol's (1992) writing about Civil War pensions, Trattner offers a reminder that federal government involvement in matters we might broadly define as "social welfare" did not emerge fresh during the New Deal, but neither substantiates a claim that the American welfare state was more precocious than is generally believed. There were, after all, benefits paid even to Revolutionary War veterans, and institutions established for their care. However, Civil War pensions were not part of a federal role in general social welfare or an assertion of federal responsibility, but a narrowly circumscribed, short-lived effort to pay a debt incurred during wartime and to solidify the power of the Republican party (see Bensel 2000). See Henderson (1897, 476) for a contemporaneous appraisal of federal and states' roles in nineteenth century relief provision. That said, the study of the history of poor relief in the South, still in its infancy, may prove my claim wrong. Green (1999), for example, argued that during and after the Civil War the federal government was a significant provider of relief in the South.

12. Phillips 1990, Table 2; see also Amin 2000, Phillips 2002.

13. In Painter 1987, 125.

14. Painter 1987, xx.

15. Collins and Yeskel 2000, 54–57; www.census.gov.

16. Phillips 2002, 122–23.

17. More recently, George W. Bush's advisor Karl Rove compares himself to Hannah (see Moore and Slater 2003).

18. Tabb 2001, 38.

19. George 1879, 7.

20. Berk 1994; Roy 1997; Sklar 1988; see Weinstein 1968 for post-1900 implications.

21. Chandler 1990.

22. See Gramsci 1971, esp. section II.2; Carnoy 1984.

23. Amin 2000; Tabb 2001; Castells 1980; Mishel, Bernstein, and Schmitt 2003, see esp. Figure 1I.

24. Hofstadter 1944, 204.

222 · NOTES TO PAGES 22–29

25. Hofstadter 1944, 44; Fine 1956, 98.
26. Lowell 1887, 138.
27. S. O'Connor 2001; Trattner 1994, 118.
28. Hall 1892, 120–21.
29. Fine 1956, 97.
30. Geremek 1994, 222.
31. In Waugh 2001.
32. Stewart 1911, 144–45.
33. Riis 1890, 191.
34. Rector 1998, 2000, 2001. See also Douglas J. Besharov, "We're Feeding the Poor as if They're Starving," *Washington Post* (12/8/2002).
35. Or "suffering with." Ebeling 1995, 64.
36. Hofstadter 1944, 203.
37. Gingrich 1996.
38. Mead 1996.
39. Kaus 1992, 136; *LAH* 1886 vol. 1, no. 3: 127–129.
40. NCCC 1892, 211.
41. Rector 2000.
42. Mead 1994, 339.
43. Mead 1993; 1997; 1998.
44. Schwartz 2001; see also Schwartz 2000.
45. Himmelfarb 1994.
46. Ebeling 1995, 63.
47. Olasky 1992, 5. Of those who explicitly advocated a return to a Gilded Age or Victorian charity—Schwartz, Himmelfarb, Olasky, and to a lesser extent Mead, Rector, and Murray—only Schwartz and Mead acknowledged that private voluntary agencies had been unable to provide for those in need once their cities were confronted with the depression of 1893–98. Olasky asserted that nineteenth-century reformers succeeded and should serve as a model, but failed to offer evidence to support the claim. Himmelfarb escaped this dilemma by concerning herself with the *spirit* of the age, with Victorian virtues, leaving matters of policy, programs, and outcomes largely outside her discussion—it is what nineteenth-century American reformers might call "moral tone" with which she concerned herself. Gingrich (1995), instead of looking specifically to the Gilded Age as a model, proposed that we return to "the values and principles of American Civilization," or to pre–New Deal understandings of the role of the state. Murray and Rector seemed to have in mind some mythologized 1950s, when communities of self-reliant individuals and voluntary associations supposedly did what government would do later. Schwartz, Olasky, and Himmelfarb, who paid most attention to the Gilded Age, said curiously little about the assaults on out-relief that are the focus here.
48. Hunter 1904, 63.
49. In Albelda, Folbre, and the Center for Popular Economics, 1996, 92.
50. Speech delivered to the Heritage Foundation, Lecture no. 539, 8/4/1995. Brace also told lurid tales of the multigenerational paupers he said he encountered (Brace 1880). Lowell reported of poorhouse inmates, "These women and their children, and hundreds more like them, costing the hard-working inhabitants

of the state annually thousands of dollars for their maintenance, corrupting those who are thrown into companionship with them, and sowing disease and death among the people, are the direct outcome of our system. . . . To begin at the beginning, what right had we to permit them to be born of parents who are depraved in body and mind? What right have we today to allow men and women who are diseased and vicious to reproduce their kind?" (Lowell 1879, 193). By 1877, Lowell had launched what would be a ten-year fight to establish "reformatories" for women: to separate them from the male population, to relieve local officials from the care of "vagrant and degraded women," and to "provide work for them, as appropriate, instead of allowing them to degrade themselves and infect others in almshouses." The reformatories she proposed would incarcerate for up to five years women under thirty who were arrested for misdemeanors (petty larceny, public drunkenness, prostitution) or those who had borne more than one illegitimate child, and here they could "be taught to be women." Even if she could not reform them, she said, she could at least protect society from them, and keep them from reproducing (Stewart 1911, 89 ff.).

51. Himmelfarb (1995b) argued in the *Wall Street Journal* that the culture of poverty had metastasized into a "culture of social pathology." Lewis (1968) is perhaps the most articulate and well-known chronicler of the poverty culture, although the idea of a separate culture among poor people was hardly new with him, nor was it original to Edward Banfield's 1958 book, *Moral Basis of a Backward Society*; even the phrase predates them both. Robert Hunter reported in 1904 that George K. Holmes described "an enormous culture bed of poverty" (Hunter 1904, 43).

52. Though in a form that misread Lewis' point—that the culture of poverty was an adaptive response to social conditions largely beyond the control of the poor and that it contained the seeds of revolutionary resistance.

53. It may have been Dwight MacDonald's (1963) *New Yorker* review of Harrington and of Galbraith (1958) that created the perception that *The Other America* was a radical work. In fact, culture-of-poverty interpretations pervade it, offering faint echoes of Hunter (1904) or Riis (1890; see, e.g., p. 10–11).

54. For a review of culture of poverty and underclass debates, see Katz 1989, 1993; A. O'Connor 2001.

55. Kusmer 1973, 661.

56. Almy 1900, 138.

57. NCCC 1892, 211.

58. Lowell 1894, 66.

59. Gladden 1891.

60. Brace 1880.

61. Schram and Soss 2000; CBS, *60 Minutes,* "Depressed and on Welfare," 11/10/2002.

62. In Bremner 1956b, 170.

63. Gilder 1981, 30.

64. Niskanen 1996.

65. Bishop 1902, 608.

66. King 1893, 456.

67. In Mead 1997, Ch. 9.
68. In Bendich 1966, 92.
69. Nill et al. 1891, 42–43.
70. NCCC 1897, 156.
71. Nill et al. 1891, 43.
72. *Congressional Record* 3/24/1995, H3766, H3772; see also H3884.
73. Murray 1984, 18. Others have well described the ways in which the AFDC rolls became identified with black women and how that contributed to its political vulnerability and, more generally, the operations of race in welfare policy making and implementation. See Quadagno 1994; Brown 1999; Gilens 1999; Neubeck and Cazenave 2001; Schram 2002, Chs. 5 and 6; Schram, Soss, and Fording 2003.
74. NCCC 1877, 57–58.
75. NCCC 1893, 113.
76. Rector 2000.
77. By 2000, 34 states had used TANF funds for teen pregnancy programs, and all but Oklahoma had begun a pro-marriage program, although in three of the five states that received the PRA's "illegitimacy bonus," no dedicated program or special activity was undertaken to reduce out-of-wedlock births or abortion (Greenberg et al. 2000).
78. Murray 1994.
79. Bennett in Weaver 2000, 151.
80. *Los Angeles Times* 10/1/1995, "Under Her Father's Watch . . ."
81. In Clement 1992, 42–43.
82. NCCC 1879 in Goodman 1983, 661.
83. Gilder focuses more upon the behavior of men (black men, typically) than do other anti-relief agitators. "The key problem of the welfare culture is not unemployed women with illegitimate children," he wrote, "it is the women's skewed and traumatic relationships with men and boys. In a reversal of the usual pattern in civilized societies, the women have the income and the ties to government authority and support. The men are economically and socially subordinate." And, even worse, "All programs addressed to relieve the condition or upgrade the employability of welfare mothers will only ensconce more fully these welfare 'queens' on their leisured thrones and render the men still more optional, desperate, feral and single." They need to be "tamed by marriage." Not that women are blameless in Gilder's world. In fact, most efforts to force their employment are doomed, he says, because "these women are slovenly, incompetent, and sexually promiscuous." What's more, "the very idea that women with small children should work outside the home is perverse" (Gilder 1995). Compare this last point with Lowell 1884, 108–9; Devine 1904, 44; and Feder 1936, 136.
84. See *Chicago Tribune,* 12/18/1994, "The World According to Speaker Newt."
85. See also Trachtenberg 1982. Before Alger came to New York to work and live with Brace and the lads at the Five Points Mission, he resigned his ministry for having committed, as he later confessed to Henry James Sr., the "abominable and revolting crime of unnatural familiarity with *boys*" (S. O'Connor 2001,

231) [italics in original]. Many of the moralists at the center of both ages' relief dramas did not live as they commanded others to.

86. Miller 1949; however, mobility was sometimes much greater in the West (Thernstrom, in Pope 2000).

87. Mishel, Bernstein, and Boushey 2003, Chs. 2 and 7.

88. For a fine contemporary account, see Ehrenreich 2001.

89. Gilder 1981, 79.

90. Mead 1996; Mead 1994, 323. Many studies confirm what those who know poor women know—they are as likely to be resourceful, hardworking, and committed to a better life for their children as any. See Edin and Lein 1997; Newman 1999; Hays 2003.

91. Mead 1990, 49.

92. Ebeling 1995, 69.

93. Murray 1984, 186.

94. *New York Times* 7/25/2000.

95. Geremek 1994, 215.

96. But see Schram 1995; Williams 1996.

97. Weaver 1998, 375; see also Weaver 2000; Patterson 2000; Mead 2000.

98. Williams 1996; Covington 1997.

99. Zaller 1992.

100. Shapiro et al. 1987.

101. Gilens 1999.

102. Scholz and Levine 2001, 195; Schneider and Jacoby 2002.

103. Low in Warner 1894, 169; see also Devine 1898, 187; Frankel 1903, 320; Watson 1922, 55; Feder 1936, 46.

104. Mead would object that "it is implausible to argue that the public's hostility to traditional welfare is to any important extent the creation of elites" because, in part, "the public is likeliest to defer to elites in areas of policy that are technical or remote from everyday experience, such as economic regulation or arms control. Social problems are more everyday. People respond to them out of their own lives. These views may be right or wrong, but elites and the media do not control these opinions more than marginally" (Mead 2000). But what in their own lives do people have to respond to, and how does this differ among classes? For people with no direct experience with AFDC, how would they understand it directly as Mead proposes? Besides, people interpret social problems through more than their personal experience (Edelman 1964, see esp. Ch. 9; Stone 1997; Schneider and Ingram 1997; Yee 1996; Lewis 2001), and they have been taught by public intellectuals, politicians, and the media for three decades to interpret them in certain ways. More to the point, perhaps, is that people are generally of two minds when it comes to welfare: they may defer to elites on abstract policy goals, but may not do so when considering specific proposals (Feldman and Zaller 1992). Americans are ambivalent about welfare, and while polling may be good at measuring opinion, it is much less effective at measuring beliefs (Converse 1964; Weaver 2000, Ch. 7; Lewis 2001). I assert that such ambivalence can be and has been manipulated as one part of a political strategy.

105. Jacobs and Shapiro 2000, xiv, xv.

106. To wit: Weaver's analysis of the politics of the PRA (2000) and Lui's studies of nineteenth-century New York relief abolition (1993, 1995a, 1995b), to take two of the best examples, offer persuasive accounts of how competition between parties, competition within parties, and election-year politics shaped reform, and I align myself with many of their arguments. My complaint is that Weaver and Lui each comes too late to the story. Weaver is right, for example, that Clinton's campaign pledge to "end welfare as we know it" was important and helped set in motion one chain of micro-political events, but how did it come to pass that policy debate and party politics had changed so much that a Democratic president sought election (and won) and sought reelection (and won) at least in part by promising to undo (and then undoing) significant elements of what his New Deal and Great Society predecessors had built? Why did so many Democrats abandon their party's defense of welfare and adopt policies that Ronald Reagan had been unable to enact? Similarly, Lui does not tell us why relief was withdrawn while other, more lucrative forms of patronage were not. We must explain why only at these particular junctures in political time old theories about the danger and waste of poor relief rose to prominence and were enacted as regressive policy, just as others have shown how such theories were overcome to expand relief during other eras.

107. Geremek 1994; Piven and Cloward 1971.
108. See Katz 1986; Piven and Cloward 1971; Trattner 1994.
109. Schmidt 2002.
110. See Pierson 2001.
111. Similarly, one factor important to regressive change in post-industrial (neo-) liberal welfare state regimes has been the rise of "neoliberal economic orthodoxy" (Swank 2002).
112. Mead 2002.
113. Stone 1997.
114. Piven and Cloward (1987, 7) called it *The Great Relief Hoax*.

2. Rise of the Reformer

1. Allen 1992; Burch 1997; Burris 1992; Edsall 1984; Ferguson and Rodgers 1986; Hardisty 1999; Judis 2000; Martin 1998; Ricci 1993; Saloma 1984; Smith 1990; Su, Neustadt, and Clawson 1992; Useem 1984.
2. See data at www.acf.dhhs.gov.
3. Keyssar 1986, 149.
4. Rodgers 1974, ch. 6.
5. Painter 1987.
6. This is the dilemma at the root of James O'Connor's *Fiscal Crisis of the State:* how to please capital by keeping public welfare expenditures low while preserving order and maintaining electoral power by extending benefits to the poor and working classes.
7. This is almost identical to the percentage on relief the next time fears of a relief explosion would lead to an attack against it. In 1974, 6.9 percent of the U.S. population received non-insurance-based public assistance.

8. Hannon 1984a; Hannon 1984b; Kiesling and Margo 1997.
9. From $524,943 to $976,560; indoor relief expenditures grew even more, from $351,820 in 1860 to $1,731,677 in 1870 (Katz 1986, Table 2.1).
10. See *Brooklyn Daily Eagle,* June 15, 1868, for example.
11. Clement 1992, Tables 1 and 2.
12. As they had begun to do in larger cities since the 1830s (see Johnson 1978; Wilenz 1984).
13. Beckert 2001, Chs. 8 and 9. See also Rosenzweig 1983; Trachtenberg 1982; Hays 1965; see Weinstein 1968 for similar activity located earlier in the Gilded Age.
14. Rezneck 1950, 501.
15. Lee 1937, 437 ff.
16. NCCC 1901, 112. For further examples: in the files of the New York COS there is a small scrap of paper showing that someone was tracking the positions of each city newspaper on the pending bill to abolish free coal; Lowell wrote to her sister-in-law in 1894, "Certainly the modern newspaper is a very 'mixed good.' The view a reporter takes of things is generally the wrong view, but it helps to make public opinion"; and the NCCC of 1891 observed that dealings with the poor were only part of the mission of the COS, that it must be conducted in concert with "the general education of the community" (CSS Box 108; Stewart 1911, 70; NCCC 1891, 27).
17. Sklar 1988, 15.
18. Wiebe 1962, 21.
19. Kellogg 1893; Bigelow 1878.
20. Watson 1922, 399.
21. Gurteen 1882.
22. Devine 1904, Part II; Devine, "Draft," CSS Box 92; Devine manuscript, CSS Box 108.
23. Bremner 1956a; Trattner 1994.
24. Katz 1986; Piven and Cloward 1987; Boyer 1978.
25. DeForest 1891, 2.
26. Johnson 1923, 53; Watson 1922, 7.
27. Lowell 1884, 89; Waugh 1997.
28. Accusations that this was to acquire power and resources for COSs and their leaders grew increasingly frequent by the turn of the century. During debate over the reinstatement of free coal distribution in 1898, Devine was compelled to explicitly deny any profit motive in his opposition to coal relief (*New York Commercial Advertiser,* 2/10/1898, in CSS Box 108). *Charities Review* offered this suggestive report (1894, 408) of a relief skirmish in Ohio: "The Associated Charities of Canton have found themselves cramped for funds for over a year, and during that time have been endeavoring to get possession of the Hartford poor fund, the interest of which amounts to over $2,500 a year. The sum has been distributed by councilmen, there being a law governing it. The council refused to turn over the money to the Associated Charities, and the ladies went to Columbus and got a bill passed, compelling them to do so."
29. Barnett 1899.
30. Devine 1904, 82.

31. Gurteen 1882; Watson 1922, 38ff.
32. Henderson, unusual but not alone among reformers, saw virtue in each form of relief. "It is generally agreed that personal and private charity surpasses official charity in spontaneity, versatility, adaptability, idealism, religious fervor. It is thought that official charity surpasses private charity in completeness, adequacy, equality of burdens, and in the control of criminal tendencies often mixed up with pauperism" (Henderson 1894b, 233).
33. See NCCC 1886, 171ff; NCCC 1887, 130; see also Warner 1894a, 30.
34. Hyslop 1894. Yet one 1896 study of COS records (in Devine 1904) found that 44 percent of all applicants for whom "lack of employment" was cited as cause of their need had been replaced by another (presumably lower-paid or more compliant) worker; in only 17 percent of such cases could the COS attribute the worker's termination to "character weakness."
35. Johnson 1923, 56.
36. In Ringenback 1973, 100.
37. Bremmer 1956a, 53.
38. "Free Coal Bill. Mr. Harburger Denounces Charitable Associations. Says High-Salaried Officials Stand in Way of Relief for Poor Persons," *Commercial Advertiser,* 1/31/1898, CSS Box 108.
39. NCCC 1883, 75.
40. "Charity organization is no longer on the defensive," boasted *Charities Review* in 1892 (p. 233), "it no longer needs to explain. Its principles are well-nigh universally adopted among thinking men and women."
41. In Watson 1922, 15.
42. Mather 1710, 58–59, 78–79.
43. New York Society for the Prevention of Pauperism 1818, in Rockman 2003, 49–56.
44. Riis 1890, 35.
45. NYAICP, esp. nos. 1–3.
46. Bruere in Watson 1922, 78.
47. In Watson 1922, 84.
48. NYAICP nos. 1 and 21.
49. Watson 1922, 81, 89.
50. Watson 1922, 175, 179. In other cities, agencies that would later adopt COS methods had earlier roots, like the Lawrence City Mission of 1859. Many "COSs" were not actually called Charity Organization Societies, and were more often Associated Charities. Still others were Societies for Organizing Charities, United Charities, Federal Charities, and so on. Some, as Watson noted, were COSs in name only, while others closed, abandoned COS principles, or fell into disuse shortly after having been established (Watson 1922, 347, 104). The convention, begun by movement contemporaries and continued in scholarship of the period, has been to refer to all such organizations as COSs. I will continue to do so here. There were other mutual aid societies—ethnic, religious, trade—that would to varying degrees adopt COS methods; few are included here.
51. Watson 1922, 179–86.
52. On Gurteen, see Gurteen 1894; Gurteen 1882; "Stephen Humphreys Gur-

teen," *CR* vol. III, no. 8, 1898 (Oct.); "Gurteen," *Encyclopedia of Social Work*, 19th ed., vol. 3, 1995.

53. *CR* vol. III, no. 8, 1898 (Oct.)

54. NCCC passim; Sage 1914; NYCOS 1896; Watson 1922; Warner 1894; Warner 1908; Gurteen 1882; Feder 1936.

55. While there was no COS in Atlanta by the turn of the century, for example, and the New Orleans organization was inactive, there were "strong" COSs in the southern cities of Louisville, Memphis, Nashville, Chattanooga, Richmond, Wilmington (North Carolina), and Charleston (South Carolina) (Ayers 1895). Smaller cities (Burlington, Iowa; Taunton and Brookline, Massachusetts; and Little Rock, Arkansas) and western ones (Salt Lake City, Dallas, Portland, Oakland, and Los Angeles) also could boast active societies. Even some small towns like Tivoli, New York (1896 population of 1,300), Haddonfield, New Jersey (population 3,000), and Bryn Mawr, Pennsylvania (population 876) had established a COS.

56. See NCCC 1897, 142; Gurteen 1894, 365–66. For Gurteen, one of the functions of such a national society would have been to help redistribute labor supply throughout the country or within regions. By 1914, the Russell Sage Foundation recorded the presence of COSs in Canada, Austria-Hungary, Belgium, Denmark, Egypt, France, Germany, Great Britain (Africa, Australasia, England and Wales, India, Ireland, Scotland), Greece, Holland, Italy, Russia, Sweden and Norway, Switzerland, and Turkey.

57. Parenti 1999, see Ch. 2.

58. Lowi 1987, 106.

59. Edsall 1984; Judis 2000; Ferguson and Rodgers 1986; Useem 1984; Vogel 1989.

60. Castells 1980, 95.

61. Piven and Cloward 1971, 183; Fording 1997.

62. Katz 1989, 113.

63. Vogel 1989, 54; see also Smith 2000.

64. In Su, Neustadt, and Clawson 1992.

65. Saloma 1984, 67.

66. In Judis 2000, 116; read the memorandum at mediatransparency.org/stories/powellmanifesto.htm.

67. Judis 2000, 117; Powell memorandum (see note 66); Edwards 1998.

68. Karen Paget traced the modern conservative resurgence to the day in 1969 when Paul Weyrich was accidentally invited to a liberal political strategy meeting, where he saw revealed the possibilities to exert influence, change opinions, and remake policy. "Weyrich now thanks the left, the Lord, and Joe Coors—in that order—for providing the inspiration and the wherewithal to begin building what today is known as the 'new conservative labyrinth,' " she reported (Paget 1998). Coors provided him with a substantial portion of the initial funds for the Heritage Foundation and its precursor organization, Analysis and Research Association. Upon his death Coors's brother Bill told the *New York Times* (3/17/2003): "He was conservative as they come. I mean, he was a little bit right of Attila the Hun."

69. Judis 2000, 112.

70. See Su, Neustadt, and Clawson 1992 for a discussion of this last point.

71. See Judis 2000; Vogel 1989.
72. Peschek 1987.
73. Plotke (1992) criticized this kind of explanation as too economically determinative (in its crudest form, it argues that declining profits caused business as a class to launch an assault on regulation, taxes, and unions). The timing of declining profits and mobilization doesn't support the thesis, he argued (but see Castells, 1980, Figure 9), and the best predictor of activism, Plotke found, was the *size* of business, not its profitability (Martin 1998 also emphasized the different influences in our decentralized polity of large and small business). Moreover, that business would focus on combating regulation was not the logical choice given the economic data available to them at the time. Instead, he claimed, "widespread concern with regulation was a political interpretation of economic problems." That is, the arguments business used as strategy should not be confused with their diagnosis, and perhaps businesses concluded that "opposing social and economic regulation would have greater appeal than conventional anti-union complaints or efforts to reduce corporate taxes." Other data also suggest that regulatory concern, not profit declines, best correlates with business mobilization (Su, Neustadt, and Clawson 1992). For my purposes, it does not matter whether Su and colleagues and Plotke, or Useem, Vogel, Edsall, and Ferguson and Rodgers are closer to the truth—all agree that across sectors businesses large and small, capital-intensive and labor-intensive, perceived a need to intervene in public policy and sought to alter the power of labor and the state. There is not, to my knowledge, any informed observer who disputes that sometime in the early 1970s, American corporate leaders became newly determined to act to influence public policy. And as Tabb (2001, 83) wrote, it is ultimately "arbitrary" what date or event we choose as marker, for "the point is that in these years something we associate with globalization became evident and something we call the postwar era dominated by the national Keynesian welfare state came to an end." Castells (1980) placed the first important stirrings of a corporate mobilization more than a decade earlier than most (but reported that it ran into labor and political resistance it was unable to overcome until the 1970s). Saloma (1984) saw the first important stirrings in the early 1950s. Others credibly pointed to Barry Goldwater's presidential bid and a concurrent suburban mobilization as the birth of the late-century conservative resurgence (see Perlstein 2001, McGirr 2001). I have marked 1973 as the onset but could have chosen another date, or no particular date. In Tabb's sense, it is arbitrary.
74. Rosenbloom 2002.
75. Noble 1997, 14.
76. See Edsall 1984; Ferguson and Rodgers 1986.
77. Ahlstrom 1972, 1086.
78. Lipset and Raab 1981.
79. Ahlstrom 1972, 1079.
80. Weber, 1904–05.
81. Wuthnow 1988, 112. Not all were politically conservative, I should emphasize. As McAdam (1982) showed, for example, the expansion of the black church

(along with colleges and the NAACP) in the twentieth century constituted an essential institutional resource to help advance the civil rights movement.

82. Wuthnow 1988.

83. Diamond 1998; see also Diamond 1995.

84. See Smith 1990, Ricci 1993 for histories; see mediatransparency.org and Fairness and Accuracy in Reporting's *Think Tank Monitor* for ongoing documentation.

85. Rich and Weaver 2000.

86. Allen 1992; Domhoff 1998; Rich and Weaver 2000; Burris 1992; Peschek 1987; Judis 2000.

87. Edwards 1998.

88. Post 1997; Allen 1992.

89. Saloma 1984.

90. Peschek 1987.

91. Burris 1992.

92. Useem 1984.

93. Vogel 1989.

94. Domhoff 1998.

95. Alpert and Markusen 1980. They emphasized Brookings.

96. Allen 1992. This is a theme in certain think-tank scholarship, that policy-planning organizations have supplanted political parties and created a new form of interest group.

97. Burris 1992.

98. *New York Times* 6/11/2001, "In Virginia, Young Conservatives Learn How to Develop and Use Their Political Voices."

99. Quintero 2002.

100. Piven 1999a.

101. Smith 2000, 193.

102. In Gramscian terms, it is a war of *position* not a war of *maneuver.* See Carnoy 1984.

103. *Wall Street Journal* 1/23/1995, "Behind the Scenes: GOP's Stance Owes a Lot to Prodding From Robert Rector"; www.mediatransparency.org (2001).

104. Stefancic and Delgado 1996, 137ff; see also Brock 2002.

105. Kingdon 1995.

106. See Campbell 2002 for an overview of the state of the discipline on this matter.

107. See Greeley 1995.

108. Biography Resource Center 2003, Doc. no. BT2310014914.

109. Goodman 1983, 693–94. Goodman's analysis of the New York AICP offered similar findings: "Of the 539 men who served as managers of the agency from 1844 to 1882, 400 can be identified. The majority of the chief office-holders (321 men) consisted of merchants, manufacturers, shopkeepers and craftsmen. The remaining 79 managers consisted of 32 doctors, 16 laborers, 14 lawyers, 8 teachers, 7 politicians, 1 editor and 1 minister." (Perhaps the presence of non-professional working men among leadership of the AICP helps account for its "demise" into a relief-giving institution, much derided by the COS until they began systematically working together in the 1890s. In 1939 the COS and

AICP combined and became the Community Service Society of New York.) Most, if not all, were Protestant. Most of whom they served were foreign-born and Roman Catholic. The AICP's founders "were all six merchants and businessmen of some standing—one owned one of the largest US shipping firms, another the largest financial institution in the city." Even the Society for the Prevention of Pauperism represented many of the same interests: of the eighty-nine men who served as managers from 1817 to 1823, all were "conservative individuals representing the commercial and professional class of Manhattan . . . the occupations of sixty-nine of them have been identified and included thirty-four businessmen, four clergymen, five politicians, nine attorneys, two teachers, eight mechanics, six doctors and one editor." Heale (1976) presents a consistent accounting, with minor differences.

110. Kusmer 1973, Table I and 674 (he found data on 89 percent of these directors).
111. Gurteen 1894. The New York State Charities Aid Association also had similar membership, consisting of "New York City's elite—merchants, industrialists, ministers, lawyers, professors, and physicians," including Frederick Law Olmsted, E.L. Godkin, Theodore Roosevelt Sr., Charles Loring Brace, Josephine Shaw Lowell, and Louisa Schulyer (Stanley 1992, 1275).
112. Waugh 1997, 114.
113. Piven and Cloward 1987, 14–15; Trattner 1994, 96.
114. Rauch 1975.
115. Bremner 1956b, 171.
116. Kusmer 1973, 673ff.
117. It was he who received an oft-cited letter from a clergyman with the accusation that "your society, with its board of trustees made up of steel magnates, coal operators, and employers is not really interested in charity. If it were, it would stop the twelve-hour day; it would increase wages and put an end to the cruel killing and maiming of men. It is interested in getting its own wreckage out of sight. It isn't pleasant to see it begging on the streets" (Bremner 1956a, 54).
118. Ross 1914.
119. See CR 1894, 362; NCCC 1895, 62; Greeley 1995, 127–32.
120. Stewart 1911, 129.
121. There was not one upper class, of course, but many upper classes. William Dean Howells's novel The Rise of Silas Lapham offers one glimpse of the conflict between old and new money. Their attitudes toward each other differed as their interests differed; so too did their attitudes toward the poor—instead of the noblesse oblige of the old aristocracy, the rising manufacturing classes often demonstrated a contempt for the idle poor that had much in common with their contempt for the idle rich (see Lowell on this, for example). Whether we subscribe to Hammack's (1982) typology of five turn-of-the-century elites (the Protestants of wealth, cultivation, or ancestry, the German Christians, and the German Jews), McCabe's (1882) four-tiered upper class (professionals, Knickerbockers, the cultured, and the newly rich), or Beckert's (2001) more unified bourgeoisie, all remind us that attitudes toward the poor could differ among the non-poor in ways that affected the material well-being of the lower classes. The "old" charity that the COSs condemned, while rooted in the church and its indiscriminate giving, was still practiced by the old aris-

tocracy—perhaps one of the reasons that many, if not most, had little to do with the COSs and the "new" charity (Leiby 1984). Hammack (1982, 77) noted that only one of forty-three COS directors was invited to Mrs. Astor's 1892 Ball for the Four Hundred. And those wealthy people who did seek out the assistance of organized charity, for example, to respond to pleas they received from poor people—"begging letters"—did not always follow the COS's advice, and offered charity even when advised against it (see Greeley 1995).

122. Devine 1898.

123. Katz 1986; Boyer 1978. Some visitors may even have compelled labor from their poor clients, having them serve as domestics in their own homes (Stewart 1911, 149). Julia Rauch (1976) argued that visitors were themselves being used because they "provided a cheap source of labor for male philanthropists unwilling to support professional social workers."

124. In Wagner 2000, 63.

125. Henderson 1894b, 226.

126. In Becker 1961, 391.

127. Perhaps little changed in the following century: Piven and Cloward (1971, 176) report New York State findings that more people received AFDC when there were fewer professionally trained social workers serving as caseworkers.

128. Addams 1899, 164.

129. Addams 1910, 167.

130. In many cities charity organization also worked with the chamber of commerce or the merchants' association to decide which charities were "responsible" enough to receive public contributions and which should not survive; their charities endorsement committees or community chests evaluated charities and published reports on those they condoned and those to which no one should contribute (their late-twentieth-century counterparts were the National Charities Information Bureau and the Better Business Bureau's Philanthropic Advisory Service). By 1910 charities endorsement was managed, to varying degrees, by "commercial organizations" in Buffalo, Cincinnati, Cleveland, Denver, Grand Rapids, Indianapolis, Lincoln, Los Angeles, Milwaukee, Omaha, Peoria, Philadelphia, Pittsburgh, San Francisco, Seattle, Wheeling, Worcester, and Youngstown, and throughout Louisiana (Watson 1922, 421–22; Feder 1936, 209–10; Green 1999, 93). Felton said of her endorsement committee in San Francisco, which was instituted by the merchants' association "to investigate all charitable enterprises applying to it for endorsement and to issue its official card to such as are doing honest and efficient work," that it "has been bitterly criticized by every organization refused endorsement. That such criticism has passed almost unnoticed is due to the fact that the merchants generally consider the endorsement committee as a merchants committee—a committee made up of their own members, whose impartiality is beyond question." Three of its members were appointed by the Merchants' Association, two by the Associated Charities, and two by other charities. *Charities and the Commons* wrote that "so effective has been its work that not only members of the Chamber but the whole community relies upon it. Without its card, an organization cannot raise funds sufficient for maintenance" (*CR* 1909, vol. 21). That is, through the endorsement committees, the Chamber of Com-

merce could drive charities whose methods they disapproved out of business, in their own "impartial" manner. Watson (1922, 222) described this as part of the COSs' "overlordship of charity," secured with the support of local business.

131. See NCCC 1874.

132. Davis 1874.

133. NCCC 1883, 16.

134. In Gettleman 1963, 320.

135. Denver COS in Watson 1922, 240.

136. Gettleman 1963, 317 n. 21.

137. Gurteen 1882, 213.

138. Evans 1889, 28.

139. NCCC 1904, 165.

140. Ringenback 1973, 146–47.

141. Watson 1922, 111 (italics added).

142. NCCC 1910, 247.

143. Gurteen 1882, 129.

144. See Feder 1936, 199–22 for a similar tale in 1894 Indianapolis.

145. By 1900, the annual budget for the COS in New York was $56,000 ($15,751 of which was devoted to salaries and other administrative expenses), $22,500 in Boston ($17,000 for administration), $10,719 in Baltimore (all of which was administrative), and $8,096 in Buffalo ($2,595 for administration) (Munsterberg 1902, 681). Most others operated on significantly smaller revenues. A few were endowed: Buffalo had investments in 1892 totaling $308,873, and Bryn Mawr, Pennsylvania, had nearly $92,000 (Warner 1894, Table XXXII).

146. In its first fourteen years, for example, the Buffalo COS dealt with only 8,235 cases; from the 1880s to 1893, the Boston COS rarely had more than 1,000 cases per year; even New York recorded only a total of 18,100 cases from 1889 to 1898, for an average of under 2,000 cases per year in a decade of deep depression; and Baltimore counted 6,395 cases from 1888 to 1895 (Warner 1894, Table IV; Warner 1908, 47ff.).

147. In some substantially smaller cities, visitor-to-cases ratios were lower (1:2 in Columbus, 1:3 in Poughkeepsie, 1:4 in East Saginaw), but most cities for which data are available had around one visitor for every twenty cases and one for every few hundred paupers (nearly one for four hundred in New Haven, Chicago, and New York). By contrast, the average visitor handled fifty cases in Buffalo, sixty-six in New Haven, fifty-five in Louisville, and seventy-two in Davenport. In the same year, Boston had twenty-seven paid agents and administrative staff, Philadelphia had twenty-five, and New York had twenty-three; no other cities seem to have had even half as many (NCCC 1887, 134 Table 1).

148. Watson 1922; Greeley 1995. COSs often also operated woodyards for men and laundries and other small businesses for women as "work tests" to determine who was worthy of relief; they provided not only cheap labor but could sometimes provide revenue. By 1895, seventeen COSs operated a woodyard or a workroom of some kind; Louisville's made a profit that year (NCCC 1895, 95). In 1890, Chicago's was a consistent source of revenue for the COS, though most either broke even or recouped 50–75 percent of their expenses (Warner

1890, 5; NCCC 1895, 70). New York's woodyard sales totaled $32,462 in 1897 (*CR* 1897, 782).

149. Howells 1885; Waugh 1997.
150. Warner 1908, 380–81.
151. Munsterberg 1902, 506–7.
152. Ross 1914.
153. Addams 1910, 190. A case in point: while winters were always gruesomely difficult for many of the poor, only when distress reached the middle classes did this realization seem to hit, as an editorial in the usually anti-relief *Brooklyn Daily Eagle* (2/11/1899) during the harsh winter of 1898–99 makes clear: "No stronger evidence of the fact that there is widespread suffering among the poor can reasonably be asked for than the knowledge that in thousands of usually comfortable homes the cold weather is causing great discomforts. . . . If you, my reader, in your well carpeted rooms . . . furnace fires blazing . . . —if you and yours complain bitterly of the cold, how must it be with your less fortunate fellows."
154. See also Polsky 1991, Ch. 1; Bender 1975.
155. Half from manufacturing and mining; 18 percent from banking and finance; and 20 percent from utilities, retail, and other (Burris 1992).
156. The American Enterprise Institute and Brookings were among the policy-planning organizations most "interlocked" with the corporate elite (Domhoff 1998; Callahan 1999a; Burris 1992; see also Allen 1992). Heritage and the National Association of Manufacturers were among the least interlocked (Domhoff 1998; Burris 1992). While 64.6 percent of the American Enterprise Institute's funding was from Fortune 500 firms, 48.9 percent of Heritage's was (Post 1997). While Heritage received its early funding from many of the same foundations that supported the American Enterprise Institute (in 1980 both received more than half their individual contributions from executives of large corporations, says Post 1997), it historically sought significant portions of its funds from individual donations, possibly because it was so politically active. By 1986, it was raising 37 percent of its budget from individuals (Allen 1992), and represented a different set of anti-relief interests—hence stronger ties to the religious right than to the neoliberal right, which afforded it the freedom (or created for it the necessity) to focus more upon the sexual and marital aspects of welfare reform. Similarly, the ultraconservative nature of the National Association of Manufacturers—once affiliated with the John Birch Society, among others, it lost influence as it grew more conservative, reported Burris (1992)—made it a less useful vehicle for interests that were seeking to build consensus among and across corporate interests and to use such institutions to persuade the public that their analysis was "objective" and "scientific," which was essential if they were to be credible and persuasive (Lewis 2001). This helps account for why it ceded a role in welfare reform to the Chamber of Commerce (see below).
157. Burris 1992. Domhoff (1998, 57, 193) has argued that the National Federation of Independent Businesses suffered the same fate and came to be dominated by big business, not the smaller concerns it purported to represent.
158. Smith 2000.

159. Covington 1997.
160. The Foundation Center, data at fdncenter.org.
161. Data at mediatransparency.org (June 2003). In its early years, from 1977 to 1986, the Heritage Foundation received 91 percent of its total funding from only twelve sources; the figures were 51.6 percent for AEI, 90.8 percent for the Manhattan Institute and 85.2 percent for Hoover. For the same period, 9 percent of all American foundations provided 35 percent of all foundation grants to these institutions (Allen 1992).
162. See Allen 1992.
163. Covington in Paget 1998.
164. Swomley 1996.
165. People for the American Way 1996.
166. Scherer 2002.
167. Lowry 1999.
168. People for the American Way 1996. Hall (2000) argued that even the foundation associations, the Council on Foundations and the Independent Sector, had undergone a "dramatic" turn to the right and focused increasingly upon "professional and corporate issues."
169. In 1973 Weyrich also founded the American Legislative Exchange Council (ALEC), which was supported by corporate contributions and grants from Scaife, Coors, Bradley and Olin–affiliated philanthropies (Callahan 1998; National Resources Defense Council 2002). ALEC's literature noted that their "credo is that business can, should, and must be an ally of [state] legislators," and that it "provides for the private sector to work in a one-on-one relationship with state legislators to develop public policies that are pro-growth, pro-business and pro-freedom." Early members included Henry Hyde, Tommy Thompson, and John Engler (National Resources Defense Council 2002). It shared office space with Heritage, whose own Project on Federalism and the States extended the foundation's activity to state-level policies. ALEC, in turn, created the Madison Group, a national coordinating organization of state-level foundations and think tanks (National Committee for Responsive Philanthropy 1991). Similarly, the State Policy Network, founded in 1992, with Olin, Bradley, and Koch money, had forty member organizations by 2001, including the Pacific Research Institute (California), the Mackinac Center for Public Policy (Michigan), and the Heartland Institute (Chicago), with combined 1999 budgets of $6 million, much from hundreds of corporate donors seeking to influence state policy and change policy debate in the manner in which they have influenced national policy (Callahan 2001). As one Pennsylvania state policy organization director said to Heritage in 1989, "Ideas are ammunition, the bullets of a political movement, but let us not forget that to fire those bullets effectively we need a full arsenal of weapons at the state level, just as we need them at the federal level." The Heartland Institute, created by local businessmen as a means of influencing local policy and advocating free-market policies, went so far as to name its newsletter *Intellectual Ammunition.* By 1991, Heartland had affiliates in Cleveland, St. Louis, Kansas City, and Milwaukee (National Committee for Responsive Philanthropy 1991; People for the American Way 1996). Family-focused groups have also founded state-level policy

organizations; Gary Bauer and Focus on the Family's James Dobson helped establish them in thirty-eight states by 1995 (*National Journal* 10/28/1995).

170. The argument that follows owes something to Heale's (1976) analysis of the mid-nineteenth century.

171. Not all reformers opposed state intervention in all matters of relief. Gilder was willing to use its power to compel changes in marriage and reproductive behavior that would restore black men to their "rightful" role as dominant over women; Mead and Kaus would do so to require work. Mead argued that welfare did not regulate the poor but should, with a state that "seeks order rather than justice" by creating new obligations for its citizens (Mead 1998; 2000). Olasky (1992; 1996; 1997) advocated a near complete withdrawal of government from welfare provision and proposed a Welfare Replacement Act that would have cut taxes and offered incentives to contribute to churches and other charities. Himmelfarb (1996) hesitated to support workfare programs for fear that *any* government guarantee of support would promote dependency. Lowell (Stewart 1911) also expressed this concern but sanctioned the use of police and prisons to better punish the poor, and supported state institutions that would better segregate, house, and employ them; she might be said to have advocated an old paternalism that anticipated (or is at the root of) elements of Mead's new paternalism. But Lowell was much more determined to remove public agencies from relief provision than Mead. Murray (1984; 1994; 1998) emphasized private provision too, though his reasons were more connected with perverse incentives theses (and he conceded the possible need to establish group homes for unwed mothers and orphanages for the children of unfit ones). Gingrich (1995) also emphasized the superiority of the private voluntary sector, whether celebrating Boys' Town and the Spencer Tracy movie romanticizing it or harking back, as so many so often do, to Tocqueville's few short pages on American associations in *Democracy in America*. But while Gingrich would decentralize and privatize state power (especially economic power), he argued for a centralized moral culture, a single set of appropriate values.

3. Reform: Then Neither Should She Eat

1. Folks 1898; Devine 1898; Almy 1899; Almy 1900; NCCC 1892, 243; NCCC 1893, 99; Henderson et al. 1894.

2. Whether there was a *depression* in the 1880s is in some dispute, as is its duration. I follow Rezneck (1956).

3. Katz 1986, 41; see also Bremner 1956a and 1956b; Mohl 1983; Patterson 1994; Piven and Cloward 1971, 1983, 1987; Trattner 1994.

4. Kauffman and Kiesling 1997.

5. Watson 1922, 212–13.

6. Katz 1986, 41; Rockman 2003.

7. Huggins 1971, 70, 26.

8. Katz 1986, 47–54; Kaplan 1978; Lui 1993, 1995a, 1995b.

9. Watson 1922, 191.

10. Warner 1908, 242.

11. NCCC 1903, 379. Ruth Scannell's 1938 history of the New York COS (CSS Box 128) similarly credits the COS with defeating "formidable" late-century efforts to reinstate relief after it was abolished by the Greater New York Charter.

12. Kellogg 1893, 60.

13. Devine 1904, 303 (italics added).

14. Watson 1922, 399 n. 1 (italics added).

15. The vast majority of all COSs that had failed or lapsed by the turn of the century were in cities with populations below forty thousand.

16. New Orleans, the District of Columbia, Minneapolis, Columbus, St. Joseph, Atlanta, and Reading.

17. Baltimore, New York, Castleton (Staten Island), Philadelphia, Atlanta, and Indianapolis.

18. The mere absence of a formal COS in any city should not be read as an indication that charity organization ideas did not have influence there. Many would-be reformers in cities without a COS would have had ample opportunity to hear organizationists speak about their principles and hear them recount the successes of their efforts as they toured the United States, including the South, to proselytize (Green 1999, 85). The charity journals produced by some of the larger cities were widely circulated. The stories of COS successes, and especially reports of the abolition of relief in Brooklyn and Philadelphia, inspired activists in many cities: Indianapolis, for example, may have launched its anti-relief campaign in direct response to these perceived successes (Ziliak 1996a, 56–57), and Ohio organized both its public and private charities and began to restrict relief, one of its representatives said, solely because of the example offered by the NCCC and its members (NCCC 1893, 7).

19. Almy 1899; Katz 1986. Some at the time did argue that one of the functions of relief was to keep workers present throughout the winter so that they would be available come spring (see e.g., NCCC 1883, 183), but given a relative abundance of cheap labor in many cities throughout this period, there was likely minimal need for relief to fulfill this function, and very few made this argument.

20. But campaigns against out-relief were nonetheless more prominent in the North, where wages by 1890 were higher and labor markets tighter than in the South (Rosenbloom 2002).

21. Warner 1908, 227.

22. Hunter 1897, 692.

23. It is at this point that some of you will be wondering why I am not using more sophisticated methods to analyze these data, offering a regression table showing the relative influence of various factors upon relief withdrawal. That was my original hope, but, as I note in the acknowledgments, this cruder method is all the data collected permit.

24. "Out-door relief appears to be now an integral part of our poor law system everywhere, excepting in some of the Southern States, where it is unknown," wrote Low (1881, 145).

25. NCCC 1900, 259–61. The general secretary of the Portland, Oregon, COS said in 1901, "The attempt was made in the first place, twelve years ago, to make

this strictly a charity-organization society, but a few years in that direction demonstrated the necessity of combining relief work with the other. We have, I think, succeeded in doing this without giving place to the evil effects that are usually supposed to arise from such a combination. Outdoor relief has been greatly diminished, begging practically abolished, and a good degree of cooperation secured among churches, societies, and benevolent individuals. The county commissioners contemplate discontinuing outdoor relief and have followed our example in requiring work from able-bodied persons asking relief. The situation is not all that could be desired, but improves from year to year" (Hubbard 1901).

26. NCCC 1879, 98.
27. Low 1881.
28. Warner 1894, 54.
29. Rosenbloom 2002, Table 2.1.
30. See *CR* 1894, 409.
31. In Low 1881.
32. Bremner 1956b.
33. Katz 1986; Hannon 1984a, 1984b; Kiesling and Margo 1997.
34. Gunckel 1897, 756.
35. Schneider and Deutch 1969; Goodman 1983; Feder 1936.
36. Almy 1899 (Detroit offered little cash relief, but substantial in-kind assistance).
37. Monkkonen 1993.
38. Katz 1986, 45–50, 57. Others also emphasize the ways in which outdoor relief was used as a patronage tool (see Skocpol 1992, 96; Orloff 1988, 50).
39. Low 1879, 202ff.
40. NCCC 1898, 247.
41. *CR* 1899, vol. 9, no. 4, 136.
42. For one review of state practices, see Henderson 1898.
43. Riordan 1994, 64. Such antipathy between relief officials and charity reformers is commonplace in accounts from the era.
44. In Feder 1936, 22.
45. Kennedy 1992, 104–5.
46. Lui 1993; 1995a, 348, 354–55, 388; 1995b.
47. Kaplan 1978.
48. Pellew 1878, 64.
49. Kauffman and Kiesling 1997.
50. Goodman 1983, 636.
51. By 1887 the COS had helped pass state-wide laws restricting relief, although many were ignored by local overseers reluctant to relinquish control. By 1894 there were still 360 agencies—not including churches and individuals—that offered some form of relief. And, as Kaplan observes, the lack of public relief afforded Tammany an opportunity during the Depression to step in with money, coal, jobs, and money for burials (Branscombe 1943; Kaplan 1978).
52. And despite Lui's claims, the COS was largely responsible for the later failure to reinstate free coal in New York. The COS succeeded, though they acted behind the scenes, using their formidable connections to quietly change policy. During debate over the greater New York charter of 1897–98, the COS had a

sympathetic legislator insert a provision that would finally prohibit *all* outdoor relief in the new city, including coal. The charter was ratified, and the provision was apparently little noticed. Once the discovery was made, bills were introduced to reinstate free coal. The COS testified against them. Yet as Homer Folks reported,

> The representatives of the charitable societies were shown scant courtesy by the assembly committee. They were evidently looked upon as hardhearted, visionary enthusiasts, probably of doubtful moral character. The bills were promptly reported favorably by the assembly committee, passed the assembly with practical unanimity, and the struggle was renewed before the senate. Meanwhile spring was coming on, and the charitable societies had been proving themselves fully able to meet the need during the winter. The Republicans in the senate may have thought that the power to distribute free coal might be made a valuable perquisite in the hands of a Tammany administration in New York city. The attitude of the charitable societies in opposing the bill, and in offering to furnish coal themselves when needed, afforded at least a plausible reason for refusing to pass the bill (Folks 1901, 268ff; Devine 1898 confirms the salient facts).

The bill died in the state senate, as it did again in 1899, 1900, and 1901, all with COS opposition apparently central to the outcome. The COS was active in the defeat of these efforts to reinstate free coal, although, as Folks suggested, it may be that the COS served as cover for Republican state senators who wanted to limit free coal to limit the patronage power of Tammany Democrats (an account consistent with Kaplan's history). Some years later, during the anthracite coal strike of the early 1900s, the COS as well as the AICP, United Hebrew Charities, the State Charities Aid Association, and the Society of St. Vincent de Paul all voiced their opposition to expanded coal delivery: "The city's generosity would be perverted to the profit of operators and speculators who are now taking advantage of our necessity," they wrote (letter to Sen. Horace White, chair, Senate Committee on Committees, 1/17/1903, CSS Box 108). They prevailed.

53. See Clement 1992, Table 2.
54. Rauch 1976, 57.
55. Watson 1922, 187ff.
56. First Annual Report 1879 in Watson 1922, 547ff.
57. Rauch 1976, 57–58.
58. Watson 1922, 187ff; Devine 1904, 300–3; Watson 1922, 193.
59. Rauch 1976, 57–58.
60. Kusmer 1973.
61. Hunter 1902, 77.
62. Watson 1922, 224; Hunter 1902.
63. Johnson 1923.
64. See Biography Resource Center 2003, Doc. no. BT2310010307; "Alexander Johnson," *American National Biography Online,* 2000.
65. Watson 1922.

66. Chicago Relief and Aid Society, 16th Annual Report, in Feder 1936, 57; see also Trusdell in NCCC 1895, 66–71.

67. Flanagan 2002. This may have been so that the directors of relief and aid could control which companies received contracts for relief supplies: directors' companies earned $343,287 from such deals (Flanagan 2002, 28).

68. Almy 1899, 26. While Watson (1922) records the Associated Charities as having been established in 1881, he argued that it had minimal influence until after 1900; Sage (1914) records its establishment as 1900.

69. In fact, such reductions in public out-relief that are evident occurred before the COS came into being: while 4,590 families shared in $95,000 in relief in 1875, it declined steadily until 1877, then precipitously after a strict work test was implemented, so that by 1880 1,200 families shared in $17,000 in relief (Low 1881, 152).

70. Watson 1922, 400n, 65, 72–74.

71. Feder 1936, 48, 54; Watson 1922.

72. Indiana may have been the first to codify COS principles on a state-wide basis in 1899 (Warner 1908, 234).

73. Huggins 1971, 69.

74. Watson 1922; Devine 1904; Warner 1908; Huggins 1971.

75. *LAH* 1888; *LAH* 1889; Warner 1894; Devine 1904.

76. Warner 1894, 172.

77. Devine 1904, 304–5.

78. In fact, per-capita cash relief in Boston increased substantially in the late nineteenth century. From 1877 to 1900, *total* Boston expenditures for outdoor relief declined from $80,342 to $64,502. The number of recipients declined too, from 6,662 to 2,863, so that per-family averages received rose from $12.12 to $22.53. From 1880 to 1890, the total expenditures of the Boston Overseers of the Poor (a subset of total relief expenditures) declined from $34,459 to $22,682. But these data also reveal that those declines all occurred in the funding allocated for in-kind relief for fuel and food; funding for immediate cash relief actually *doubled* from 1880 to 1890—from about $230.00 to $418.00 per family (Devine 1904, 303–8; *LAH* 1890 vol. 5, 700).

79. Devine 1904, 309 (italics added).

80. NCCC 1895, 63.

81. Devine 1904, 282.

82. Paul Pierson (2000b) would write some one hundred years later, "Different welfare state configurations are the products of complex conjunctural causation, with multiple factors working together over extended periods of time to generate dramatically different outcomes. There is no theoretical justification for arguing that a 10% shift in the value of one variable or another will have a simple direct effect on outcomes." In other words, there can be no monocausal explanations for welfare state development and expansion, despite scholars' attempts to correlate single factors such as GNP, labor party power, or political culture to explain variations across states. Nor, by extension, should we reasonably hope that variation in local relief policies across some three decades of the nineteenth century could be sufficiently explained by such factors as their size,

the harshness of their winters, the racial or ethnic populations of their cities, or even general levels of protest.

83. Rezneck 1950, 499.
84. In Gutman 1965, 254.
85. George 1883, in Ahlstrom 1972, 732.
86. Gilje 1996, 118.
87. Katz 1986, 186.
88. In Cahn 1972, 158.
89. In Hatheway 1995.
90. Mohl 1983, 38–39.
91. Piven and Cloward 1971, 3.
92. Piven and Cloward 1983, 131.
93. NCCC 1893, 104.
94. Piven and Cloward 1977, Ch. 1.
95. Kellogg 1894, 27.
96. Gutman 1965.
97. In Gutman 1965, 256.
98. Schneider and Deutch 1969; Goodman 1983; Feder 1936.
99. Gutman 1965.
100. Gurteen 1882, 20.
101. Stewart 1911, 151.
102. Katz 1986, 54.
103. Almy 1899; Almy 1900.
104. Warner 1908, 241.
105. Katz 1986; Keyssar 1986; NCCC 1895, 67.
106. Hammack 1982, 113.
107. Lui 1995a.
108. Gutman 1965, 265.
109. Mandler 1990, 24. But he also cautions us not to assume simply because bourgeois citizens attached a stigma to charity that that is reason to presume that working-class or other persons in need did so.
110. Kellogg 1894, 24.
111. Boyer 1978, 125–127.
112. Feder 1936, 51–56. This was an unwitting precursor to Piven and Cloward's "flood-the-rolls" strategy. See *The Nation* 5/2/1966; see also *New York Times* 8/1/1968.
113. Gurteen 1882, 124.
114. Gurteen 1882; Almy 1900; Rezneck 1953; Munsterberg 1902.
115. NCCC 1900, 142.
116. See Watson 1922, 179ff; Gurteen 1882, 129. Buffalo did, however, successfully restrict cash relief, but failed to reduce its "lavish" in-kind aid.
117. Keyssar 1986, 246.
118. A Striker 1877.
119. NCCC 1897, 272.
120. Brooks 1894, 361–62.
121. In Feder 1936, 155.
122. Greeley 1995, 313.

123. Watson 1922, 266.
124. Closson 1894, passim.
125. This is a "feedback" phenomenon observed in analysis of modern welfare states, too. Pierson (1996) argued that welfare cutbacks can strengthen support for and ultimately expand the welfare state. Piven and Cloward (1982, Chs. 5 and 6) made related arguments.
126. Ziliak 1997. "As the public expenditures per relieved household were taken to the relatively low level of $3.40 per year by 1890, private expenditures rose to $15.10, ironically approaching the 'lavish' public expenditures in Boston, and exceeding that in Brooklyn" (see Ziliak 1996a, 1996b). However, *total* per capita public relief expenditures were still higher in Boston in 1897 ($1.379), which did not abolish outdoor relief, than in cities that did, including New York ($1.081), Baltimore ($1.068), St. Louis ($0.933), Philadelphia ($0.824), and San Francisco ($0.812), and were substantially higher than Atlanta ($0.406), Memphis ($0.234), New Orleans ($0.148), Denver ($0.146), Kansas City, Missouri ($0.108), Brooklyn ($0.047), Salt Lake City ($0.013), and Louisville ($0.012)—all cities that also abolished public out-relief. Similarly, Boston boasted the highest per capita private outdoor relief expenditures in 1897 ($0.261), followed by Cambridge ($0.247), which reduced but never abolished relief. For other cities private expenditures were $0.178 in New York, $0.163 in San Francisco, $0.076 in Baltimore, $0.063 in Chicago, $0.050 in Indianapolis, and $0.047 in Brooklyn (my calculations from Folks 1898; NYCOS 1896; Gibson and Lennon 1999).

4. Reform Redux: Dethroning the Welfare Queen

1. Schattschneider 1960, 66 (italics in original).
2. Markets are neither natural nor free; see Polanyi 1944. There is much to this resistance to establishing a right to relief, for rights have power beyond their legal status. As Martha Minow wrote: "Rights pronounced by courts become possessions of the dispossessed . . . legal language, like a song, can be hummed by someone who did not write it and changed by those for whom it was not intended" (Minow in McCann 1992, 733). A legally established or culturally accepted right has power even if its obligations remain unenforced: to confer rights is to concede power. In 1970 the Supreme Court in *Goldberg v. Kelly* had come close to identifying a property right in welfare, as Yale law professor Charles Reich had urged (Reich 1964). Justice Brennan, in a footnote to the majority opinion in *Goldberg,* wrote, "It may be realistic today to regard welfare entitlements as more like 'property' than a 'gratuity.' Much of the existing wealth in this country takes the form of rights that do not fall within traditional common-law concepts of property. . . . We have come to recognize that forces not within the control of the poor contribute to their poverty." He continued, "Public assistance, then, is not mere charity, but a means to 'promote the general welfare, and secure the Blessings of Liberty to ourselves and our Posterity.' " But, alas, he retreated and rejected the implications of his own claims: "We, no less than the dissenters, recognize the importance of not im-

posing upon the States or the Federal Government in this developing field of law any procedural requirements beyond those demanded by rudimentary due process." The potential consequences, had such a right been conferred, are profound. We have retreated further still: for discussion of the failure of even relief recipients to employ the language of rights, see Gilliom 2001, Ch. 3; Sarat 1990; see also Soss 2002.

3. Neuhaus and Berger 1976.
4. I do not attempt to document state policy changes conducted under HHS waivers, nor do I attempt to summarize state-by-state variation in the implementation of the PRA. See instead Williams 1994; Weaver 2000; Winston 2002; and the State and Welfare Rules Databases of the Urban Institute, www.urban.org.
5. Albelda, Folbre, and the Center for Popular Economics 1996, 88. This is a complicated question, however, that reveals one perennial problem in polling on welfare issues; if by "welfare" respondents included Social Security, Medicare, and Medicaid, the response is accurate. If, instead, they associate "welfare" only with AFDC and food stamps (as most usually do), it is inaccurate. At its pre-PRA peak in 1995, federal AFDC spending was $17 billion, and combined federal and state spending was $25 billion; in the same year, defense spending was $272 billion.
6. See acf.dhhs.gov/news/stats.
7. Edelman 1997, 44; Katz 1989, 68.
8. Thomas and Sawhill 2001.
9. Abramovitz 1988.
10. See Schram 2002, Ch. 6, for an analysis of the racial composition of welfare rolls that refutes the conventional wisdom of the left while eschewing the racist conclusions of the right.
11. See Edin and Lein 1997.
12. See Ziliak 2002 for a concise summary of the "constants" of welfare throughout American history—from the duration of relief receipt, the value of benefits, "migrations" from welfare to work, and poorhouse populations.
13. Weaver 2000, see Ch. 7.
14. Ellwood 1988, 4 (italics added).
15. Personal Responsibility and Work Opportunity Reconciliation Act of 1996; Super et al. 1996.
16. Peschek 1987, 27.
17. Allen 1992.
18. Burris 1992; Allen 1992.
19. Peschek 1987; Allen 1992.
20. Saloma 1984, 16–17; Peschek 1987, 32.
21. Allen 1992.
22. Burris 1992; Saloma 1984, 15. By the time George W. Bush assumed the presidency, the status of these institutions as power brokers and sources for leadership and policy ideas was unquestionable: the administration asked Heritage to review all Clinton administration executive orders and recommend targets for repeal (Berkowitz 2001b), and Heritage, the American Enterprise Institute, Hudson, and Cato activists quickly found homes throughout the admin-

istration, including numerous senior posts, notably the secretary of labor, director of the Office of Personnel Management, and director of speechwriting (Heritage), chairman of the Council of Economic Advisers and secretary of the Treasury (American Enterprise Institute), numerous members of the Committee to Strengthen Social Security (Cato), and the directors of the Office of Management and Budget and the Office of Family Services at HHS (Hudson). See "Conservative Movement Moves In," at mediatransparency.org/move ment_goes.htm (2/23/2003); see also *Economist* 2/15/2003.

23. Trattner 1994, 354–59.
24. Brodkin 1995, 216.
25. Katz 1986, 295–99; Hout 1997.
26. Katz 1986, 295–99.
27. As Sidney Blumenthal (1986) noted, Murray's argument that the War on Poverty had failed contradicted the previously favored conservative thesis offered by Martin Anderson (1978), a Nixon and Reagan domestic policy advisor from Hoover, that the War on Poverty had finally been won. Both came to the same conclusion, however, that the War on Poverty must therefore be ended.
28. National Governors Association 1988.
29. Trattner 1994; Brodkin 1995; Weaver 2000; Winston 2002.
30. Weaver 2000.
31. Williams 1996.
32. Weaver 2000.
33. Some such innovations actually have earlier roots. At the end of the nineteenth century, Buffalo demanded that the children of the poor attend school in order for the family to receive relief (Feder 1936, 205; see also NCCC 1888, 145–46). Some few years later New York began fingerprinting all tramps and vagrants (Watson 1922, 301), as it did again in the late 1990s. The NCCC (1903; see also Devine 1904, 280) worried at length about the means to remedy the "desertion" by fathers of women and children who turned to relief providers, insisting that "the obligation to provide for the family must be recognized voluntarily or compulsorily enforced." Buffalo opened a crèche in 1880, providing child care to working women for a fee of 5 cents per day (NCCC 1886, 179), as did many other cities.
34. See Hays 2001, 186: "the debate was more wide-open to divergent viewpoints than later welfare debates, because there were fewer assumptions widely shared by all of the participants." During debate over the FSA, Moynihan's position was arguably closer to that of the Reagan administration than his Democratic colleagues; by debate over the PRA, he was among the loudest voices in opposition. Moynihan's position had not changed; rather, the political center had shifted so far to the right that he appeared liberal by comparison.
35. Wilson 1996, 49.
36. Dreier, Mollenkopf, and Swanstrom 2001, 26.
37. Patterson 1994, 233.
38. Mishel, Bernstein, and Schmitt 2003, Table 2.41; Katz 1986, 303.
39. Mishel, Bernstein, and Schmitt 1997, 334. Edin and Lein (1997) and Newman (1999) demonstrated that while work often offered less security and fewer re-

wards than welfare, many women worked nonetheless "because it made them feel better about themselves" (see also Wilson 1996; Piven 1998b).

40. Mead 1994, 328.
41. Mishel, Bernstein, and Schmitt 1997, 149.
42. Mishel, Bernstein, and Schmitt 1997, 11.
43. Brodkin 1995, 218.
44. *New York Times* 7/15/1994.
45. *New York Times* 12/8/1996.
46. *New York Times* 10/20/1994.
47. *New York Times* 11/13/1994.
48. Kaus 1992, xiv.
49. In Heclo 2000.
50. Mead 1986, 40.
51. Gingrich 1995; 1996.
52. Rector 2000. This was a favorite tactic of Rector's (see 1998, 2000, 2001), to argue that, in his words, "although material hardship does occur in America, it is rare. The bulk of the 'poor' live in material conditions considerably more comfortable or even well-off than just a few generations ago." He reports that significant percentages of poor Americans own homes, cars, color televisions (it is that they are *color* televisions that always seems most galling to him), VCRs, dishwashers, and microwaves. He notes, "Most 'poor' Americans today are better housed and better fed and own more personal property than average Americans throughout much of this century." That many poor people today may live in less squalor than a resident of one of the turn-of-the-century tenements Riis's photographs made famous is a meaningless trick of analysis for actual poor people living in actual conditions of material poverty and of relative poverty. But as a political tactic it is shrewd—as political scientist Deborah Stone has so well put it, in politics "interpretations are more powerful than facts" (Stone 1997, 28). Should Rector succeed, he could interpret away a large portion of American poverty.
53. Gilder 1981, 12.
54. Murray 1984.
55. See Albelda, Folbre, and the Center for Popular Economics 1996; Ackerman 1999. Rector would later play the game again and bring his total to $7.9 trillion (Rector and Fagan 2001) (by 2003, it was $8.29 trillion). Rightly noting that total welfare spending had increased and not declined after the passage of the PRA (see Chapter 5), Rector urged that "steps must be taken to help policymakers and the public understand the vast size of the welfare system and to limit its future growth" (Rector 2000). He did just that. In testimony about the reauthorization of the PRA before the U.S. House of Representatives, he argued that the federal government operated some seventy welfare programs, and that for fiscal year 2000, total state and federal spending on welfare totaled $434 billion. "Welfare spending," he told the committee, "is so large it is difficult to comprehend. On average, the annual cost of the welfare system amounts to around $5,600 in taxes from each household that paid federal income tax in 2000." Still, even while Rector included expenditures we should exclude from an estimate of total "welfare" costs, his tally amounted to 4.4 per-

cent of the total budget. While hardly an insignificant sum, he fails to make the case that this amount per se should inspire concern. See Rector 2001, Appendix II, for his list of welfare programs. Martin Anderson (1978) made this argument earlier, in much the same way; see Anderson's Appendix A for his list; note that he distinguishes for the reader between income transfer and welfare programs. Still, Anderson wrote, "By the end of 1977 the war on poverty will have cost more than World War II."

56. Noble 1997, 94.
57. Stefancic and Delgado 1996.
58. Piven 1998a.
59. Weaver 2000; *New York Times* 4/22/1994; *Wall Street Journal* 1/23/1995, "Behind the Scenes: GOP's Stance Owes a Lot to Prodding from Robert Rector."
60. *Economist* 6/18/1994.
61. *L.A. Times* 8/21/1994, "Merchants of Virtue."
62. See *New York Times* 4/22/1994.
63. Williams 1996.
64. *National Journal* 10/28/1995, "Lobbying: All in the Family."
65. *Weekly Standard* 8/5/1996.
66. See *Washington Times* 7/1/1995, "Wobbly Shoves on Welfare"; 1/17/1995, "How Deep the GOP Divide on Welfare"; 11/22/1994, " 'Moderates' Could Derail GOP Agenda"; and 4/14/1994, "Kemp Urges GOP to Drop Welfare Bill, Fight 'Soft' Reforms," for examples.
67. In Weaver 2000, 156.
68. Callahan 1999a.
69. Edwards 1998.
70. See Alterman 1999; Moore and Slater 2003; mediatransparency.org/people/ marvin_olasky.htm; Biography Resource Center 2003, Doc. no. H1000111991.
71. Blumenthal 1986.
72. *Gannett News Service* 11/21/2001.
73. Haskins 2001.
74. In People for the American Way 1996.
75. Callahan 1999a.
76. In Swomley 1996.
77. Callahan 1998.
78. mediatransparency.org, "The Feeding Trough: Wisconsin's National Model for Welfare Reform" (5/1997).
79. mediatransparency.org, "Wisconsin's Exploding Prison Population: The Bradley Connection" (9/2000).
80. Weaver 2000, Table 6-2. Winston (2002) and Hays (2001, Ch. 4) also analyzed hearings on the PRA, and their findings are consistent with Weaver's and with the claim that *ostensibly* liberal voices were well represented in formal congressional debate.
81. Winston 2002, 80–81.
82. Hays 2001, Table 4-11.
83. It is now known as the American Public Human Services Association.
84. Winston 2002, 82.
85. Schneier and Gross 1993; Hall 1996.

86. Turner was an influential reformer in Wisconsin (1993–1997) and later in New York City; he pioneered workfare programs for both. He subsequently became a fellow at the Heritage Foundation. Jason DeParle (*New York Times,* 1/20/1998) reports that as a high school student Turner designed welfare-to-work programs. For fun.

87. Winston 2002, Table 3-3. They testified eight times each. Next, in order, were Manpower Demonstration Research Corporation (seven times), Catholic Charities and Child Welfare League of America (five), Lawrence Mead, Center on Budget and Policy Priorities, Center for Law and Social Policy, and the National Organization for Women's Legal Defense and Education Fund (four), and, at three each, Children's Defense Fund, American Civil Liberties Union, AFSCME (American Foundation of State, County and Municipal Employees), California Department of Health and Human Services, Michigan Department of Social Services, Gov. Engler, Gov. Thompson, and the Riverside, California Department of Social Services.

88. See *Chronicle of Philanthropy* 8/9/2001.

89. Heclo 2000; see also *Washington Times* 1/9/1995, "Guest Lists for Hearings on Hill Undergo Sweeping Change, Too."

90. Marshall Wittman in *Wall Street Journal* 1/23/1995, "Behind the Scenes: GOP's Stance Owes a Lot to Prodding From Robert Rector."

91. Winston 2002, Ch. 3. This is the most revealing look yet at who was involved in the drafting of the PRA.

92. Rich and Weaver 2000.

93. Rich and Weaver 2000.

94. Dolny 1996. I include Brookings among conservative organizations, although Smith and others characterize it as without consistent ideological identity; across all issues, that may be true, but it was not true for welfare policy in my judgment. And, as a former Brookings man who moved to the American Enterprise Institute said of both: "It's probably true that both are moving to the middle, but the middle is moving to the right" (Peschek 1987, 31). See also Husseini 1998 on Brookings as conservative.

95. Smith 2000.

96. Dolny 1997. See more recent data at Dolny 2003.

97. Paget 1998; see Dolny 1998.

98. Flanders and Jackson 1995.

99. Schneider and Jacoby 2002.

100. And more blamed immigrants—39 percent of poorer respondents (versus 27 percent for higher-income respondents) cited immigration as a major cause of poverty. There were a few differences of note, however: 52 percent of poorer respondents (versus 27 percent) identified a shortage of jobs as a major cause; 64 percent (versus 50 percent) thought the quality of those jobs themselves to be a factor; and 69 percent (versus 54 percent) blamed medical expenses. Differences by race were even more pronounced, even when controlled for income, with whites less likely to attribute poverty to structural causes.

101. Weaver 2000, Ch. 7; Albelda, Folbre, and the Center for Popular Economics 1996; NPR et al. 2001. But again we should not conclude too much from these

short-term fluctuations in polled opinion: even in 1969 one survey reported that 84 percent of respondents thought "there are too many people receiving welfare money who should be working," and over half thought "lack of thrift" or "lack of effort" were principal causes of poverty (Feagin 1975, Ch. 4). General antipathy to welfare and welfare recipients has been a constant, short-term fluctuations notwithstanding.

102. Lewis 2001; Converse 1964.
103. Fried and Harris 2001; see also Jacobs and Shapiro 2000.
104. Schneider and Jacoby 2002.
105. Edelman 1997, 47.
106. Mink 1998, 147.
107. See Post 1997, n. 18. By contrast, the National Association of Manufacturers and the Chamber of Commerce were sharply divided over Nixon's Family Assistance Plan; their agreement over the PRA marks the success of the Chamber's position (see Hays 2001, 190).
108. Winston 2002, 92.
109. Post 1997.
110. United States Chamber of Commerce, Aug. 1995.
111. In Post 1997.
112. United States Chamber of Commerce, Aug. 1994.
113. *Business Week* 6/13/1994.
114. United States Chamber of Commerce, Aug. 1994.
115. United States Chamber of Commerce, June 1995; Nov. 1995.
116. United States Chamber of Commerce, June 1995.
117. *Economist* 6/18/1994.
118. See Weicher 1995.
119. Hein 1999a; Hein 1999b.
120. Jonas 2001; Jonas 1999.
121. Jonas 1999.
122. And continued to. In 1997 the U.S. Chamber of Commerce and National Association of Manufacturers joined to create Workforce Innovation Networks, which was designed to shape TANF implementation and reauthorization to suit their labor needs. See "Building a Nation That Works: Designing TANF for the Workplace," Workforce Innovation Networks, June 2002.
123. For a review of these issues in the context of New Deal business power, see Hacker and Pierson 2002.
124. See Hansen and Mitchell 2000.
125. Schattschneider 1960.
126. *American Spectator* 6/1994.
127. Dick Morris, Bruce Reed, Mickey Kantor, and Rahm Immanuel, says Stephanopoulos (1999, 420–421). He reports that while Morris insisted to Clinton that if he vetoed the PRA he would lose the election by three percentage points, Stephanopoulos instead projected "a quick five- or six-point drop" that would "never cost [them] the race." One post-PRA poll revealed that only 13 percent of respondents even knew that Clinton had signed the bill (Lewis 2001, 193). Morris (1997, 298–305) reports that he told Clinton that signing the PRA

would help him win a fifteen-point margin of victory (he won by eight) and "usher in a sixties-like era of commitment to helping poor people."

128. United States Chamber of Commerce, Aug. 1994.

5. Results of Reforms

1. See Clement 1992; Keyssar 1986; Hickey 2003, 90. Compare with twentieth-century survival strategies in Edin and Lein 1997; Zedlewski et al. 2003.
2. "U.S. Welfare Caseloads Information," www.acf.dhhs.gov/news/stats.
3. Haskins and Primus 2001.
4. Haskins 2000; Jarchow 2002.
5. Blank 2001; Besharov and Germanis 2001.
6. Murray (1998) offered this: "My interpretation of the trends in welfare rolls is that the rhetoric worked. The welfare population includes a fairly large number of women who could work if they wanted to badly enough, and all the hoopla moved some portion of these women to act."
7. Federation of Protestant Welfare Agencies 2000.
8. *New York Times* 8/12/2000.
9. Kaplan in Oliphant 2000.
10. Soss et al. 2001; Fording in Schram, Soss, and Fording. 2003. Kalil, Seefeldt, and Wang 2002 confirm that being African American and lacking a high school diploma predicted sanctions in Michigan.
11. Soss et al. 2001; see also Fording 2001 on the incarceration question.
12. That said, states that had provided more generous AFDC benefits were less likely to impose harsh penalties in their TANF programs.
13. Oliphant 2000.
14. Haskins, Sawhill, and Weaver 2001a; Loprest 2002; Cancian et al. 2002.
15. Allen and Kirby 2000; see Waller and Berube 2002 for the urban concentration of longer-term cases.
16. See www.acf.dhhs.gov; Lichter and Jayakody 2002.
17. Lowell 1884, 63.
18. Kellogg 1893, 60.
19. Warner 1908, 235.
20. See Feder 1936, 79.
21. NCCC 1893, 102.
22. Moving between 27,000 and 33,000; it then grew from 38,771 in 1883 to 42,664 in 1888 and to 48,921 in 1889. Given the growth in population over this same period, from 942,000 in 1870 to 1.5 million in 1890, these increases are of little note (Kauffman and Kiesling 2001; Katz 1986, Table 2.2).
23. Butler 1906, 763ff.
24. NCCC 1887, 84–92, Sched. B.
25. Kauffman and Kiesling 1997, 446.
26. See also Katz 1983.
27. NCCC 1891, 265. Between 1874 and 1875, some 16 percent of New York almshouse inmates were children, 16.5 percent were "old and destitute," 25 percent were blind, deaf, epileptic, feeble-minded, or otherwise "temporarily

or permanently disabled," and 32 percent were classified as insane (Warner 1894b, 57), but by the mid-1880s most New York almshouses were devoid of children (Hannon 1997, 425–27) and most others states had done the same by the mid-1890s (Folks 1894, 124–26). By 1903, only 7 percent of all the institutionalized "insane" were in an almshouse (Warner 1908, 196ff). By the turn of the century, poorhouses were a last refuge for old people who had little value in the labor market (see Katz 1983); by 1904 more than 40 percent of almshouse inmates were over sixty years old (Warner 1908, 196ff).

28. Abel 1998.
29. Katz 1986; Folks 1894, 124–26.
30. Hannon 1997, 427.
31. Folks 1901, 272.
32. S. O'Connor 2001.
33. Stewart 1911, 244ff.
34. Fetter 1901, 377.
35. Devine 1904, 109.
36. NCCC 1883, 38.
37. NCCC 1890, 403.
38. Rothman 1971.
39. See sentencingproject.org.
40. Lowell 1884, 62–65.
41. Rothman 1971.
42. While 24 percent had a "common" education, 21 percent had a "fair" education, and 16 percent a "good" education (Ebert 1999).
43. Ebert 1999.
44. In Ebert 1999.
45. Rothman 1980.
46. Ebert 1999.
47. Scull 1977.
48. Ebert 1999; Rothman 1980.
49. That said, I do not find evidence to suggest that nineteenth-century reformers were engaged in deceit, or attempting to hide bad outcomes; their analyses of post-reform events suggest, instead, that they did not understand that what they were measuring could not offer data on what they sought to explain. They were trapped by what Schram and Soss (2000) described regarding evaluations of recent reforms as "a political climate that privileges some facts and interpretations over others:" because the few arguments that reformers encountered against abolishing outdoor relief often pointed to the rise in indoor costs it caused, addressing that critique was how pro-abolition reformers sought to defend their policies.
50. Mishel, Bernstein, and Boushey 2003. Similarly, it is true that since the PRA the growth in out-of-wedlock childbirth, single-parent families, and divorce has slowed, and births to unmarried women ages fifteen to nineteen have declined (although the percentage of all births to unmarried teenagers rose after the passage of the PRA) (Oliphant 2000). But the relationship between these trends and the PRA is unclear (see Lichter and Jayakody 2002 for a review of the literature). Teen birthrates, for example, have been declining since the

1950s (Allan Guttmacher Institute Issue Brief, "Teen Pregnancy: Trends and Lessons Learned," 2002). Regardless, while abortion rates overall were down, those among very poor women and women on Medicaid rose from 1994 to 2000 (Jones, Darrach, and Henshaw 2002).

51. Center on Budget and Policy Priorities 9/24/2002, "Census Data Show Increase in Extent and Severity of Poverty and Decline in Household Income," www.cbpp.org.
52. U.S. Census Bureau, "Income and Poverty 2002—Press Briefing," 9/26/2003, www.census.gov. If we include those who were "near-poor," with income 100–125 percent of the official poverty line, the total is 16.5 percent.
53. Greenberg et al. 2000; Haskins 2000; National Campaign for Jobs and Income Support 2001; Jarchow 2002. Cancian et al. 2000 find 80 percent of Wisconsin leavers employed "at some point in their first year after exit." Note that women have historically cycled on and off the rolls, in and out of the workforce—this was not a new development of reform (see Mishel, Bernstein, and Boushey 1997, 334).
54. Greenberg et al. 2000; National Campaign for Jobs and Income Support 2001; Boushey 2001; Cancian et al. 2002.
55. Economic Policy Institute Issue Brief no. 191, 4/11/2003.
56. Haskins 2000.
57. See Hays 2003.
58. Greenberg et al. 2000; National Campaign for Jobs and Income Support 2001.
59. Children's Defense Fund in Haskins 2000.
60. National Campaign for Jobs and Income Support 2001; Boushey 2001.
61. *Brookings Review* 2001.
62. Lichter and Jayakody 2002; Greenberg et al. 2000.
63. National Campaign for Jobs and Income Support 2001.
64. U.S. Census Bureau in Lichter and Jayakody 2002.
65. Pimpare 2000; Paxson and Waldfogel 2002; *New York Times* 8/7/2001, "Surprising Results." Other studies found no correlation between such ill effects and work (see Lichter and Jayakody 2002; National Institutes of Health 3/6/2003, "Mothers' Leaving Welfare Had No Effects on Preschoolers").
66. Children's Defense Fund, 4/30/2003, "Number of Black Children in Extreme Poverty Hits Record High."
67. Note, however, that the relationship between some indicators of rising need and welfare reform has not been established.
68. National Campaign for Jobs and Income Support 2001.
69. *New York Times* 8/1/2001, "Use of Shelters by Families Sets Record in New York"; *New York Times,* 2/13/2002, "Many More Children Calling New York City Shelters Home"; see also *New York Times* 2/7/2001, "Shelter Population Reaches Highest Level Since 1980's."
70. *New York Times* 2/13/2002; *New York Newsday* 2/20/2003; www.coalition-forthehomeless.org (Feb. 2003).
71. Fendt, Mulligan-Hansel, and White 2001.
72. National Campaign for Jobs and Income Support 2001; U.S. Conference of Mayors, Reports on Hunger and Homelessness in American Cities, 2001, 2002, and 2003, www.usmayors.org.

73. Associated Press 11/2/2003.
74. Loprest 1999.
75. *Chronicle of Philanthropy* 8/9/2001.
76. Fendt, Mulligan-Hansel, and White 2001. By July 2003, food-stamp caseloads were rising again (see cbpp.org 12/12/2003).
77. *Boston Globe* 5/8/2002, "Study Finds More Infants Going Hungry." See also Cook et al. 2002.
78. Piven and Cloward 1971; Katz 1986, 15.
79. NCCC 1890, 76.
80. Davis 1874, 10.
81. From 1860 to 1864, when it averaged 20.46 percent, to 10.24 percent from 1870 to 1874, to 9.98 percent from 1880 to 1884, and 6.7 percent from 1890 to 1894 (Hannon 1997, Table 4).
82. From .460 in 1860–1864 to .898 in 1890–1894 (Hannon 1997, Table 4).
83. From 10.99 from 1860 to 1864 to 31.10 from 1870 to 1874 and to 29.29 from 1880 to 1884, finally hitting 46.75 from 1890 to 1895 (Hannon 1997, Table 4).
84. In Woods 1895, 367.
85. NCCC 1887, Sched. B.
86. Except for a small amount for aid to the blind. NCCC 1901, 132; Fetter 1901, 363 shows slightly different figures.
87. Warner 1908, 405.
88. Clement 1992, Tables 1 and 2.
89. Warner 1894, 339; Warner 1908, 403.
90. Katz 1986, 111.
91. Fetter 1901, 371–72; Fetter 1901, Table II.
92. *CR* 1899 vol. 9, no. 2, 79. As were many COSs; Denver's, for example, received just shy of half its 1895 budget from the city (NCCC 1895, 57).
93. In twelve states (Colorado, Virginia, Michigan, Rhode Island, Delaware, New Jersey, Alabama, Minnesota, Ohio, Iowa, Indiana, and Utah), combined public and private subsidies were minimal and totaled less than $10,000. In eleven states (Illinois, Vermont, Georgia, North Carolina, New Hampshire, Massachusetts, Wisconsin, Louisiana, Missouri, Oregon, and Kansas) combined subsides ranged from a high of $63,796 in Illinois to a low of $14,400 in Kansas; most subsidies except in Oregon and Kansas were local (Green 1999 shows that in New Orleans the number of institutions receiving subsidies for poor relief rose from twelve in 1870 to fifty by 1933, and that it was political considerations that most accounted for their receipt). But in other states, subsidies were much higher. For Connecticut, state subsidies were $101,750 and local were $24,500; D.C. reported $200,000 in local subsidies; for Maryland, there were $96,000 in state and $185,000 in local payments and California reported $410,000 in state subsidies to private charities. For all those states above total state and local subsidies amounted to $1,486,215, roughly 14 percent of the total for the year. The other 86 percent of all public subsidies for private charities were from only two states—New York ($3,645,000—94 percent local) and Pennsylvania ($5,853,500—98 percent state) (Fetter 1901, passim).
94. Green 1999, 83.
95. Barbour 1901, 125.

96. Munsterberg 1902, 678–79.

97. Gingrich 1994.

98. U.S. GAO 8/1998, "Welfare Reform: Early Fiscal Effects of the TANF Block Grant."

99. Center on Budget and Policy Priorities 11/1/2001 and 10/30/2002, www.cbpp.org. Thus, total TANF expenditures in fiscal year 2002 were $18.749 billion. However, if reauthorization of the PRA in 2004 locks in the TANF block grant at the same amount, the real value of the grant by 2008 would decline by perhaps one-fourth.

100. Haskins, Sawhill, and Weaver 2001b.

101. Greenberg et al. 2000; National Campaign for Jobs and Income Support 2001; Haskins, Sawhill, and Weaver 2001a.

102. *City Limits* 12/1999, "The New Math."

103. GAO 8/1998.

104. Urban Institute 2002; Center on Budget and Policy Priorities, cbpp.org, 10/30/2002; Center for Law and Social Policy, "How States Used TANF and MOE Funds in FY 2002," clasp.org, 7/2003.

105. Blank and Schmidt 2000.

106. McConnell et al. 2003. Under AFDC, certain eligibility determination procedures were not permitted to be contracted to non-governmental organizations, but there are no such limitations under TANF; in June 2002 Florida received a waiver to use contractors to determine food stamp eligibility, too (ibid.).

107. *City Limits* 5/2001, "The Great Training Robbery."

108. *New York Times* 1/5/2002.

109. American Federation of State, County and Municipal Employees, "Private Profits/Public Needs: Milwaukee Private W-2 Agency Contract Surplus Distribution" and "Safety Net for Sale: The Driving Forces Behind Privatization," www.afscme.org (12/8/2001).

110. *Washington Post* 5/7/2001.

111. *Washington Post* 9/20/1999.

112. See *Los Angeles Times* 6/20/2000.

113. *Milwaukee Journal Sentinel* 5/10/2000.

114. *New York Times* 10/25/2000; see also Berkowitz 2001a; *Village Voice* 6/18–24/2003.

115. "Maximus," at Public Service Workers Project, polarisinstitute.org (12/06/2002).

116. *Financial Times* 12/22/1997; McConnell et al. 2003.

117. *New York Times* 2/7/1996.

118. See, for one example, *New York Times* 4/11/2001.

119. "EDS," at Public Service Workers Project, polarisinstitute.org (12/06/2002).

120. "Accenture," at Public Service Workers Project, polarisinstitute.org (12/06/2002).

121. Weaver 2000.

122. Berlin 2000.

123. Haskins 2000.

124. Haskins, Sawhill, and Weaver 2001a.

125. This has the peculiar effect of re-creating the worst effects of the Speenhamland system of aid in wages that led to the creation of the English Poor Law Commission and the New Poor Law of 1834. However, by 1998 the Bush administration's Internal Revenue Service was enacting and proposing new rules that would reduce EITC participation among eligible low-income families.

126. Solow 1998.

127. Piven 1999a, 1999b.

128. Esping-Andersen 1990; Piven 1999a; see also Piven 1999b; Pierson 2001. This is, however, the "retrenchment" that James O'Connor (1973) would predict.

129. Potts 2001.

130. Lowell 1884.

131. See Piven and Cloward 1971; Solow 1998; Hout 1997; Peck 2001. See Whitaker and Time (2001) for evidence that states with higher AFDC benefits also had higher per-capita incomes. Hout (1997) also offered confirmation of Piven and Cloward (1971) and Piven (1998) by demonstrating that, state by state, the lower the welfare benefits the lower the wages for women with a high school diploma or less—low benefits hold less attraction to potential recipients (there is truth to the "perversity thesis," as I have said), who instead enter the low-wage labor market, further depressing wages. For the mid 1800s, Kiesling and Margo (1997) found instead an inverse relationship between the "pauperism level" and the "real unskilled wage." Hunter (1897) undertook to debate this issue with Hyslop, who in the June 1897 *Forum* claimed, as I do, that out-relief increases wages.

132. Stewart 1911, 191.

133. In one study of families in Washington, D.C. (Forman 1906), one-fourth to one-fifth of the population "moves along the poverty line" because food expenses fluctuated, unforeseen expenses cropped up, and employment was unpredictable. Many experienced a monthly food shortage when rent was due (in the twentieth century a similar dilemma was referred to as the choice to "heat or eat"). Half spent half their income on food and as much as 25 percent on installment payments for chairs, tables, stoves, and other goods. Hunter (1904, 51–55, 58) showed that in New York rent alone could be up to 40 percent of monthly income and "laborers of the poorest class pass backward and forward over they poverty line." See Stanley (1992, 1272–73) for how "laborers repeatedly crossed back and forth from depending on wages to depending on alms, from inside to outside the wage contract. For them the beggar was neither a deviant nor a disingenuous figure, but one who personified, in an extreme way, the dependence and compulsion implicit in the wage contract itself."

134. Tilly 1996; Solow 1998; Hout 1997.

135. See *New York Times* 4/20/2000, "Poverty Snaring Families Once Thought Immune."

136. Bartik 1999; Bartik 2002; Solow 1998; Bernstein 1999.

137. Marchevsky and Theoharis 2000.

138. *City Limits* 11/1998, "Homeless Help Wanted."

139. Community Voices Heard 2000.

140. In Piven 1998b.

141. *New York Times* 4/8/2000.

142. See *Financial Times* 12/22/1997.
143. Peck 2001, 6.
144. Ziliak 1997. Kane (1987, 414) argued further that enforced work takes away choices from women who already have few, and may make them reluctant to work even if they would have chosen to do so in the absence of coercion.
145. Weisman and Kasmir 1994; Muhlhausen 2002.
146. Blank 2001.
147. O'Neill and Hill 2001.
148. Blank 2001.
149. NCCC 1894, 303.
150. Closson 1894, 476.
151. NCCC 1898, 9.
152. Kauffman and Kiesling 2001.
153. Almy 1899, 71.
154. Clement 1992, 49ff.
155. Watson 1922, 283.
156. Feder 1936, 138–39.
157. Watson 1922, 263–65; see also Burgess 1962, 262.
158. Feder 1936, 325ff.
159. Gunckel 1897, 755; NCCC 1896, 17.
160. Hunter 1904, 60–62.
161. Second Harvest 2001; *New York Times* 11/14/2001.
162. Fendt, Mulligan-Hansel, and White 2001.
163. Chapter 7 in Schram 2002.

6. The Squeegee Guy and the Tramp

1. The problem was the reverse for comparative welfare state studies, which only recently have included women (see Orloff 1996; O'Connor 1996; Sainsbury 1996; Sainsbury 1999). Most late-nineteenth-century poor-relief recipients were women (see Katz 1986, 1983); men constituted at best less than 20 percent of *applicants* in New York and 13 percent in New Haven (Warner 1894, Table XII). Very few were likely to have been deemed "worthy."
2. Forbath 1989; Orren 1991.
3. See Warner 1908, 235, 228–29; Warner 1894, 173; Ayers 1895, 262.
4. Piven and Cloward 1971, 149, 3–4.
5. NCCC 1877, 112.
6. Riis 1890, 188.
7. These terms were typically used interchangeably, but for definitions and distinctions, see McCook 1893, 58; Devine 1904, 82–85.
8. NCCC 1877, 104.
9. NCCC 1879, 25. Including those of 1871, 1876, and 1879 in Pennsylvania; 1874 and 1877 in Illinois; and 1880 and 1885 in New York, where the State Charities Aid Association was especially involved in anti-begging and tramp laws.
10. Beard and Beard 1944, 320.
11. Stanley 1992; Ringenbach 1973.

12. Closson 1895b; Millis 1897.
13. NCCC 1903, 414ff. "The one noticeable thing about the length of a sentence," reported Millis (1897), "is that it is long in the New England states and gradually shortens as one travels toward the west and south, where the maximum is almost always fixed at ninety days." The sheriff's fees in some jurisdictions could add years to those sentences, reported Blackmon (2001).
14. Millis 1897.
15. Stanley 1992, 1279.
16. *CR* 1900, 162.
17. NCCC 1890, 403. All data on nineteenth-century jail and prison populations must be viewed with some skepticism and should be considered approximations. What is nonetheless clear and most relevant here is that the increase in incarceration was substantial in the late century.
18. McCabe 1882. As Lowell said in 1876: "One of the most important and most dangerous causes of the increase of crime, pauperism and insanity is the unrestricted liberty allowed vagrant and degraded women" (in Watson 1922, 237 n. 2).
19. Howland 1922, Table I.
20. Brace 1880.
21. Feder 1936, 64–65.
22. Rothman 1971.
23. Timothy Lynch, 2/23/2000, "Population Bomb Behind Bars," Cato Institute, www.cato.org/dailys/02-23-00.html.
24. Friedman 1993, 460; Cole 1999; Mauer 1999; Platt 2001; Sentencing Project, "Does the Punishment Fit the Crime," www.sentencingproject.org (5/1993); Sentencing Project, "Facts About Prisons and Prisoners," www.sentencing project.org (8/2001 and 4/2003).
25. Foscarinis 1996.
26. Parenti 1999, 8–12. Note that the PRA allowed states to forever deny food stamp or TANF benefits to anyone convicted of a drug felony.
27. Parenti 1999, Ch. 3.
28. Bennett, DiIulio, and Walters 1996.
29. Mauer 1999, Ch. 4.
30. Poor men faced yet another difficulty in the late twentieth century when state-level general assistance programs were cut. By 1998, sixteen states did not offer state aid to those ineligible for TANF or other federal benefits. Of those that did, nearly half imposed a work test, eight states offered in-kind aid only, and ten imposed time limits. Most restricted benefits to "severely poor," disabled, elderly, "and otherwise unemployable individuals." In twenty-seven states benefits averaged less than 40 percent of the poverty line, and in all states but seven the value of benefits had declined since 1996 (Gallagher et al. 1999). When combined with rules changes in SSI and food stamps that reduced the value of those benefits and made them harder to obtain, the late-century reform era left men with very few sources of public relief, substantially less even than those available to women.
31. Teir 1998.
32. See National Law Center on Homelessness and Poverty 1991.

33. For the above see American Bar Association 1993; Ellickson 1996; Foscarinis 1996; Foscarinis, Cunningham-Bowers, and Brown 1999; Barta 1999; National Law Center on Homelessness and Poverty 1999, 1996, 1994, 1993; Brosch 1998; Howard and Gajilan 1998; Teir 1998; *The Nation* 3/10/1997, "In Fact"; *Christian Science Monitor* 2/24/1997, "L.A. Debates $500 Fine for Begging"; *Washington Post* 6/17/2002, "Moving Far Off Welfare"; *Newsweek* 1/17/1994, "These Guys Do Windows."

34. *New York Times* 1/9/2002.

35. Wilson and Kelling 1982; Kelling and Coles 1996.

36. *Christian Science Monitor* 2/24/1997, "L.A. Debates $500 Fine for Begging."

37. Stanley 1992, 1274.

38. In Gettleman 1963, 316.

39. In Stanley 1992, 1271.

40. Mason 1891.

41. NCCC 1903, 414ff.

42. Waugh 1997.

43. *CR,* passim.

44. Warner 1908, 252–53.

45. Gurteen 1882, 62.

46. Ringenback 1973, 57.

47. Warner 1908, 256; see also Warner 1894.

48. Ayers 1895, 263.

49. Stewart 1911, 327.

50. Katz 1986.

51. Stewart 1911, 446–50, 458.

52. See Rezneck 1953, 333.

53. In Ringenback 1973, 44.

54. Barbour 1894, 11.

55. McCook 1893, 1895.

56. NCCC 1877, 126.

57. NCCC 1877, 106.

58. Warner 1908, 247.

59. McCook 1895; Warner 1908, 247. As Chapter 5 showed for relief costs in the wake of reform, it would appear that while public expenses for the "care" of tramps grew $1.5 million from 1895 to 1905, per-capita expenditures sharply declined.

60. Keyssar 1986, 141.

61. Feder 1936, 162.

62. NCCC 1898, 449.

63. Brinkerhoff 1887, 106ff.

64. Lewis 1887, 113–15.

65. NCCC 1898, 53–55.

66. Blackmon 2001.

67. Shelden 1993, 615–17.

68. Lewis 1887.

69. NCCC 1880, xxiv.

70. Blackmon 2001.

71. See Rothman 1971; Ebert 1999.
72. American Federation of State, County and Municipal Employees, "The Evidence Is Clear: Crime Shouldn't Pay," www.afscme.org (12/8/2001).
73. U.S. Department of Justice, Bureau of Justice Statistics 4/2003, "Prison and Jail Inmates at Midyear 2002."
74. *Wall Street Journal* 5/7/2003.
75. Dyer 2000.
76. *Seattle Weekly* 1/2/2002, "Prison Coffee."
77. Petchesky 1993. See also "Board of Managers of Letchworth Village" in Breckinridge 1927.
78. See Dyer 2000.
79. Weiss 2001; see also *Village Voice* 8/14–20/2002, "Watch on the INS: Detainess Equals Dollars."
80. Karen Olsson, *Mother Jones,* Sep./Oct. 2002, "Ghostwriting the Law."
81. Ellickson 1996 n. 75.
82. In Baltimore *Daily Record* 10/27/1995.
83. *Kiplinger's Personal Finance Magazine* 1/1998, "Time's Expired on Panhandling."
84. Foscarinis, Cunningham-Bowers, and Brown 1999.
85. National Law Center on Homelessness and Poverty 1999.
86. National Law Center on Homelessness and Poverty 1994.
87. National Law Center on Homelessness and Poverty 1996.
88. National Law Center on Homelessness and Poverty 1991, 1993, 1994, 1996, 1999.
89. *Economist* 7/6/1996; *Economist* 2/26/1994.
90. *Crain's Cleveland Business* 7/5/1999.
91. *Crain's Detroit Business* 7/26/1999.
92. *Crain's Chicago Business* 3/22/1993, 2/22/1993.
93. *American Banker* 6/10/1994.
94. Brosch 1998.
95. *Journal-World* 6/14/1996, "Lawrence, Kan., Merchants Unite Against Downtown Panhandling."
96. Baltimore *Daily Record* 10/27/1995.
97. *Arizona Republic* 9/8/1996.
98. *Buffalo News* 3/30/1995.
99. See National Law Center on Homelessness and Poverty 1991, 1993, 1994, 1996, 1999.
100. *New York Times* 2/14/2002, "Loitering Behind the Clean Streets." One of the differences between such policies in the late nineteenth and twentieth centuries was the twentieth-century courts' willingness to intercede on behalf of the poor; many such laws were struck down on First, Fourth, Eighth, and Fourteenth Amendment grounds as violations of speech, search and seizure, cruel and unusual punishment, and equal protection guarantees, respectively; other courts were able to use state constitutions, some of which (New York most especially, and even Florida) offered greater protections to poor people than the federal Constitution. But as the trend toward new anti-vagrancy laws and enforcement continued throughout the 1990s, many cities began artfully

drafting their laws and amending old statutes to withstand legal challenges, while some municipalities simply ignored court orders (see National Law Center on Homelessness and Poverty 1991, 1993, 1994, 1996, 1999 for case law summaries; see Orren 1991 for a discussion of nineteenth-century courts' unwillingness to intercede in similar matters).

101. National Law Center on Homelessness and Poverty 1993.
102. Foscarinis 1996.
103. National Coalition for the Homeless, "Fact Sheets," www.nationalhomeless. org/numbers (12/2001). This is a pattern in evidence since at least the 1700s in Britain—"usually following demobilisation from the army and navy, the number of beggars increased dramatically" (Marriott 2000).
104. See Teir 1998 n. 23.
105. Crown 1993.
106. National Law Center on Homelessness and Poverty 1993.
107. Crown 1993.
108. See *New York Times* 8/12–17/2002.
109. Fording 2001. Note in this regard that in 2003, while George W. Bush and the 108th Congress continued an assault on the welfare state and a redistribution of wealth and power away from the poor and working classes, the government simultaneously undertook, with a "war on terror" as the rationale, a bold effort to increase federal powers of surveillance, detention, and a concomitant restriction on constitutional freedoms. Regressive redistribution may well need such repression.
110. Beckett and Western 2001. Similarly, states with higher numbers of blacks and Hispanics (and more Republican elected officials), all else being equal, had higher imprisonment rates (Jacobs and Carmichael 2001), and cities with higher unemployment rates were more likely to incarcerate unemployed men of the "rabble class" before their trial (D'Alessio and Stolzenberg 2002).
111. Sentencingproject.org 3/2003, "Felony Disenfranchisement Laws in the United States."
112. Zinn 1999, Ch. 24. As he says sardonically about welfare, "How skillful to tax the middle class to pay for the relief of the poor, building resentment on top of humiliation!"

7. Poverty and Propaganda

1. Gordon 1998.
2. Frankel 1903, 317–18.
3. Claire Tousley, "Report," CSS Box 128.
4. Watson 1922, 325.
5. But I nonetheless wonder how to here separate philosophy from necessity— after the onset of the 1893 depression and the great new needs that arose, the moral education that was the hallmark of the COS project was likely much too labor-intensive and time-consuming for many COSs, especially given the lack most had of sufficient staff and visitors (NCCC 1887, 134; Warner 1894, 373). Some COSs may have turned back to relief because it was cheaper and easier;

it may have been the only way to act given the constraints they operated under. Hubbard (1901) reported that fifty-one of seventy-five societies surveyed offered relief from their own funds by the turn of the century, and thirteen others did so during "emergencies" because there was no public relief in their cities, no private relief society or no cooperative arrangement with them through which they might secure aid for their cases. He concluded, "Relief-giving was omitted from the work of the first charity-organization society for special reasons, but the conditions do not seem to have made it possible for the societies in the United States to follow the original plan with success." Or the general turn of the COS to relief giving may have been the result of its structural and organizational failings. As Greeley (1995, Ch. 3) demonstrated, the dearth of friendly visitors in New York and the difficulty they had securing adequate participation from the volunteers who served on the District Committee tended to devolve responsibility upon the paid agents—generally low-paid, working-class women whose function was originally conceived as clerk and assistant. Because they were less exposed to and perhaps little sympathetic to COS philosophy, they were more liberal with relief than the Central Committee wished.

6. Frankel 1903, 322.
7. Tousley, CSS Box 128.
8. See esp. Greeley 1995.
9. Schattschneider 1960, 70.
10. Riker in Brady 1992, 42.
11. Lui 1993, 1995a, 1995b.
12. Seccombe, James, and Walters 1998; Hays 2003.
13. Piven and Cloward 1971; Piven 1998b; see also Edelman 1964.
14. See Lewis 2001. And about much else (see Converse 1964).
15. George 1999.
16. Pierson 2001; Pierson 1996; Piven and Cloward 1982.
17. Kristol 1995. Brock (2002, 144–45) identified Kristol's opposition to Clinton's health care reform proposal as rooted in Kristol's "[fear] that a new middle-class entitlement would seal Clinton's hold over crucial swing voters."
18. And those who urge a return to private charity through "faith-based" organizations should read the reformers of the Gilded Age. They, like many today, urged discrimination in relief giving, limited cash assistance, and moral education, each tailored to the specific needs of each individual, but it was for precisely this reason they argued that church-based philanthrophy was ineffective, for it would fail to refuse relief to those members ill-deserving of it, and might be tempted to extend "pauperizing" relief in order to attract adherents. Wrote Fetter (1901, 366): "It must be noted, however, that there is much idealizing of this religious control, and that few subsidized institutions accomplish the results the ideal would require, while it is by no means impossible to arrive at these results by other agencies, or in institutions publicly controlled." Moreover, as Kennedy (2001) argued, the "Charitable Choice" provision of the PRA advocated a public-private partnership that was not new. A 1965 survey of 406 religious organizations in twenty-one cities found that 70 percent had some kind of service contract with government; in 1994 government funding

accounted for 65 percent of Catholic Charities' $2 billion budget. The Salvation Army has been a long-standing recipient of government funding despite its very "pervasively sectarian" approach. Charitable Choice is based on the assumption that faith-based organizations are more effective and efficient. "However," notes Kennedy (2001; see also Press 2001, *New York Times* 4/24/2001, "Church-based Projects Lack Data on Results"), "there is no empirical data available either to support or rebut that presumption." Preliminary findings in May 2003 from a Kennedy study at Indiana University ("Charitable Choice: First Results From Three States," at ccr.urbancenter.iupui.edu/index.html) found that faith-based organizations were no more effective than others in helping welfare recipients find jobs, but that the jobs they did help recipients find were less likely to offer health insurance. Evidence for the superiority of faith-based service provision is still missing.

19. *Washington Post* 8/4/1996.
20. See Weaver 2000; NPR et al. 2001.
21. See also Gans 1995; Schram and Soss, in Schram 2002.
22. Gurteen 1882, 30.
23. Lee in Ebeling 1995, 100.
24. Zaller 1992.
25. Piven 1998a.

Acknowledgments

1. Katz 1986, 341 n. 13; see also Katz 2001, 58: "outdoor relief remains the least-studied facet of American welfare history."
2. Piven and Cloward 1987, n. 6.

SELECT BIBLIOGRAPHY

KEY TO ABBREVIATIONS:

CR: Charities Review
CSS: Archives of the Community Service Society of New York
LAH: Lend-a-Hand
NCCC: Proceedings of the National Conference on Charities and Corrections
NYAICP: Annual Reports of the New York Association for Improving the Condition of the Poor
NYCOS: Annual Reports of the New York Charity Organization Society
Sage: Charity Organization Department of the Russell Sage Foundation

Note: Citations show date of original publication followed, as necessary, by date of edition used.

A Striker. 1877. "Fair Wages." *North American Review* 125 (Sep.): 322–26.
Abel, Emily K. 1998. "Valuing Care: Turn-of-the-Century Conflicts Between Charity Workers and Women Clients." *Journal of Women's History* 10, no. 3 (Autumn): 32–52.
Abramovitz, Mimi. 1988 [1996]. *Regulating the Lives of Women: Social Welfare Policy from Colonial Times to the Present.* Boston: South End Press.
Addams, Jane. 1899. "The Subtle Problems of Charity." *Atlantic Monthly* LXXXIII: 163–78.
Addams, Jane. 1910 [1961]. *Twenty Years at Hull-House.* New York: Signet Classics.
Ahlstrom, Sydney E. 1972. *A Religious History of the American People.* New Haven: Yale University Press.
Albelda, Randy, Nancy Folbre, and the Center for Popular Economics. 1996. *The War on the Poor: A Defense Manual.* New York: New Press.
Alger, Horatio. 1868, 1890 [1985]. *Ragged Dick* and *Struggling Upward.* New York: Penguin.
Allen, Katherine, and Maria Kirby. 2000. "Unfinished Business: Why Cities Matter

to Welfare Reform." Brookings Institution, Center on Urban and Metropolitan Policy, Survey Series (Jul.).

Allen, Michael. 1992. "Elite Social Movement Organizations and the State: The Rise of the Conservative Policy-Planning Network." *Research in Politics and Society* 4: 87–109.

Almy, Frederic. 1899. "The Relation Between Public and Private Outdoor Relief." Parts I and II. *CR* IX, no. 1 (Mar.): 22–33 and no. 2 (Apr.): 65–71.

Almy, Frederic. 1900. "Public or Private Outdoor Relief." *NCCC:* 134–45.

Alpert, Irvine, and Ann Markusen. 1980. "Think Tanks and Capitalist Policy." In G. William Domhoff, ed., *Power Structure Research*. New York: Sage.

Alterman, Eric. 1999. "The 'Right' Books and Big Ideas." *The Nation* (Nov. 22).

American Bar Association. 1993. "Aggressive Panhandling Laws." *American Bar Association Journal* 79, no. 40 (Jun.).

Amin, Samir. 2000. "The Political Economy of the Twentieth Century." *Monthly Review* 52 (Jun.).

Anderson, Martin. 1978. *Welfare: The Political Economy of Welfare Reform in the United States*. Washington, DC.: Hoover Institution.

Auletta, Ken. 1982 [2000]. *The Underclass*. New York: Penguin.

Ayres, Philip W. 1895. "Charity Organization in Southern Cities." *CR* IV: 259–64.

Barbour, Levi. 1894. "The Value of State Boards." *NCCC:* 9–15.

Barbour, Levi, et al. 1901. "Subsidies." *NCCC:* 118–31.

Barnett, Samuel. 1899. "Charity Versus Outdoor Relief." *The Nineteenth Century* 46 (Nov.): 818–26.

Barta, Peter A. 1999. "Giuliani, Broken Windows and the Right to Beg." *Georgetown Journal of Poverty Law & Policy* 6, no. 165 (summer).

Bartik, Timothy J. 1999. "Displacement and Wage Effects of Welfare Reform." W.E. Upjohn Institute for Employment Research (Jan.).

Bartik, Timothy J. 2002. "Instrumental Variable Estimates of the Labor Market Spillover Effects of Welfare Reform." W.E. Upjohn Institute for Employment Research, Staff Working Paper no. 02-078 (Apr.).

Beard, Charles A., and Mary Beard. 1944. *A Basic History of the United States*. New York: Doubleday.

Becker, Dorothy G. 1961. "The Visitor to the New York City Poor, 1843–1920." *Social Service Review* 35 (Dec.): 382–96.

Beckert, Sven. 2001. *The Monied Metropolis: New York City and the Consolidation of the American Bourgeoisie, 1850–1896.* New York: Cambridge University Press.

Beckett, Katherine, and Bruce Western. 2001. "Governing Social Marginality: Welfare, Incarceration, and the Transformation of State Policy." *Punishment & Society* 3, no. 1: 43–59.

Bender, Thomas. 1975 [1991]. *Toward an Urban Vision: Ideas and Institutions in Nineteenth Century America*. Baltimore: Johns Hopkins University Press.

Bendich, Albert M. 1966. "Privacy, Poverty and the Constitution." In Jacobus tenBroek, ed., *The Law of the Poor*. San Francisco: Chandler.

Bennett, William J., John DiIulio Jr., and John P. Walters. 1996. *Body Count: Moral Poverty and How to Win America's War Against Crime and Drugs*. New York: Simon & Schuster.

Bensel, Richard Franklin. 2000. *The Political Economy of American Industrialization, 1877–1900.* New York: Cambridge University Press.

Berk, Gerald. 1994. *Alternative Tracks: The Constitution of American Industrial Order, 1865–1917.* Baltimore: Johns Hopkins University Press.

Berkowitz, Bill. 2001a. "Prospecting Among the Poor: Welfare Privatization." Applied Research Center, Oakland (May).

Berkowitz, Bill. 2001b. "The Heritage Foundation Soars." *Z Magazine* (Jun.).

Berlin, Gordon. 2000. "Redesigning the Safety Net for the Working Poor, the Hard to Employ, and Those At-Risk." Manpower Demonstration Research Corp. (Feb.). Draft paper presented at the City University of New York forum "Rethinking the Urban Agenda" (Mar. 2). See also John Mollenkopf and Ken Emerson, eds., *Rethinking the Urban Agenda: Reinvigorating the Liberal Tradition in New York and Urban America.* New York: Century Foundation Press, 2001.

Bernstein, Jared. 1999. "Welfare Reform and the Low-Wage Labor Market: Employment, Wages and Wage Policies." In John E. Hansan and Robert Morris, eds., *Welfare Reform, 1996–2000: Is There a Safety Net?* Westport, CT: Auburn House.

Besharov, Douglas J., and Peter Germanis. 2001. "Welfare Reform After Five Years." Acton Institute, *Policy Forum* 1 (Oct.).

Biography Resource Center. 2003. Gale Group, www.galenet.com/servlet/BioRC.

Bishop, Samuel H. 1902. "The New Movement in Charity." *American Journal of Sociology* 7, no. 5 (Mar.): 595–610.

Blackmon, Douglas A. 2001. "Hard Time: From Alabama's Past, Capitalism and Racism in a Cruel Partnership." *Wall Street Journal* (Jul. 16): A1.

Blank, Rebecca M. 2001. "Declining Caseloads/Increased Work: What Can We Conclude About the Effects of Welfare Reform?" Federal Reserve Bank of New York, *Economic Policy Review* (Sep.).

Blank, Rebecca M., and Lucie Schmidt. 2000. "Work and Wages." Paper delivered at the New World of Welfare Conference (Dec.). See also Rebecca Blank, Ron Haskins, and Jennifer Phillips, eds., *The New World of Welfare.* Washington, DC: Brookings Institution, 2002.

Block, Fred. 2003. "The Dubious Lessons of the Old and New Poor Laws." Draft paper delivered at the American Political Science Association annual meeting, Philadelphia (Aug.).

Blumenthal, Sidney. 1986. "The Second Coming." Chapter 12 in *The Rise of the Counter Establishment,* reprinted by the Potowmack Institute, www.potowmack.org/sidblum.html (11/19/02).

Bonaparte, Charles T. 1892. "What a Charity Organization Society Can Do and What It Cannot." *CR* I, no. 5 (Mar.): 201–9.

Boushey, Heather. 2001. Testimony before the U.S. House of Representatives Committee on Education and the Workforce, Subcommittee on 21st Century Competitiveness (Sep. 20).

Boyer, Paul. 1978 [1997]. *Urban Masses and Moral Order in America, 1820–1920.* Cambridge, MA: Harvard University Press.

Brace, Charles Loring. 1876. "The 'Placing Out' Plan for Homeless and Vagrant Children." *NCCC:* 135–50 (with discussion).

Brace, Charles Loring. 1880 [1967]. *The Dangerous Classes of New York and Twenty Years' Work Among Them.* Montclair, NJ: Patterson Smith.

Brady, David. 1992. "Incrementalism in the People's Branch: The Constitution and the Development of the Policy-making Process." In Peter F. Nardulli, ed., *The Constitution and American Political Development.* Urbana: University of Illinois Press.

Brandt, Lillian. 1908. "The Causes of Poverty." *Political Science Quarterly* 23, no. 4 (Dec.): 637–51.

Branscombe, Martha. 1943. *The Courts and the Poor Laws in New York State, 1784–1929.* Chicago: University of Chicago Press.

Breckinridge, Sophonisba P. 1927 [1938]. *Public Welfare Administration in the United States: Select Documents.* Chicago: University of Chicago Press.

Bremner, Robert H. 1956a [1972]. *From the Depths: The Discovery of Poverty in the United States.* New York: New York University Press.

Bremner, Robert H. 1956b. " 'Scientific Philanthropy,' 1873–93." *Social Service Review* 30, no. 2 (Jun.): 168–73.

Brinkerhoff, General R. 1887. "The Convict Contract Labor System." *NCCC:* 106–12.

Brinkerhoff, General R. 1894. "Boards of State Charities as Boards of Control." *NCCC:* 15–19.

Brock, David. 2002. *Blinded by the Right: The Conscience of an Ex-Conservative.* New York: Crown.

Brodkin, Evelyn. 1995. "The War Against Welfare." *Dissent* (spring).

Brookings Review. 2001. "Welfare Reform and Beyond." Brookings Institution (summer).

Brooks, John Graham. 1894. "The Question of the Unemployed in Massachusetts." *Economic Journal* 4, no. 14 (Jun.): 361–65.

Brosch, Eric. 1998. "No Place Like Home." *Harper's Magazine* 296, no. 1775 (Apr.).

Brown, Michael K. 1999. *Race, Money, and the American Welfare State.* Ithaca: Cornell University Press.

Bruno, Frank J. 1948. *Trends in Social Work as Reflected in the Proceedings of the National Conference of Social Work, 1874–1946.* New York: Columbia University Press.

Burch, Philip H. 1997. "Reagan, Bush, and Right-Wing Politics: Elites, Think-Tanks, Power and Policy." *Research in Political Economy* 16: 91–174.

Burgess, Charles O. 1962. "The Newspaper as Charity Worker: Poor Relief in New York City, 1893–1894." *New York History* (Jul.): 249–68.

Burnham, Walter Dean. 1970. *Critical Elections and the Mainsprings of American Politics.* New York: Norton.

Burris, Val. 1992. "Elite Policy Planning Networks in the United States." *Research in Politics and Society* 4.

Butler, Amos. W. 1906. "A Decade of Official Poor-Relief in Indiana." *American Journal of Sociology* 11, no. 6 (May): 763–83.

Cahn, William. 1972. *A Pictorial History of American Labor.* New York: Crown.

Calhoun, Charles, ed. 1996. *The Gilded Age: Essays on the Origins of Modern America.* Delaware: Scholarly Resources.

Callahan, David. 1998. "State Think Tanks on the Move." *The Nation* (Oct. 12).

Callahan, David. 1999a. "$1 Billion for Ideas: Conservative Think Tanks in the 1990s." National Committee for Responsive Philanthropy (Mar.).

Callahan, David. 1999b. "$1 Billion for Conservative Ideas." *The Nation* (Apr. 26).
Callahan, David. 2001. "Clash in the States." *American Prospect* 12, no. 11 (Jun. 18).
Campbell, John L. 2002. "Ideas, Politics, and Public Policy." *Annual Review of Sociology* 28: 21–38.
Cancian, Maria, Robert H. Haveman, Daniel R. Meyer, and Barbara Wolf. 2002. "Before and After TANF: Economic Well-Being of Women Leaving Welfare." *Social Service Review* 76, no. 4 (Dec.).
Carnoy, Martin. 1984. *The State and Political Theory.* Princeton: Princeton University Press.
Castells, Manuel. 1980. *The Economic Crisis and American Society.* Princeton: Princeton University Press.
Chandler, Alfred D. 1990. *Scale and Scope: The Dynamics of Industrial Capitalism.* Cambridge, MA: Harvard University Press.
Charity Organization Department of the Russell Sage Foundation. 1914. *Directory of Charity Organization Societies of the United States and Canada,* 6th ed. (Mar.).
Charity Organization Society of the City of New York. 1896. *New York Charities Directory,* 7th ed.
Clement, Priscilla Ferguson. 1992. "Nineteenth-Century Welfare Policy, Programs, and Poor Women: Philadelphia as a Case Study." *Feminist Studies* 18, no. 1 (spring): 35–58.
Closson, Carlos C. 1894. "The Unemployed in American Cities." Parts I and II. *Quarterly Journal of Economics* 8 (Jan. and Jul.): 168–217, 453–77.
Closson, Carlos C. 1895a. "Notes on the History of 'Unemployment' and Relief Measures in the United States." *Journal of Political Economy* 3, no. 4 (Sep.): 461–69.
Closson, Carlos C. 1895b. "Review of 'Report of the Massachusetts Board to Investigate the Subject of the Unemployed.'" *Journal of Political Economy* 3, no. 4 (Sep.): 492–97.
Cole, David. 1999. *No Equal Justice: Race and Class in the American Criminal Justice System.* New York: New Press.
Collins, Chuck, and Felice Yeskel. 2000. *Economic Apartheid in America: A Primer on Economic Inequality and Insecurity.* New York: New Press.
Commons, John R. 1893. "The Church and the Problem of Poverty in Cities." *CR* II, no. 7 (May): 347–56.
Community Voices Heard. 2000. "The Work Experience Program (WEP): New York City's Public Sweatshop Economy." www.cvhaction.org.
Converse, Philip E. 1964. "The Nature of Belief Systems in Mass Publics." In David E. Apter, ed., *Ideology and Discontent.* London: Free Press of Glencoe.
Cook, John T., Deborah A. Frank, Carol Berkowitz, et al. 2002. "Welfare Reform and the Health of Young Children." *Archives of Pediatric Adolescent Medicine* 156: 678–84.
Covington, Sally. 1997. "Moving a Public Policy Agenda: The Strategic Philanthropy of Conservative Foundations." National Committee for Responsive Philanthropy (Jul.).

D'Alessio, Stewart J., and Lisa Stolzenberg. 2002. "A Multilevel Analysis of the Relationship Between Labor Surplus and Pretrial Incarceration." *Social Problems* 49, no. 2: 178–93.

Davis, R.T. 1874. "Pauperism in the City of New York." Paper read at the annual meeting of the American Social Science Association (May 22) in NCCC 1874. (Also in *Journal of Social Science,* 1874, vol. 6: 60–99.)

deForest, Robert W. 1891. "What Is Charity Organization?" *CR* I, no. 1 (Nov.):1–5.

Devine, Edward T. 1898. "Public Outdoor Relief." Parts I and II. *CR* VIII: 129–37, 186–99.

Devine, Edward T. 1904 [1971]. *The Principles of Relief.* New York: Arno Press.

Diamond, Sara. 1995. *Roads to Dominion: Right-Wing Movements and Political Power in the United States.* New York: Guilford.

Diamond, Sara. 1998. *Not by Politics Alone: The Enduring Influence of the Christian Right.* New York: Guilford.

Dolny, Michael. 1996. "The Think Tank Spectrum." *Extra!* (May/Jun.).

Dolny, Michael. 1997. "New Survey on Think Tanks." *Extra!* (Jul./Aug.).

Dolny, Michael. 1998. "What's in a Label?" *Extra!* (May/Jun.).

Dolny, Michael. 2003. "Spectrum Narrows Further in 2002." *Extra!* (Jul./Aug.).

Domhoff, G. William. 1998. *Who Rules America? Power and Politics in the Year 2000,* 3rd ed. Mountain View, NJ: Mayfield.

Dreier, Peter, John Mollenkopf, and Todd Swanstrom. 2001. *Place Matters: Metropolitics for the Twenty-first Century.* Lawrence: University Press of Kansas.

Dugdale, R.L. 1877. "Hereditary Pauperism, as Illustrated in the 'Juke' Family." *NCCC:* 81–95.

Dyer, Joel. 2000. *The Perpetual Prisoner Machine: How America Profits from Crime.* Boulder: Westview.

Ebeling, Richard M., ed. 1995. *American Perestroika: The Demise of the Welfare State.* Vol. 23, Ludwig von Mises Lecture Series. Michigan: Hilldale College Press.

Ebert, Thomas G. 1999. *A Social History of the Asylum.* Bristol, IN: Wyndham Hall.

Edelman, Murray. 1964 [1985]. *The Symbolic Uses of Politics.* Urbana: University of Illinois Press.

Edelman, Peter. 1997. "The Worst Thing Bill Clinton Has Done." *The Atlantic Monthly* (Mar.).

Edin, Kathryn, and Laura Lein. 1997. *Making Ends Meet: How Single Mothers Survive Welfare and Low-Wage Work.* New York: Russell Sage.

Edsall, Thomas Byrne. 1984. *The New Politics of Inequality.* New York: Norton.

Edwards, Lee. 1998. Chapter 1 of *The Power of Ideas: The Heritage Foundation at 25 Years.* Ottowa, IL: Jameson Books. Reprinted in *New York Times Book Review* online (May 10, 1998).

Ehrenreich, Barbara. 2001. *Nickel and Dimed: On (Not) Getting By in America.* New York: Henry Holt.

Ellickson, Robert C. 1996. "Controlling Chronic Misconduct in City Space: Of Panhandlers, Skid Rows, and Public-Space Zoning." *Yale Law Journal* 105, no. 1165 (Mar.).

Ellwood, David T. 1988. *Poor Support: Poverty in the American Family.* New York: Basic.

Ellwood, David T. 1996. "When Bad Things Happen to Good Policies; Welfare Reform as I Knew It." *American Prospect* (May/Jun.).

Esping-Andersen, Gøsta. 1990. *The Three World of Welfare Capitalism.* Princeton: Princeton University Press.

Evans, Mrs. Glendower. 1889. "Scientific Charity." *NCCC:* 24–35.

Feagin, Joe R. 1975. *Subordinating the Poor: Welfare and American Beliefs.* New Jersey: Prentice Hall.

Feder, Leah Hannah. 1936. *Unemployment Relief in Periods of Depression.* New York: Russell Sage.

Federation of Protestant Welfare Agencies. 2000. "Downside: The Human Consequences of the Giuliani Administration's Welfare Caseload Cuts" (Nov.).

Feldman, Stanley, and John Zaller. 1992. "The Political Culture of Ambivalence: Ideological Responses to the Welfare State." *American Journal of Political Science* 36, no. 1: 268–307.

Felton, Katherine C. 1905. "The Charities Endorsement Committee." *NCCC:* 350–58.

Fendt, Pamela S., Kathleen Mulligan-Hansel, and Marcus A. White. 2001. "Passing the Buck: W-2 and Emergency Services in Milwaukee County." Institute for Wisconsin's Future et al., www.wisconsinsfuture.org.

Ferguson, Thomas, and Joel Rogers. 1986. *Right Turn: The Decline of the Democrats and the Future of American Politics.* New York: Hill and Wang.

Fetter, Frank A. 1901. "The Subsidizing of Private Charities." *American Journal of Sociology* 7, no. 3 (Nov.): 359–85.

Fine, Sidney. 1956 [1967]. *Laissez Faire and the General-Welfare State.* Ann Arbor: University of Michigan Press.

Flanagan, Maureen A. 2002. *Seeing with Their Hearts: Chicago Women and the Vision of the Good City, 1871–1933.* Princeton: Princeton University Press.

Flanders, Laura, and Janine Jackson. 1995. "Public Enemy Number One? Media's Welfare Debate Is a War on Poor Women." *Extra!* (Mar./Apr.).

Folks, Homer. 1894. "The Removal of Children from Almshouses." *NCCC:* 119–32.

Folks, Homer. 1898. "Municipal Charities in the United States." *NCCC:* 113–83.

Folks, Homer. 1901. "The Charities Chapter of the Greater New York Charter." *American Journal of Sociology* 7, no. 2 (Sep.): 262–76.

Forbath, William E. 1989. "The Shaping of the American Labor Movement." *Harvard Law Review* 102, no. 6 (Apr.).

Fording, Richard C. 1997. "The Conditional Effects of Violence as a Political Tactic: Mass Insurgency, Welfare Generosity, and Electoral Context in the American States." *American Journal of Political Science* 41, no. 1 (Jan.).

Fording, Richard C. 2001. "The Political Response to Black Insurgency: A Critical Test of Competing Theories of the State." *American Political Science Review* 95, no. 1 (Mar.).

Foscarinis, Maria. 1996. "Downward Spiral: Homelessness and its Criminalization." *Yale Law & Policy Review* 14, no. 1.

Foscarinis, Maria, Kelly Cunningham-Bowers, and Kristen E. Brown. 1999. "Out of Sight—Out of Mind? The Continuing Trend Toward the Criminalization of Homelessness." *Georgetown Journal of Poverty Law and Policy* 6, no. 145 (summer).

Frankel, Lee. 1903. "The Uses of Material Relief." *NCCC:* 317–28.

Fraser, Nancy, and Linda Gordon. 1994. "A Genealogy of Dependency: Tracing a Keyword of the U.S. Welfare State." *Signs* 19, no. 2 (winter): 309–37.

Fried, Amy, and Douglas B. Harris. 2001. "On Red Capes and Charging Bulls: How and Why Conservative Politicians and Interest Groups Promoted Public Anger." In John R. Hibbing and Elizabeth Theiss-Morse, eds., *What Is It About Government That Americans Dislike?* New York: Cambridge University Press.

Friedman, Lawrence M. 1993. *Crime and Punishment in American History.* New York: Basic Books.

Friedman, Milton. 1962 [1982]. *Capitalism and Freedom.* Chicago: University of Chicago Press.

Galbraith, John Kenneth. 1958. *The Affluent Society.* Boston: Houghton Mifflin.

Gallagher, L. Jerome, Cori E. Uccello, Alicia B. Pierce, and Erin B. Reidy. 1999. "State General Assistance Programs." Urban Institute (Apr.).

Gans, Herbert J. 1995. *The War Against the Poor.* New York: Basic Books.

George, Henry. 1879 [1992]. *Progress and Poverty.* New York: Robert Schalkenbach Foundation.

George, Susan. 1999. "A Short History of Neoliberalism." Paper delivered at the Conference on Economic Sovereignty in a Globalizing World (Mar. 24–26).

Geremek, Bronislaw. 1994. *Poverty: A History.* Oxford: Blackwell.

Gettleman, Marvin E. 1963. "Charity and Social Classes in the United States, 1874–1900." Parts I and II. *American Journal of Economics and Sociology* 22: 313–29, 417–26.

Gibson, Campbell. 1998. "Population of the 100 Largest Cities and Other Urban Places in the United States: 1790 to 1990." Washington, DC: U.S. Bureau of the Census, Population Division Working Paper no. 27 (Jun.).

Gibson, Campbell, and Emily Lennon. 1999. "Historical Census Statistics on the Foreign-born Population of the United States: 1850–1990." Washington, DC: U.S. Bureau of the Census, Population Division Working Paper no. 29 (Feb.).

Gilder, George. 1981 [1993]. *Wealth and Poverty.* San Francisco: ICS.

Gilder, George. 1995. "End Welfare Reform as We Know It." *American Spectator* 28, no. 6 (Jun.).

Gilens, Martin. 1999. *Why Americans Hate Welfare: Race, Media and the Politics of Antipoverty Strategy.* Chicago: University of Chicago Press.

Gilje, Paul A. 1996. *Rioting in America.* Bloomington: Indiana University Press.

Gilliom, John. 2001. *Overseers of the Poor: Surveillance, Resistance, and the Limits of Privacy.* Chicago: University of Chicago Press.

Gindin, Sam, and Leo Panitch. 2002. "Rethinking Crisis." *Monthly Review* 54, no. 6 (Nov.).

Gingrich, Newt. 1995. "Renewing American Civilization." *Futurist* 29, no. 4 (Jul./Aug.).

Gingrich, Newt. 1996. "Rethinking Our Approach to Poverty." *National Forum* 76, no. 3 (summer).

Gingrich, Newt, et al. 1994. *Contract with America: The Bold Plan by Rep. Newt Gingrich, Rep. Dick Armey, and the House Republicans to Change the Nation.* New York: Times Books. See also www.house.gov/house/Contract/CONTRACT.html.

Gladden, Washington. 1891. "The Plain Path of Reform." *CR* I: 251–56.

Glenn, John. 1891. "Co-Operation Against Beggary." *CR* I: 67–72.

Goldberg, Gertrude Schaffner, and Sheila D. Collins. 2001. *Washington's New Poor Law: Welfare "Reform" and the Roads Not Taken, 1935 to the Present.* New York: Apex.

Goodman, Robert Warren. 1983. "A Study of Humanitarian Philanthropy in an American Urban Community: The History of Four Social Welfare Agencies in New York City 1783–1905." Ph.D. dissertation, Rutgers University.

Gordon, Linda. 1994. *Pitied but Not Entitled: Single Mothers and the History of Welfare.* Cambridge, MA: Harvard University Press.

Gordon, Linda. 1998. "Share-Holders in Relief: The Political Culture of the Public Sector." Working Paper, Russell Sage Foundation.

Gramsci, Antonio. 1971. *Selections from the Prison Notebooks.* Ed. and trans., Quentin Hoare. New York: International Publishers.

Greeley, Dawn. 1995. "Beyond Benevolence: Gender, Class and the Development of Scientific Charity in New York City, 1882–1935." Ph.D. dissertation, State University of New York at Stony Brook.

Green, Elna C. 1999. "Introduction" and "National Trends, Regional Differences, Local Circumstances: Social Welfare in New Orleans, 1870s–1920s." In Elna C. Green, ed., *Before the New Deal: Social Welfare in the South, 1890–1930.* Athens: University of Georgia Press.

Greenberg, Mark, Jodie Levin-Epstein, Rutledge Hutson, et al. 2000. "Welfare Reauthorization: An Early Guide to the Issues." Washington, DC: Center for Law and Social Policy (Jul.).

Gunckel, Lewis B. 1897. "Outdoor Relief in Ohio." *CR* VII: 755–63.

Gurteen, S. Humphreys. 1882. *A Handbook of Charity Organization.* Buffalo: Courier.

Gurteen, S. Humphreys. 1894. "Beginnings of Charity Organization in America." *LAH* XIII: 352–67.

Gutman, Herbert G. 1965. "The Failure of the Movement by the Unemployed for Public Works in 1873." *Political Science Quarterly* 80, no. 2 (Jun.): 254–76.

Hacker, Jacob S., and Paul Pierson. 2002. "Business Power and Social Policy: Employers and the Formation of the American Welfare State." *Politics and Society* 30, no. 2 (June): 277–325.

Hall, Bolton. 1892. "The Effect of Taxation Upon Pauperism." *CR* 1, no. 3 (Jan.): 115–21.

Hall, Peter Dobkin. 2000. "Philanthropy, the Welfare State, and the Transformation of American Public and Private Institutions, 1945–2000." Working Paper no. 5, Hauser Center for Nonprofit Organizations, Harvard University (Nov.).

Hall, Richard L. 1996. *Participation in Congress.* New Haven: Yale University Press.

Hammack, David C. 1982 [1987]. *Power and Society: Greater New York at the Turn of the Century.* New York: Columbia University Press.

Hannon, Joan Underhill. 1984a. "Poverty in the Antebellum Northeast: The View from New York State's Poor Relief Rolls." *Journal of Economic History* 44, no. 4 (Dec.): 1007–32.

Hannon, Joan Underhill. 1984b. "The Generosity of Antebellum Poor Relief." *Journal of Economic History* 44, no. 3 (Sep.): 810–21.

Hannon, Joan Underhill. 1997. "Shutting Down Welfare: Two Cases from America's Past." *Quarterly Review of Economics and Finance* 37, no. 2 (summer): 419–38.

Hansen, Wendy L., and Neil J. Mitchell. 2000. "Disaggregating and Explaining Corporate Political Activity: Domestic and Foreign Corporations in National Politics." *American Political Science Review* 94, no. 4 (Dec.): 891–903.

Hardisty, Jean. 1999. *Mobilizing Resentment: Conservative Resurgence from the John Birch Society to the Promise Keepers.* Boston: Beacon.

Harrington, Michael. 1962 [1997]. *The Other America: Poverty in the United States.* New York: Touchstone.

Haskins, Ron. 2000. "The Second Most Important Issue: Effects of Welfare Reform on Family Income and Poverty." Paper presented at the New World of Welfare conference (Dec.). See also Rebecca Blank, Ron Haskins, and Jennifer Phillips, eds., *The New World of Welfare.* Washington, DC: Brookings Institution, 2002.

Haskins, Ron. 2001. "The Welfare Reform Law of 1996: What Has Been Accomplished? What Remains to be Done?" Acton Institute, *Policy Forum* 2 (Oct.)

Haskins, Ron, and Wendell Primus. 2001. "Welfare Reform and Poverty." Brookings Institution, *Policy Brief* 4 (Jul.).

Haskins, Ron, Isabel Sawhill, and Kent Weaver. 2001a. "Welfare Reform: An Overview of Effects to Date." Brookings Institution, *Policy Brief* 1 (Jan.).

Haskins, Ron, Isabel Sawhill, and Kent Weaver. 2001b. "Welfare Reform Reauthorization: An Overview of Problems and Issues." Brookings Institution, *Policy Brief* 2 (Jan.).

Hatheway, Jay. 1995. "The Puritan Covenant II: Anti-Modernism and the 'Contract with America.' " *The Humanist* 55, no. 4 (Jul.).

Hays, R. Allen. 2001. *Who Speaks for the Poor?* New York: Routledge.

Hays, Samuel P. 1965. "The Politics of Reform in Municipal Government in the Progressive Era." *Pacific Northwest Quarterly* 55.

Hays, Sharon. 2003. *Flat Broke with Children: Women in the Age of Welfare Reform.* New York: Oxford University Press.

Heale, M.J. 1976. "From City Fathers to Social Critics: Humanitarianism and Government in New York, 1790–1860." *Journal of American History* 63, no. 1 (Jun.): 21–44.

Heclo, Hugh. 1974. *Modern Social Politics in Britain and Sweden: From Relief to Income Maintenance.* New Haven: Yale University Press.

Heclo, Hugh. 2000. "The Politics of Welfare Reform." Paper presented at the New World of Welfare conference (Dec.). See also Rebecca Blank, Ron Haskins, and Jennifer Phillips, eds., *The New World of Welfare.* Washington, DC: Brookings Institution, 2002.

Hein, Jay. 1999a. "Florida Leads States in War on Poverty." Welfare Policy Center of the Hudson Institute (Nov. 20).

Hein, Jay. 1999b. "Market-Oriented Welfare Services." Hudson Institute, *American Outlook* (fall).

Henderson, C.R. 1898. "Politics in Public Institutions of Charity and Correction." *American Journal of Sociology* 4, no. 2 (Sep.): 202–34.

Henderson, C.R., et al. 1894. "Outdoor Relief: Conditions, Methods and Statistics." *NCCC:* 106–18.

Henderson, Charles R. 1894b. "Public Relief and Private Charity." *CR* III (Mar.): 226–35.

Henderson, Charles R. 1897. "Poor Laws of the United States." *CR* VI: 476–92.

Hernes, Helga Maria. 1987. *Welfare State and Woman Power: Essays in State Feminism*. Oslo: Norwegian University Press.

Hickey, Georgina. 2003. *Hope and Danger in the New South City: Working-Class Women and Urban Development in Atlanta, 1890–1940*. Athens: University of Georgia Press.

Himmelfarb, Gertrude. 1992. *Poverty and Compassion: The Moral Imagination of the Late Victorians*. New York: Vintage.

Himmelfarb, Gertrude. 1994. "A De-Moralized Society: The British/American Experience." Reprinted in Mark Gerson, ed., *The Essential Neo-Conservative Reader*. Reading, MA: Addison-Wesley, 1996.

Himmelfarb, Gertrude. 1995a. *The DeMoralization of Society: From Victorian Virtues to Modern Values*. New York: Knopf.

Himmelfarb, Gertrude. 1995b. "Beyond Social Policy: ReMoralizing America." *Wall Street Journal* (Feb. 7).

Himmelfarb, Gertrude. 1996. "Welfare as a Moral Problem." *Harvard Journal of Law and Public Policy* 19, no. 3.

Himmelfarb, Gertrude. 1997. "The Age of Philanthropy." *Wilson Quarterly* 21, no. 2 (spring).

Hoffmann, Frederick L. 1907. "Statistics of Poverty and Pauperism." *NCCC:* 132–54.

Hofstadter, Richard. 1944 [1992]. *Social Darwinism in American Thought*. Boston: Beacon.

Hout, Michael. 1997. "Inequality at the Margins: The Effects of Welfare, the Minimum Wage, and Tax Credits on Low-Wage Labor Markets." Russell Sage Foundation (Mar.).

Howells, William Dean. 1885 [1983]. *The Rise of Silas Lapham*. New York: Signet Classic.

Howland, Katherine E. 1922. "A Statistical Study of Poor Relief in Massachusetts." *Journal of the American Statistical Association* 18, no. 140 (Dec.): 480–89.

Hubbard, C.M. 1901. "Relation of C.O.S. to Relief Societies and Relief Giving." *American Journal of Sociology* 6: 783–89.

Huggins, Nathan Irvin. 1971. *Protestants Against Poverty: Boston's Charities, 1870–1900*. Westport, CT: Greenwood Publishing.

Hunter, Robert. 1897. "Outdoor Relief in the West." *CR* VII: 687–692.

Hunter, Robert. 1902. "Relation Between Social Settlements and Charity Organization." *Journal of Political Economy* 11, no. 1 (Dec.): 75–88.

Hunter, Robert. 1904. *Poverty*. New York: Grosset & Dunlap.

Husseini, Sam. 1998. "Brookings: The Establishment's Think Tank." *Extra!* (Nov./Dec.).

Hyslop, James H. 1894. "Charity Organization and Labor Bureaus." *CR* IV: 1–16.

Jacobs, Davis, and Jason T. Carmichael. 2001. "The Politics of Punishment Across Time and Space: A Pooled Time-Series Analysis of Imprisonment Rates." *Social Forces* 80, no. 1 (Sep.).

Jacobs, Lawrence R., and Robert Y. Shapiro. 1998. "The Politicization of Public Opinion: The Fight for the Pulpit." In Margaret Weir, ed., *The Social Divide: Political Parties and the Future of Activist Government*. Washington, DC: Brookings Institution.

Jacobs, Lawrence R., and Robert Y. Shapiro. 2000. *Politicians Don't Pander: Political Manipulation and the Loss of Democratic Responsiveness*. Chicago: University of Chicago Press.

Jarchow, Courtney. 2002."Employment Experience of TANF Recipients." National Conference of State Legislatures (May).

Johnson, Alexander. 1899. "Concerning Certain Wise Limits to Charity Organization Society Work." *American Journal of Sociology* 5, no. 3 (Nov.): 322–28.

Johnson, Alexander. 1923. *Adventures in Social Welfare: Being Reminiscences of Things, Thoughts and Folks During Forty Years of Social Work*. Fort Wayne, IN: Author.

Johnson, Paul E. 1978. *A Shopkeeper's Millennium: Society and Revivals in Rochester, New York, 1815–1837*. New York: Hill and Wang.

Johnson, W. Alex. 1884. "The Dangers Attending Almsgiving by Charity Organization Societies." *NCCC:* 77–80.

Jonas, Donald K. 1999. "The Business of Welfare Reform in Florida." Welfare Policy Center of the Hudson Institute (Oct. 6).

Jonas, Donald K. 2001. "The New Golden Rule." Welfare Policy Center of the Hudson Institute.

Jones, Rachel K., Jacqueline E. Darroch, and Stanley K. Henshaw. 2002. "Patterns in the Socioeconomic Characteristics of Women Obtaining Abortions in 2000–2001." *Perspectives on Sexual and Reproductive Health* 34, no. 5 (Sep./Oct.).

Judis, John B. 2000. *The Paradox of American Democracy: Elites, Special Interests, and the Betrayal of Public Trust*. New York: Pantheon.

Kalil, Ariel, Kristin S. Seefeldt, and Hui-chen Wang. 2002. "Sanctions and Material Hardship Under TANF." *Social Service Review* 76, no. 4 (Dec.).

Kane, Thomas J. 1987. "Giving Back Control: Long-Term Poverty and Motivation." *Social Service Review* (Sep.).

Kaplan, Barry J. 1978. "Reformers and Charity: The Abolition of Public Outdoor Relief in New York City, 1870–1898." *Social Service Review* 52, no. 2 (Jun.): 202–14.

Katz, Michael B. 1983. *Poverty and Policy in American History*. New York: Academic Press.

Katz, Michael B. 1986 [1996]. *In the Shadow of the Poorhouse: A Social History of Welfare in America*. New York: Basic.

Katz, Michael B. 1989. *The Undeserving Poor: From the War on Poverty to the War on Welfare*. New York: Pantheon.

Katz, Michael B. 2001. *The Price of Citizenship: Redefining the American Welfare State*. New York: Metropolitan Books.

Katz, Michael B., ed. 1993. *The "Underclass" Debate: Views from History*. Princeton: Princeton University Press.

Kauffman, Kyle D., and L. Lynne Kiesling. 1997. "Was There a Nineteenth Century Welfare Magnet in the United States? Preliminary Results from New York

City and Brooklyn." *Quarterly Review of Economics and Finance* 37, no. 2 (summer): 439–48.

Kauffman, Kyle D., and L. Lynne Kiesling. 2001. Unpublished data set. (Compiled from annual reports of the New York Secretary of State on Statistics of the Poor and the annual reports of the New York State Board of Charities, 1870–1889, as reported in Kauffman and Kiesling 1997.)

Kaus, Mickey. 1992 [1995]. *The End of Equality.* New York: Basic Books.

Kelling, George L., and Catherine M. Coles. 1996. *Fixing Broken Windows: Restoring Order and Reducing Crime in Our Communities.* New York: Touchstone.

Kellogg, Charles D., et al. 1893. "Charity Organization in the United States: Report of the Committee on History of Charity Organization." *NCCC:* 52–94, with appendices.

Kellogg, Charles D. 1894. "The Situation in New York During the Winter of 1893–1894." *NCCC:* 21–30.

Kennedy, Lawrence W. 1992. *Planning the City Upon a Hill.* Amherst: University of Massachusetts Press.

Kennedy, Sheila S. 2001. "Taking Contracting to Church: Using Faith-Based Organizations to Deliver Social Services." Paper presented at the annual meeting of the American Political Science Association, San Francisco (Aug./Sep.).

Keyssar, Alexander. 1986. *Out of Work: The First Century of Unemployment in Massachusetts.* New York: Cambridge University Press.

Kiesling, L. Lynne, and Robert A. Margo. 1997. "Explaining the Rise in Antebellum Pauperism, 1850–1860: New Evidence." *Quarterly Review of Economics and Finance* 37, no. 2 (summer): 405–18.

King, Moses. 1893 [1972]. *King's Handbook of New York City,* 2nd ed. New York: Benjamin Blom.

Kingdon, John W. 1995. *Agendas, Alternatives, and Public Policies,* 2nd ed. New York: HarperCollins.

Kittay, Eva Feder. 1998. "Welfare, Dependency and a Public Ethic of Care." *Social Justice* (spring).

Korpi, Walter. 1983. *The Democratic Class Struggle.* London: Routledge.

Kristol, Irving. 1978. "Human Nature and Social Reform." Reprinted in Mark Gerson, ed., *The Essential Neo-Conservative Reader.* Reading, MA: Addison-Wesley, 1996.

Kristol, Irving. 1993. "A Conservative Welfare State." *Wall Street Journal* (Jun. 14).

Kristol, Irving. 1997. "The Lost Soul of the Welfare State." American Enterprise Institute, *On the Issues* (Mar.).

Kristol, William. 1995. "The Politics of Liberty, the Sociology of Virtue." Reprinted in Mark Gerson, ed., *The Essential Neo-Conservative Reader.* Reading, MA: Addison-Wesley, 1996.

Kusmer, Kenneth L. 1973. "The Functions of Organized Charity in the Progressive Era: Chicago as a Case Study." *Journal of American History* 9, no. 3 (Dec.): 657–78.

Lee, Alfred McClung. 1937 [1973]. *The Daily Newspaper in America: The Evolution of a Social Instrument.* New York: Octagon Books.

Leiby, James. 1984. "Charity Organization Reconsidered." *Social Service Review* 54, no. 4 (Dec.): 523–38.

Lewis, Justin. 2001. *Constructing Public Opinion: How Political Elites Do What They Like and Why We Seem to Go Along with It*. New York: Columbia University Press.

Lewis, Oscar. 1968. "The Culture of Poverty." Reprinted in *The Study of Slum Culture—Backgrounds for La Vida*. New York: Random House.

Lewis, W.T. 1887. "Convict Labor from a Manufacturer's Stand-Point." *NCCC:* 113–15.

Lichter, Daniel T., and Rukamalie Jayakody. 2002. "Welfare Reform: How Do We Measure Success?" *Annual Review of Sociology* 28: 117–41.

Lipset, Seymour Martin. 1996. *American Exceptionalism: A Double-Edged Sword*. New York: Norton.

Lipset, Seymour Martin, and Earl Raab. 1981. "The Election and the Evangelicals." *Commentary* (Mar.).

Loprest, Pamela J. 2002. "Who Returns to Welfare?" Urban Institute, no. B-49 in the series "New Federalism: National Survey of American Families" (Sep. 1).

Loprest, Pamela. 1999. "Families Who Left Welfare: Who Are They and How Are They Doing?" Urban Institute Assessing the New Federalism Project, Discussion Paper 2 (Jul.).

Low, Seth. 1879. "The Problem of Pauperism in the Cities of Brooklyn and New York." *NCCC:* 200–16.

Low, Seth. 1881. "Out-Door Relief in the United States." *NCCC:* 144–54 (with discussion, 154–61).

Lowell, Josephine Shaw. 1884 [1971]. *Public Relief and Private Charity*. New York: Arno Press.

Lowell, Josephine Shaw. 1891. "Labor Organization as Affected by Law." *CR* I: 6–11.

Lowell, Mrs. C.R. 1879. "One Means of Preventing Pauperism." *NCCC:* 189–200.

Lowell, Mrs. C.R. 1887. "How to Adapt 'Charity Organization' Methods to Small Communities." *NCCC:* 135–143.

Lowell, Mrs. C.R. 1890. "The Economic and Moral Effects of Public Outdoor Relief." *NCCC:* 81–91.

Lowi, Theodore J. 1987. "Two Roads to Serfdom." In Frederick C. Lane, ed., *Current Issues in Public Administration*. New York: Bedford/St. Martin's, 1999.

Lowry, Robert C. 1999. "Foundation Patronage Toward Citizen Groups and Think Tanks: Who Gets Grants?" *Journal of Politics* 61, no. 3 (Aug.): 758–76.

Lui, Adonica Y. 1993. "Party Machines, State Structure, and Social Policies: The Abolition of Public Outdoor Relief in New York City, 1874–1898." Ph.D. dissertation, Harvard University.

Lui, Adonica Y. 1995a. "The Machine and Social Policies: Tammany Hall and the Politics of Public Outdoor Relief, New York City, 1874–1898." *Studies in American Political Development* 9 (fall): 386–403.

Lui, Adonica Y. 1995b. "Political and Institutional Constraints of Reform: The Charity Reformers' Failed Campaigns Against Public Outdoor Relief, New York City, 1874–1898." *Journal of Policy History* 7, no. 3: 341–64.

MacDonald, Dwight. 1963. "Our Invisible Poor." *New Yorker* (Jan. 19).

Malthus, Thomas Robert. 1798, 1803 [1976]. *An Essay on the Principle of Population*. New York: Norton.

Mandler, Peter, ed. 1990. *The Uses of Charity: The Poor on Relief in the Nineteenth-Century Metropolis.* Philadelphia: University of Pennsylvania Press.

Marchevsky, Alejandra, and Jeanne Theoharis. 2000. "Welfare Reform, Globalization, and the Racialization of Entitlement." *American Studies* 41, nos. 2/3 (summer/fall).

Marriott, John. 2000. "Sweep Them Off the Streets." *History Today* 50, no. 8 (Aug.).

Marshall, T.H. 1950. *Citizenship and Social Class.* Cambridge: Cambridge University Press.

Martin, Cathie Jo. 1998. "Inviting Business to the Party: The Corporate Response to Social Policy." In Margaret Weir, ed., *The Social Divide: Political Parties and the Future of Activist Government.* Washington, DC: Brookings Institution.

Mason, Alfred Bishop. 1891. "Things to Do." *CR* I: 211–14.

Mather, Cotton. 1710 [1966]. *Bonifacius: An Essay Upon the Good.* Cambridge: Belknap.

Mauer, Marc, and the Sentencing Project. 1999. *Race to Incarcerate.* New York: New Press.

McAdam, Doug. 1982. *Political Processes and the Development of Black Insurgency, 1930–1970.* Chicago: University of Chicago Press.

McCabe, James D. Jr. 1882 [1984]. *New York by Gaslight.* New York: Greenwich House/Crown.

McCann, Michael W. 1992. "Reform Litigation on Trial." *Law & Social Inquiry* 17.

McColloch, Oscar C. 1888. "The Tribe of Ishmael: A Study in Social Degradation." *NCCC:* 154–59.

McConnell, Sheena, Andrew Burwick, Irma Perez-Johnson, and Pamela Winston. 2003. "Privatization in Practice: Case Studies of Contracting for TANF Case Management." Mathematica Policy Research, Inc. (Mar.).

McCook, J.J. 1895. "The Tramp Problem: What It Is and What to Do with It." *NCCC:* 288–302.

McCook, John J. 1893. "Tramps." *CR* III: 57–69.

McGirr, Lisa. 2001. *Suburban Warriors: The Origins of the New American Right.* Princeton: Princeton University Press.

Mead, Lawrence M. 1986. *Beyond Entitlement: The Social Obligations of Citizenship.* New York: Free Press.

Mead, Lawrence M. 1990. "Jobs for the Welfare Poor: Work Requirements Can Overcome the Barriers." In John A. Hird, ed., *Controversies in American Public Policy.* New York: St. Martin's.

Mead, Lawrence M. 1993. "The Poor Pre-Eminent." *Wilson Quarterly* 17, no. 3 (summer).

Mead, Lawrence M. 1994. "Poverty: How Little We Know." *Social Service Review* (Sep.).

Mead, Lawrence M. 1996. "Welfare Reform at Work." *Society* 33, no. 5 (Jul./Aug.).

Mead, Lawrence M. 1998. "Telling the Poor What to Do." *Public Interest,* no. 132 (summer).

Mead, Lawrence M. 2000. "The Politics of Conservative Welfare Reform." Paper delivered at the New World of Welfare Conference (Dec.). See also Rebecca

Blank, Ron Haskins, and Jennifer Phillips, eds., *The New World of Welfare*. Washington, DC: Brookings Institution, 2002.

Mead, Lawrence M. 2002. "State Governmental Capacity and Welfare Reform." Paper presented at the annual meeting of the American Political Science Association, Boston (Aug. 29–Sep. 1).

Mead, Lawrence M., ed. 1997. *The New Paternalism*. Washington, DC: Brookings Institution.

Miller, William. 1949. "American Historians and the Business Elite." *Journal of Economic History* 9, no. 2 (Nov.): 184–208.

Millis, Harry A. 1897. "The Law Affecting Immigrants and Tramps." *CR* VII: 587–94.

Miner, Brad. 1996. *The Concise Conservative Encyclopedia*. New York: Free Press.

Mink, Gwendolyn. 1998. "Feminism, Welfare Reform, and Welfare Justice." *Social Justice* 25, no. 1.

Mishel, Lawrence, Jared Bernstein, and Heather Boushey. 2003. *The State of Working America 2002–03*. New York: ILR Press.

Mishel, Lawrence, Jared Bernstein, and John Schmitt. 1997. *The State of Working America 1996–1997*. Economic Policy Institute. Armonk, NY: M.E. Sharpe.

Mohl, Raymond A. 1983. *The Abolition of Public Outdoor Relief, 1870–1900: A Critique of the Piven and Cloward Thesis*. In Walter I. Trattner, ed., *Social Welfare or Social Control? Some Historical Reflections on Regulating the Poor*. Knoxville: University of Tennessee Press.

Monkkonen, Eric H. 1993. "Nineteenth Century Institutions: Dealing with the Urban 'Underclass.'" In Michael B. Katz, ed., *The "Underclass" Debate: Views from History*. Princeton: Princeton University Press.

Moore, James, and Wayne Slater. 2003. *Bush's Brain: How Karl Rove Made George W. Bush Presidential*. Hoboken, NJ: John Wiley and Sons.

Morris, Dick [Richard S.]. 1997. *Behind the Oval Office*. New York: Random House.

Muhlhausen, David B. 2002. "Congress Spends Billions on Ineffective Job-Training Programs." Backgrounder no. 1597, Heritage Foundation (Sep. 30).

Munsterberg, E. 1902. "Poor Relief in the United States. View of a German Expert." Parts I and II. *American Journal of Sociology* 7, no. 4 (Jan.): 501–38 and no. 5 (Mar.): 659–86.

Murray, Charles. 1984 [1994]. *Losing Ground: American Social Policy 1950–1980*. New York: Basic Books.

Murray, Charles. 1994. "What to Do About Welfare." *Commentary* (Dec.).

Murray, Charles. 1998. "What Government Must Do." *American Enterprise* 9, no. 1 (Jan./Feb.).

National Campaign for Jobs and Income Support. 2001. "Poverty Amidst Plenty 2001: Unspent TANF Funds and Persistent Poverty." Center for Community Change, Washington, DC (Feb.).

National Committee for Responsive Philanthropy. 1991. "Special Report: Burgeoning Conservative Think Tanks" (spring).

National Governors Association. 1988. "Policy on Welfare Reform." In Richard M. Coughlin, ed., 1989, *Reforming Welfare: Lessons, Limits and Choices*. Albuquerque: University of New Mexico Press.

National Law Center on Homelessness and Poverty. 1991. "Go Directly to Jail: A Report Analyzing Local Anti-Homeless Ordinances." Washington, DC (Dec.).

National Law Center on Homelessness and Poverty. 1993. "The Right to Remain Nowhere: A Report on Anti-Homeless Laws and Litigation in 16 United States Cities." Washington, DC (Dec.).

National Law Center on Homelessness and Poverty. 1994. "No Homeless People Allowed: A Report on Anti-Homeless Laws, Litigation and Alternatives in 49 United States Cities." Washington, DC (Dec.).

National Law Center on Homelessness and Poverty. 1996. "Mean Sweeps: A Report on Anti-Homeless Laws, Litigation and Alternatives in 50 United States Cities." Washington, DC (Dec.).

National Law Center on Homelessness and Poverty. 1999. "Out of Sight—Out of Mind? A Report on Anti-Homeless Laws, Litigation and Alternatives in 50 United States Cities." Washington, DC (Jan.).

National Public Radio, the Kaiser Family Foundation, and the John F. Kennedy School of Government. 2001. "National Survey on Poverty in America." (May). npr.org/programs/specials/poll/poverty/staticresults.html.

Natural Resources Defense Council. 2002. "Corporate America's Trojan Horse in the States." www.alecwatch.org.

Neubeck, Kenneth J., and Noel A. Cazenave. 2001. *Welfare Racism: Playing the Race Card Against America's Poor.* New York: Routledge.

Neuhaus, Richard John, and Peter Berger. 1976. "To Empower People: The Role of Mediating Structures in Public Policy." Reprinted in Mark Gerson, ed., *The Essential Neo-Conservative Reader.* Reading, MA: Addison-Wesley, 1996.

Newman, Katherine S. 1999. *No Shame in My Game: The Working Poor in the Inner City.* New York: Vintage.

Nill, J. Nevin, et al. 1891. "Arguments Against Public Outdoor Relief." *NCCC:* 36–49.

Niskanen, William A. 1996. "Welfare and the Culture of Poverty." *Cato Journal* 16, no. 1 (spring/summer).

Noble, Charles. 1997. *Welfare as We Knew It: A Political History of the American Welfare State.* New York: Oxford University Press.

O'Connor, Alice. 2001. *Poverty Knowledge: Social Science, Social Policy, and the Poor in Twentieth-Century U.S. History.* Princeton: Princeton University Press.

O'Connor, James. 1973. *The Fiscal Crisis of the State.* New York: St. Martin's.

O'Connor, James. 1981. "The Fiscal Crisis of the State Revisited: A Look at Economic Crisis and Reagan's Budget Policy." *Socialist Review.*

O'Connor, Julia S. 1996. "From Women in the Welfare State to Gendering Welfare State Regimes." *Current Sociology* 44, no. 3: 59–108.

O'Connor, Stephen. 2001. *Orphan Trains: The Story of Charles Loring Brace and the Children He Saved and Failed.* Boston: Houghton Mifflin.

O'Neill, June E., and M. Anne Hill. 2001. "Gaining Ground? Measuring the Impact of Welfare Reform on Welfare and Work." Manhattan Institute, *Civic Report* 17 (Jul.).

Olasky, Marvin. 1992. *The Tragedy of American Compassion.* Washington, DC: Regnery.

Olasky, Marvin. 1994a. "History's Solutions." *National Review* 46, no. 2 (Feb. 7).

Olasky, Marvin. 1994b. "Some Dare Call It Charity." *National Review* 46, no. 18 (Sep. 26).

Olasky, Marvin. 1996. "The Right Way to Replace Welfare." *Policy Review,* no. 76 (Mar./Apr.).

Olasky, Marvin. 1997. "Welfare Reform: The End of Compassion?" *USA Today Magazine* 125, no. 2622 (Mar. 1).

Oliphant, Lisa E. 2000. "Four Years of Welfare Reform: A Progress Report." Cato Institute, *Policy Analysis* 378 (Aug. 22).

Orloff, Ann Shola. 1988. "The Political Origins of America's Belated Welfare State." In Margaret Weir, Ann Shola Orloff, and Theda Skocpol, eds., *The Politics of Social Policy in the United States.* Princeton: Princeton University Press.

Orloff, Ann. 1996. "Gender and the Welfare State." *Annual Review of Sociology* 22: 51–70.

Orren, Karen. 1991. *Belated Feudalism: Labor, the Law and Liberal Development in the United States.* New York: Cambridge University Press.

Page, Benjamin I., and Robert Y. Shapiro. 1983. "Effects of Public Opinion on Policy." *American Political Science Review* 77 (Mar.): 175–90.

Paget, Karen M. 1998. "Lessons of Right-Wing Philanthropy." *The American Prospect,* no. 40 (Sep./Oct.).

Painter, Nell Irvin. 1987. *Standing at Armageddon: The United States, 1877–1919.* New York: Norton.

Parenti, Christian. 1999 [2001]. *Lockdown America: Police and Prisons in the Age of Crisis.* London: Verso.

Parrington, Vernon Louis. 1927, 1930. *Main Currents in American Thought.* New York: Harcourt, Brace.

Parry, Robert. 1996. "Who Buys the Right? (Foundation Spending for Conservative Causes)." *The Nation* 263, no. 15 (Nov. 18).

Patterson, James T. 1994. *America's Struggle Against Poverty 1900–1994.* Cambridge, MA: Harvard University Press.

Patterson, James T. 2000. "Congress and the Welfare State: Some Historical Reflections." *Social Science History* 24, no. 2 (summer).

Paxson, Christina, and Jane Waldfogel. 2003. "Welfare Reforms, Family Resources, and Child Maltreatment." *Journal of Policy Analysis and Management* 22, no. 1 (winter).

Peck, Jamie. 2001. *Workfare States.* New York: Guilford.

Pellew, Henry E. 1878. "Out-Door Relief Administration in New York City." *NCCC:* 53–72.

People for the American Way. 1996. "Buying a Movement: Right-Wing Foundations and American Politics." www.pfaw.org/pfaw/general/default.aspx?oid=2052.

Perlstein, Rick. 2001. *Before the Storm: Barry Goldwater and the Unmaking of the American Consensus.* New York: Hill and Wang.

Peschek, Joseph G. 1987. *Policy Planning Organizations: Elite Agendas and America's Rightward Turn.* Philadelphia: Temple University Press.

Petchesky, Rosalind P. 1993. "At Hard Labor: Penal Confinement and Production in

Nineteenth-Century America." In David F. Greenberg, ed., *Crime and Capitalism: Readings in Marxist Criminology*. Philadelphia: Temple University Press.

Phillips, Kevin. 1990. *The Politics of Rich and Poor: Wealth and the American Electorate in the Reagan Aftermath*. New York: HarperPerennial.

Phillips, Kevin. 2002. *Wealth and Democracy: A Political History of the American Rich*. New York: Broadway Books.

Pierson, Paul. 1996. "The New Politics of the Welfare State." In Paul Pierson and Francis Castles, eds., *The Welfare State Reader*. Cambridge: Polity Press, 2000.

Pierson, Paul. 2000a. "Increasing Returns, Path Dependence and the Study of Politics." *American Political Science Review* 94, no. 2 (Jun.).

Pierson, Paul. 2000b. "Three Worlds of Welfare State Research." *Comparative Political Studies* 33, nos. 6/7 (Aug./Sep.).

Pierson, Paul, ed. 2001. *The New Politics of the Welfare State*. New York: Oxford University Press.

Pimpare, Stephen. 2000. "The Effects of Welfare Reform on Head Start Programs in New York and New Jersey." New York University School of Education, Head Start Quality Improvement Center (Sep.).

Piven, Frances Fox. 1998a. "Welfare and the Transformation of Electoral Politics." In Clarence Y.H. Lo and Michael Schwartz, eds., *Social Policy and the Conservative Agenda*. Malden, MA: Blackwell.

Piven, Frances Fox. 1998b. "Welfare and Work." *Social Justice* 25, no. 1.

Piven, Frances Fox. 1999a. "The Market-Friendly Welfare State." Unpublished paper. See also "Der marketfreundliche US-americanische Sozialstaat." In Sabine Lang, Margit Mayer, and Christoph Scherrer, eds., *Jobwunder USA—Model für Deutschland?* Münster: Westfälisches Dampfboot.

Piven, Frances Fox. 1999b. "The Welfare State as Work Enforcer." *Dollars and Sense*, no. 225 (Sep./Oct.).

Piven, Frances Fox, and Richard A. Cloward. 1971 [1993]. *Regulating the Poor: The Functions of Public Welfare*. New York: Vintage.

Piven, Frances Fox, and Richard A. Cloward. 1977 [1979]. *Poor People's Movements: Why They Succeed, How They Fail*. New York: Vintage.

Piven, Frances Fox, and Richard A. Cloward. 1982 [1985]. *The New Class War*. New York: Pantheon.

Piven, Frances Fox, and Richard A. Cloward. 1983. "Humanitarianism in History: A Response to the Critics." In Walter I. Trattner, ed., *Social Welfare or Social Control? Some Historical Reflections on Regulating the Poor*. Knoxville: University of Tennessee Press.

Piven, Frances Fox, and Richard A. Cloward. 1987. "The Historical Sources of the Contemporary Relief Debate." In Fred Block, Richard A. Cloward, Barbara Ehrenreich, and Frances Fox Piven, *The Mean Season*. New York: Pantheon.

Piven, Frances Fox, and Richard A. Cloward. 1989. "Welfare Doesn't Shore Up Traditional Family Roles." *Social Research* (winter).

Platt, Anthony M. 2001. "Social Insecurity: The Transformation of American Criminal Justice, 1965–2000." *Social Justice* 28, no. 1.

Plotke, David. 1992. "The Political Mobilization of Business." In Mark M. Petracca, ed., *The Politics of Interests*. Boulder: Westview.

Polanyi, Karl. 1944. *The Great Transformation.* Boston: Beacon.

Polsky, Andrew J. 1991. *The Rise of the Therapeutic State.* Princeton: Princeton University Press.

Pope, Clayne. 2000. "Inequality in the Nineteenth Century." In Stanley L. Engerman and Robert E. Gallman, eds., *The Cambridge Economic History of the United States,* vol. II: *The Long Nineteenth Century.* Cambridge: Cambridge University Press.

Post, Charles. 1997. "The Capitalist Policy Planning Network." Paper presented to the American Sociological Association.

Potts, Joel. 2001. Testimony before the U.S. House of Representatives Committee on Education and the Workforce, Subcommittee on 21st Century Competitiveness (Sep. 20).

Press, Eyal. 2001. "Lead Us Not Into Temptation." *American Prospect* 12, no. 6 (Apr. 9).

Proceedings of the Conference of [Boards of Public] Charities and *Proceedings of the National Conference [of] on Charities and Correction[s].* 1874–1907. Published by the American Social Science Association (1874–1878), A. Williams and Co., Boston (1879–1881), Midland Publishing, Madison (1882), Geo. H. Ellis, Boston (1883–1903), Press of Fred. J. Heer (1904–1906), Press of Wm. B. Burford (1907).

Quadagno, Jill S. 1984. "Welfare Capitalism and the Social Security Act of 1935." *American Sociological Review* 49, no. 5 (Oct.): 632–47.

Quadagno, Jill S. 1987. "Theories of the Welfare State." *Annual Review of Sociology* 13.

Quadagno, Jill S. 1994. *The Color of Welfare: How Racism Undermined the War on Poverty.* New York: Oxford University Press.

Quigley, William P. 1998. "Backwards into the Future: How Welfare Changes in the Millennium Resemble English Poor Law of the Middle Ages." *Stanford Law & Policy Review* 9, no. 101 (winter).

Quintero, Sofia. 2002. "Heritage's Gift Horse: What Will Foundation Gain from Training the Media?" *Extra!* (Jan./Feb.): 30.

Rauch, Julia B. 1975. "Women in Social Work: Friendly Visitors in Philadelphia, 1880." *Social Service Review* 49, no. 2 (Jun.): 241–59.

Rauch, Julia B. 1976. "The Charity Organization Movement in Philadelphia." *Social Work* 21, no. 1 (Jan.): 55–62.

Rector, Robert. 1996. "How Congress Reformed the Welfare System." Heritage Foundation.

Rector, Robert. 1998. "America Has the World's Richest Poor People." *Wall Street Journal* (Sep. 24).

Rector, Robert. 2000. "Welfare: Broadening the Reform." In Stuart M. Butler and Kim R. Holmes, eds., *Issues 2000: The Candidate's Briefing Book.* Washington, DC: Heritage Foundation.

Rector, Robert. 2001. "The Size and Scope of Means-Tested Welfare Spending." Testimony before the U.S. House of Representatives (Aug. 1).

Rector, Robert, and Patrick F. Fagan. 2001. "The Good News About Welfare Reform." Backgrounder no. 1468, Heritage Foundation (Sep. 5).

Reich, Charles. 1964. "The New Property." *Yale Law Review* 73, no. 733.

Rezneck, Samuel. 1950. "Distress, Relief, and Discontent in the United States During the Depression of 1873–78." *Journal of Political Economy* 58, no. 6 (Dec.): 494–512.

Rezneck, Samuel. 1953. "Unemployment, Unrest, and Relief in the United States During the Depression of 1893–97." *Journal of Political Economy* 61, no. 4 (Aug.): 324–45.

Rezneck, Samuel. 1956. "Patterns of Thought and Action in an American Depression, 1882–1886." *American Historical Review* 61, no. 2 (Jan.): 284–307.

Ricci, David M. 1993. *The Transformation of American Politics: The New Washington and the Rise of the Think Tanks.* New Haven: Yale University Press.

Rich, Andrew, and R. Kent Weaver. 2000. "Think Tanks in the U.S. Media." *Harvard International Journal of Press/Politics* 5, no. 4 (fall).

Riis, Jacob. 1890 [1993]. *How the Other Half Lives: Studies Among the Tenements of New York.* New York: Hill and Wang.

Ringenbach, Paul T. 1973. *Tramps and Reformers: 1873–1916, The Discovery of Unemployment in New York City.* Westport, CT: Greenwood Press.

Riordan, William L. 1905 [1994]. *Plunkitt of Tammany Hall.* New York: Bedford.

Rockman, Seth. 2003. *Welfare Reform in the Early Republic: A Brief History with Documents.* Boston: Bedford/St. Martin's.

Rodgers, Daniel T. 1974 [1979]. *The Work Ethic in Industrial America, 1850–1920.* Chicago: University of Chicago Press.

Rodgers, Daniel T. 1998. *Atlantic Crossings: Social Politics in a Progressive Age.* Cambridge, MA: Harvard University Press.

Rosenbloom, Joshua L. 2002. *Looking for Work, Searching for Workers: American Labor Markets During Industrialization.* Cambridge: Cambridge University Press.

Rosenzweig, Roy. 1983 [1985]. *Eight Hours for What We Will: Workers and Leisure in an Industrial City, 1870–1920.* Cambridge: Cambridge University Press.

Ross, Edward A. 1914. "Philanthropy with Strings." *Atlantic Monthly* CXIV (Sep.): 289–94.

Rothman, David J. 1971. *The Discovery of the Asylum: Social Order and Disorder in the New Republic.* Boston: Little, Brown.

Rothman, David J. 1980. *Conscience and Convenience: The Asylum and its Alternatives in Progressive America.* Boston: Little, Brown.

Roy, William G. 1997 [1999]. *Socializing Capital: The Rise of the Large Industrial Corporation in America.* Princeton: Princeton University Press.

Sainsbury, Diane. 1996. *Gender, Equality and Welfare States.* Cambridge: Cambridge University Press.

Sainsbury, Diane, ed. 1999. *Gender and Welfare State Regimes.* Oxford: Oxford University Press.

Saloma, John S. III. 1984. *Ominous Politics: The New Conservative Labyrinth.* New York: Hill and Wang.

Sanborn, F.B. 1877. "Statistics of Pauperism in the United States." *NCCC:* 20–28.

Sarat, Austin. 1990. "The Law Is All Over: Power, Resistance and the Legal Consciousness of the Welfare Poor." In Julie A. Nice and Louise G. Trubek, eds., *Cases and Materials on Poverty Law: Theory and Practice.* St. Paul: West, 1997.

Sawhill, Elizabeth, ed. 1995. *Welfare Reform: An Analysis of the Issues*. Washington, DC: Urban Institute Press.

Schattschneider, E.E. 1960. *The Semisovereign People*. New York: Holt Rinehart.

Scherer, Michael. 2002. "Framing the Flag." *Columbia Journalism Review*. www.cjr.org/year/02/2/scherer.asp.

Schmidt, Vivien. 2002. "Does Discourse Matter in the Politics of Welfare State Adjustment?" *Comparative Political Studies* 35, no. 2 (Mar.).

Schneider, Ann Larason, and Helen Ingram. 1997. *Policy Design for Democracy*. Lawrence: University Press of Kansas.

Schneider, David M., and Albert Deutch. 1969. *The History of Public Welfare in New York State, 1867–1940*. Montclair, NJ: Patterson Smith.

Schneier, Saundra K., and William G. Jacoby. 2002. "Elite Discourse and American Public Opinion: The Case of Welfare Spending." Paper prepared for delivery at the annual meeting of the American Political Science Association, Boston (Aug. 29–Sep. 1).

Schneier, Edward V., and Bertram Gross. 1993. *Legislative Strategy*. New York: St. Martin's.

Scholz, John Karl, and Kara Levine. 2001. "The Evolution of Income Support Policies in Recent Decades." In Sheldon Danziger and Robert Haveman, eds., *Understanding Poverty*. Cambridge, MA: Harvard University Press, 2002.

Schram, Sanford F. 1995. *Words of Welfare: The Poverty of Social Science and the Social Science of Poverty*. Minneapolis: University of Minnesota Press.

Schram, Sanford F. 2002. *Praxis for the Poor: Piven and Cloward and the Future of Social Science in Social Welfare*. New York: New York University Press.

Schram, Sanford F., Joe Soss, and Richard C. Fording, eds. 2003. *Race and the Politics of Welfare Reform*. Ann Arbor: University of Michigan Press.

Schurman, J.G. 1892. "The Growth and Character of Organized Charity." *CR* I, no. 5.

Schwartz, Joel. 2000. *Fighting Poverty with Virtue: Moral Reform and America's Urban Poor, 1825–2000*. Bloomington: Indiana University Press.

Schwartz, Joel. 2001. "About Fighting Poverty with Virtue." Message from Schwartz posted to H-STATE@h-net.msu.edu (Apr. 1).

Scull, Andrew T. 1977. "Madness and Segregative Control: The Rise of the Insane Asylum." In George T. Martin Jr. and Mayer N. Zald, eds., *Social Welfare in Society*. New York: Columbia University Press.

Seccombe, Karen, Delores James, and Kimberly Battle Walters. 1998. " 'They Think You Ain't Much of Nothing': The Social Construction of the Welfare Mother." *Journal of Marriage and the Family* 60 (Nov.): 849–65.

Second Harvest. 2001. "Hunger in America 2001" and Food for Survival, 2001, "Hunger in America 2001: The New York City Report" (Nov. 14), press releases and summaries based upon Myoung Kim, James Ohls, and Rhoda Cohen, "Hunger in America 2001," Mathematica Policy Research (Oct. 2001).

Shalev, Michael. 1983. "The Social Democratic Model and Beyond: Two 'Generations' of Comparative Research on the Welfare State." *Comparative Social Research* 6.

Shapiro, Robert Y., Kelly D. Patterson, Judith Russell, and John T. Young. 1987.

"The Polls—Employment and Social Welfare." *Public Opinion Quarterly,* vol. 51: 268–81.

Shelden, Randall G. 1993. "Convict Leasing: An Application of the Rusche-Kirchheimer Thesis to Penal Challenges in Tennessee, 1830–1915." In David F. Greenberg, ed., *Crime and Capitalism: Readings in Marxist Criminology.* Philadelphia: Temple University Press.

Simons, A.M. 1898. "A Statistical Study in Causes of Poverty." *American Journal of Sociology* 3, no. 5 (Mar.): 614–21.

Sklar, Martin J. 1988. *The Corporate Reconstruction of American Capitalism, 1890–1916: The Market, the Law, and Politics.* Cambridge: Cambridge University Press.

Skocpol, Theda. 1992. *Protecting Soldiers and Mothers: The Political Origins of Social Policy in the United States.* Cambridge: Belknap.

Smith, James A. 1990. *The Idea Brokers: Think Tanks and the Rise of the New Policy Elite.* New York: Free Press.

Smith, Mark A. 2000. *American Business and Political Power: Public Opinion, Elections, and Democracy.* Chicago: University of Chicago Press.

Solow, Robert M., et al. 1998. *Work and Welfare.* Princeton: Princeton University Press.

Soss, Joe, Sanford F. Schram, Thomas P. Vartanian, and Erin O'Brien. 2001. "Setting the Terms of Relief: Explaining State Policy Choices in the Devolution Revolution." *American Journal of Political Science* 45, no. 2 (Apr.).

Soss, Joe. 2002. *Unwanted Claims: The Politics of Participation in the U.S. Welfare System.* Ann Arbor: University of Michigan Press.

Spencer, Herbert. 1843. "The Proper Sphere of Government." In John Offer, ed., *Herbert Spencer: Political Writings.* Cambridge: Cambridge University Press, 1994.

Stanley, Amy Dru. 1992. "Beggars Can't Be Choosers: Compulsion and Contract in Postbellum America." *Journal of American History* 78, no. 4 (Mar.): 1256–93.

Stefancic, Jean, and Richard Delgado. 1996. *No Mercy: How Conservative Think Tanks and Foundations Changed America's Social Agenda.* Philadelphia: Temple University Press.

Stephanopoulos, George. 1999. *All Too Human: A Political Education.* Boston: Little, Brown.

Stewart, William Rhinelander, ed. 1911. *The Philanthropic Work of Josephine Shaw Lowell.* New York: Macmillan.

Stone, Deborah. 1997. *Policy Paradox: The Art of Political Decision Making.* New York: Norton.

Su, Tie-Ting, Alan Neustadt, and Dan Clawson. 1992. "The Coalescence of Corporate Conservatism from 1976 to 1980: The Roots of the Reagan Revolution." *Research in Politics and Society* 4.

Sumner, William Graham. 1880. "Socialism." (See also "Sociology" [1881], "The Forgotten Man" [1883], "Laissez Faire" [1886], and "The Absurd Effort to Make the World Over" [1894].) In Robert C. Bannister, ed., *On Liberty, Society, and Politics: The Essential Essays of William Graham Sumner.* Indianapolis: Liberty Fund, 1992.

Sumner, William Graham. 1887[?] "Liberty and Responsibility." In Albert Galloway Keller, ed., *Earth-Hunger and Other Essays by William Graham Sumner.* New Haven: Yale University Press, 1913.

Super, David, et al. 1996. "The New Welfare Law: Summary." Center on Budget and Policy Priorities (Aug.).

Swank, Duane H. 2002. *Global Capital, Political Institutions and Policy Change in Developed Welfare States.* Cambridge: Cambridge University Press.

Swomley, John M. 1996. "Funding for the Culture War." *Humanist* 56, no. 3 (May/Jun.).

Tabb, William K. 2001. *The Amoral Elephant: Globalization and the Struggle for Social Justice in the Twenty-First Century.* New York: Monthly Review Press.

Teir, Rob. 1998. "Restoring Order in Urban Public Spaces." *Texas Review of Law & Policy* 2, no. 256 (spring).

Thomas, Adam, and Isabel Sawhill. 2001. "For Richer or for Poorer: Marriage as an Antipoverty Strategy" (preliminary draft). Brookings Institution.

Tilly, Chris. 1996. "Workfare's Impact on the New York City Labor Market: Lower Wages and Worker Displacement." Working Paper no. 92, Russell Sage Foundation (Mar.).

Trachtenberg, Alan. 1982 [2000]. *The Incorporation of America: Culture and Society in the Gilded Age.* New York: Hill and Wang.

Trattner, Walter I. 1988. "The Federal Government and Needy Citizens in Nineteenth-Century America." *Political Science Quarterly* 103, no. 2 (summer): 347–56.

Trattner, Walter I. 1994. *From Poor Law to Welfare State: A Social History of Welfare in America,* 5th ed. New York: Free Press.

Trattner, Walter I, ed. 1983. *Social Welfare or Social Control? Some Historical Reflections on Regulating the Poor.* Knoxville: University of Tennessee Press.

United States Chamber of Commerce. 1994–1996. *Nation's Business.*

Urban Institute. 1996. "A Comparison of Selected Key Provisions of the Welfare Reform Reconciliation Act of 1996 with Current Law." Washington, DC.

Urban Institute. 2002. "Distribution of Federal and State Welfare Spending." Washington, DC (May).

Useem, Michael. 1984. *The Inner Circle: Large Corporations and the Rise of Business Political Activity.* New York: Oxford University Press.

Vogel, David. 1989. *Fluctuating Fortunes: The Political Power of Business in America.* New York: Basic Books.

Wagner, David. 2000. *What's Love Got to Do with It? Beyond the Altruistic Myths of American Charity.* New York: New Press.

Waisman, Dov, and Sharryn Kasmir. 1994. "An Analysis of Job Training Programs in the United States." Food and Hunger Hotline, New York.

Waller, Margy, and Alan Berube. 2002. "Timing Out: Long-Term Welfare Caseloads in Large Cities and Counties." The Brookings Institution Survey Series, Washington, DC (Sep.).

Warner, Amos G. 1889. "Notes on the Statistical Determination of the Causes of Poverty." *Publications of the American Statistical Association* 1, no. 5 (Mar.): 183–205.

Warner, Amos G. 1890. "Some Experiments on Behalf of the Unemployed." *Quarterly Journal of Economics* 5, no. 1 (Oct.): 1–23.

Warner, Amos G. 1894a [1971]. *American Charities.* New York: Arno Press.

Warner, Amos G. 1894b. "The Causes of Poverty Further Considered." *Publications of the American Statistical Association* 4, no. 27 (Sep.): 49–68.

Warner, Amos G. 1908. *American Charities.* Rev. by Mary Roberts Coolidge. New York: Cromwell.

Watson, Frank Dekker. 1922 [1971]. *The Charity Organization Movement in the United States: A Study in American Philanthropy.* New York: Arno Press.

Waugh, Joan. 1997. *Unsentimental Reformer: The Life of Josephine Shaw Lowell.* Cambridge, MA. Harvard University Press.

Waugh, Joan. 2001. " 'Give This Man Work!' Josephine Shaw Lowell, the Charity Organization Society of the City of New York, and the Depression of 1893." *Social Science History* 25, no. 2 (summer).

Weaver, R. Kent. 1998. "Ending Welfare as We Know It." In Margaret Weir, ed., *The Social Divide.* Washington, DC: Brookings Institution.

Weaver, R. Kent. 2000. *Ending Welfare as We Know It.* Washington, DC: Brookings Institution.

Weber, Max. 1904–05 [1997]. *The Protestant Ethic and the Spirit of Capitalism.* London: Routledge.

Weicher, John C. 1995. "The Labor Market for Welfare Recipients in the Milwaukee Metropolitan Area." Welfare Policy Center of the Hudson Institute (Jun.).

Weinstein, James. 1968. *The Corporate Ideal and the Liberal State: 1900–1918.* Boston: Beacon.

Weiss, Robert P. 2001. "Charitable Choice as a Neoliberal Welfare Strategy." *Social Justice* 28, no. 1.

Whitaker, Ingrid Phillips, and Victoria Time. 2001. "Devolution and Welfare: The Social and Legal Implications of State Inequalities for Welfare Reform in the United States." *Social Justice* 28, no. 1.

White, Julie Anne, and Joan C. Tronto. 2002. "Political Practices of Care: Needs and Rights." Draft paper presented at the annual meeting of the American Political Science Association: Boston (Aug. 29–Sep. 1).

Wiebe, Robert. 1962. *Businessmen and Reform: A Study of the Progressive Movement.* Cambridge, MA: Harvard University Press.

Wilensky, Harold. 1975. *The Welfare State and Equality.* Berkeley: University of California Press.

Wilensky, Harold, and Charles Nathan Lebeaux. 1958. *Industrial Society and Social Welfare.* New York: Russell Sage.

Wilenz, Sean. 1984. *Chants Democratic: New York City and the Rise of the American Working Class, 1788–1850.* New York: Oxford University Press.

Williams, Lucy A. 1994. "The Abuse of Section 1115 Waivers: Welfare Reform in Search of a Standard." *Yale Law & Policy Review* 12, no. 8.

Williams, Lucy. 1996. "The Right's Attack on AFDC." *Public Eye* 10, nos. 3 and 4 (fall and winter).

Wilson, James Q., and George L. Kelling. 1982. "The Police and Neighborhood Safety." *The Atlantic* (Mar.): 29–38.

Wilson, William Julius. 1996. *When Work Disappears: The World of the New Urban Poor.* New York: Vintage.

Winston, Pamela. 2002. *Welfare Policymaking in the States: The Devil in Devolution.* Washington, DC: Georgetown University Press.

Woods, Robert A., et al. 1895 [1971]. *The Poor in Great Cities.* New York: Arno Press.

Wuthnow, Robert. 1988. *The Restructuring of American Religion.* Princeton: Princeton University Press.

Yee, Albert S. 1996. "The Causal Effects of Ideas on Policies." *International Organization* 50, no. 1 (winter): 69–108.

Yule, G. Udny. 1895. "On the Correlation of Total Pauperism with Proportion of Out-Relief." *Economic Journal* 5, no. 20 (Dec.): 603–11. (See also G. Udny Yule, 1896, "On the Correlation of Total Pauperism with Proportion of Out-Relief." *Economic Journal* 6, no. 24 [Dec.]: 613–23.)

Zaller, John R. 1992. *The Nature and Origins of Mass Opinion.* Cambridge: Cambridge University Press.

Zedlewski, Sheila R., Sandi Nelson, Kathryn Edin, Heather L. Koball, Kate Pomper, and Tracy Roberts. 2003. "Families Coping Without Earnings or Government Cash Assistance." Assessing the New Federalism Occasional Paper no. 64. DC: Urban Institute (Feb. 1).

Ziliak, Stephen T. 1996a. "The End of Welfare and the Contradiction of Compassion." *Independent Review* 1, no. 1 (spring): 55–73.

Ziliak, Stephen T. 1996b. "Essays on Self-Reliance: The United States in the Era of 'Scientific Charity.' " Ph.D. dissertation, University of Iowa.

Ziliak, Stephen T. 1997. "Kicking the Malthusian Vice: Lessons from the Abolition of 'Welfare' in the Late Nineteenth Century." *Quarterly Review of Economics and Finance* 37, no. 2 (summer): 449–68.

Ziliak, Stephen T. 2002. "Some Tendencies of Social Welfare and the Problem of Interpretation." *Cato Journal* 21, no. 3 (winter): 499–513.

Zinn, Howard. 1999. *A People's History of the United States: 1492–Present.* New York: HarperCollins.

INDEX

Riis, Jacob:
  on AICPs, 51
  and police lodging houses, 181
  on street begging, 172
  on suffering and self-support, 24
Robertson, Pat, 61
Roosevelt, Franklin Delano, 38
Roosevelt, Theodore, 181
Roosevelt, Theodore, Sr., 32
*Rosencrantz and Guildenstern Are
    Dead* (Tom Stoppard), 5
Ross, Edward, 69, 75
Rouen, 38
Rove, Karl, 126
rural areas, 89

St. Paul (MN), 14
St. Vincent de Paul, 50
Salt Lake City (UT), 164, 190
Salvation Army, 181
Sanborn, F.B., 155
sanctions, 145
San Francisco (CA), 178
Santa Ana (NV), 178
Scaife, Richard Mellon, 127
Schattschneider, E.E., 112, 210
Schmidt, Vivien, 38–39
school lunch programs, 117
Schram, Sanford, 30, 211–12
Schwartz, Joel, 27, 126
Seattle (WA), 178
Shalala, Donna, 14, 136–37
Shapiro, Robert, 37
Shaw, Clay, 130, 133, 137
Sheldon, Andrea, 33
Sing Sing prison, 174

Sklar, Martin, 46–47
Slocum, William, 26, 30
"smart cards," 159
Smith, Mark, 65
social Darwinism, 21–22, 24–25
Society of St. Vincent de Paul, 166
Solow, Robert, 161, 163
Soss, Joe, 30
soup kitchens, 155, 166, 167
Spencer, Herbert, 22
"spermfare," 116
"squeegee guys," 178
Standard Oil, 45–46
Standing at Armageddon (Nell
    Painter), 44
Stanley, Amy, 179
states:
  welfare variations among, 145
Stefancic, Jean, 122
Stoppard, Tom, 5
Summer, William Graham, 19, 22,
    178
"superpredators," 176
Supplemental Security Income,
    55

Tabb, William, 20
Talent, James, 124, 125
Talmadge Amendments, 118
TANF. *See* Temporary Assistance to
    Needy Families
tax credits, 160–62
Temporary Assistance to Needy
    Families (TANF), 115–16, 145,
    146, 158, 159
Texas, 160, 185, 186

real value of, 55

relief reform affected by, 162–65

and welfare, 5, 6, 8

Walk, James, 165–66

Warner, Amos G.:

on abolition of outdoor relief, 86, 88

on cost of caring for tramps, 184

on effects of relief reform, 146

on social advancement, 75

on vagrancy, 181

War on Poverty, 1, 3, 121, 122, 125

Washington (state), 187

Watson, Frank Dekker:

on abolition of outdoor relief, 83, 86–87

on business operation of COS, 74

on creation of charity organizations, 47

on crusade for reduction of outdoor relief, 52–53

on dignity acquired by relief, 199

on division of responsibilities, 101

on success of COS, 95

on visitors to the poor, 51–52

Wayland, Francis, 171–72

Wealth and Poverty (George Gilder), 126

wealth inequalities, 19

Weaver, Kent, 128, 131–32, 140

Weber, Max, 61

welfare, 1. *See also* Aid to Families with Dependent Children; outdoor relief; relief

after depression of 1873, 6

as alternative to low-wage work, 5

benefits of, 4

defense of, 213–14

defined, 10

forward vs. backward movement in, 10

and incarceration, 191–92

19th century activism against, 6–10

percentage of Americans on, 43

reform of. *See* welfare reform

state-level administration of, 3

as trading one kind of dependency for another, 3

20th century activism against, 4–10

welfare abuse, 28–29

welfare reform, 111–41. *See also* Personal Responsibility and Work Opportunity Reconciliation Act of 1996; relief reform

and AFDC, 113–16

assumptions underlying, 10

business' role in, 135–40

and Clinton administration, 120–25

critics of, 128–35

in late 20th century, 54–59

moral interpretation of, 7

reasons for, 7

think tanks' effect on, 116–20, 125–28

welfare reform legislation. *See* Personal Responsibility and Work Opportunity Reconciliation Act of 1996